Urban Domestic Servants
in 19th-Century Canada

Claudette Lacelle

Translated from the Original French

Studies in Archaeology
Architecture and History

National Historic Parks and Sites
Environment Canada — Parks

©Minister of Supply and Services Canada 1987.

Available in Canada through authorized bookstore agents and other bookstores, or by mail from the Canadian Government Publishing Centre, Supply and Services Canada, Hull, Quebec, Canada K1A 0S9.

L'original français s'intitule **Les domestiques en milieu urbain canadien au XIXe siècle** (no de catalogue R61-2/9-36F). En vente au Canada par l'entremise de nos agents libraires agréés et autres librairies, ou par la poste au Centre d'édition du gouvernement du Canada, Approvisionnements et Services Canada, Hull, Québec, Canada K1A 0S9.

Price Canada: $15.50
Price other countries: $18.60
Price subject to change without notice.

Catalogue No.: R61-2/9-36E
ISBN: 0-660-12335-5
ISSN: 0821-1027

Published under the authority
of the Minister of the Environment,
Ottawa, 1987.

Translated by the Department of the Secretary of State.
Design: J. Brathwaite and L. Richard.
Editing: J. Brathwaite.

The opinions expressed in this report are those of the author and not necessarily those of Environment Canada.

Parks publishes the results of its research in archaeology, architecture, and history. A list of publications is available from Research Publications, Environment Canada — Parks, 1600 Liverpool Court, Ottawa, Ontario K1A 1G2.

Cover: **Canadian Illustrated News,** 6 May 1882 (Public Archives Canada, C-77137).

TABLE OF CONTENTS

1 in 6 households have any +
2/3 houses =1 servant

137 **Conclusion**

Appendices

Submitted for publication 1982, by Claudette Lacelle, Historical Research Division, National Historic Parks and Sites, Environment Canada — Parks, Ottawa.

INTRODUCTION

The context for this research into the lives of Canadian servants in the 19th century was the restoration and interpretation of historic houses by Environment Canada — Parks. This is the first time such a study has been carried out in Canada.[1] Previously no real information was available on the identities and numbers of servants, or where and how they were lodged in times gone by, and virtually nothing was known of their living and working conditions. These blanks in our knowledge have often meant that various organizations interested in restoring and interpreting historic houses have had to ignore the servants' quarters, using such areas for their own personnel or for storage,[2] being unable to provide the visiting public with important information on the life and society of the period. While in some instances research on a particular house did provide sufficient detail for servants' rooms to be taken into consideration, gleaning a few meaningful pieces of information on the servants themselves was very rare.[3] Moreover, even if such information had been plentifully available, it would have been impossible to compare that particular house with other Canadian houses in regard to domestic service — an institution whose importance over the centuries is undisputed and which has even been a measure of a family's social standing.

Given the vast scope of the project, I certainly could not cover all servants living in Canada during the 19th century and therefore concentrated on those living in urban areas and in their masters' households. This was not an arbitrary choice: it was dictated by the requirements of the department. Only urban areas have been considered because the majority of restored houses are located in such areas or belonged to city dwellers, and only those servants who both worked and lived in these houses have been included because our focus is on the residents of these historic houses.

In addition, the study has been confined to specific periods and cities. Two short periods have been chosen, one in the early part of the century — 1816-20 — the other towards the end — 1871-75. The cities chosen were those with the largest populations: Montreal and Quebec City for the first period, Toronto, Montreal, Quebec City, and Halifax for the second.

Research lasted from 1978 to 1981 and was in two stages, corresponding to the two halves of the 19th century, and two separate draft reports were issued — one in 1980, the other in 1982 — hence the two-part presentation of this material.

Contexts differ greatly from one period to the other. Indeed, how could it be otherwise given the 50-year interval between the two periods, especially when there was an unprecedented wave of immigration to Canada, as well as the birth of the industrialization and urbanization of the country, during the intervening period. The myriad transformations that Canadian cities underwent during the 19th century, especially between 1820 and 1870, are not dwelt on at length. Such a summary would, at best, be imperfect given the present state of research. However, it might be worthwhile to recall certain facts that had definite impact on daily life in homes in those days and that consequently affected servants' living and working conditions.

One major factor was common to both periods: the large cities were characterized by the coexistence of two very different populations. One was stable, permanent; the other mobile, transient. This fact is of paramount importance because it was at the level of the domestic servant that these two populations touched within a common environment and on a daily basis. Another factor common to both periods was that the houses in which masters and domestics lived represented only a fraction of town dwellings and were among the best and most comfortable in a century when the great poverty and notorious filth of the cities was loudly deplored.

Many other aspects differ from one period to the other, such as the stricter discipline imposed in the second half of the century or the changed face of the urban classes following the massive influx of immigrants. However, it was mainly the changes in the houses themselves and in lifestyles that had the most impact on those in service. For instance, the advent of central heating and running water in prosperous houses in the second half of the century basically changed more than one domestic chore. It did not always follow that such tasks as washing, cleaning, etc., were made easier; on the contrary, in more than one house such technical innovations were accompanied by new standards of cleanliness that resulted in increased rather than decreased work. Other, more incidental factors also affected daily life, such as fashionable families' habit of dining later after 1850, which meant that servants' hours were considerably longer, often at the expense of the spare time that had been available to their counterparts at the beginning of the century.

Censuses were the most helpful of all the sources consulted, but I also analyzed wills, hiring contracts, inventories of deceased persons' goods and chattels, death registers, court records, prison registers, and countless other legal documents deposited in the archives. In addition, numerous private journals and family papers were researched, together with many plans of 19th-century houses. I studied, as well as various pictorial collections, exhibition and collection catalogues and many works on the art and artists of the period.[4]

I also delved into the literature of the period — Canadian, American, and European — in its various forms.[5] The numerous works published in the past few years in the United States, Great Britain, and France dealing with 19th-century women, children, families, society, crime, work, and urban problems have also been closely studied, and recently published books on domestic service in each of these countries permitted a comparison of particular conditions there with our own conditions.

Each source had inherent limitations and did not provide all I could have wished. For instance, whereas the 1871 census was carried out uniformly across the country — a very important factor when one attempts to compare one city with another — censuses at the beginning of the century were completely unstructured and only the one taken in Quebec City in 1818 could be analyzed on the basis of individual households. Likewise, although wills and house plans were carefully drawn up in all the cities, the same could not be said of other documents, and inventories of goods and chattels in Quebec City and Montreal were far superior to those in Toronto and Halifax. In addition, although death records were found for each city, only Montreal records give the deceased's occupation sufficiently uniformly for the purposes of the study. There were other disappointments, too. Although some 200 hiring contracts for servants exist for the period from 1816 to 1820, barely a dozen were found in the Quebec City and Montreal archives for 1871 to 1875, and not a single one was found for Toronto or Halifax. In addition, pictorial collections generally contained nothing but the caricatures, fashionable in certain newspapers after 1860, that held servants up to ridicule.

Furthermore, although reading the very many foreign literary works of the period proved useful, Canadian literature is practically non-existent before the 1830s. Yet it is usually literary sources that give the best indication of what service — and being a servant — entailed at a given time. Obviously, private writings, accounts of journeys, and newspaper articles remedy the situation to some extent, but they are too few for me to judge whether the perceptions they reveal were truly Canadian or simply followed the stereotyped lines of foreign literature (mainly British and French) highly esteemed in Canada at that time. The portrait of domestic service and servants afforded by documents in the early part of the century therefore differ somewhat from the portrait that appeared in print after 1840, and a true comparison of Canadian servants and their American and European counterparts has only been possible for the second half of the century.

Finally, the extent of the problem posed by the preconceived, stereotyped ideas surrounding domestic service cannot be stressed too highly. Authors all agree that each succeeding generation considered itself less well-served than the previous one and described its servants as being in urgent need of reform, or at least control. So although such errors in perceiving service may be easy to recognize, it is nevertheless these very sources that have to be used. In addition, there is an obvious time-warp for the 20th-century historian looking at 19th-century service: it is not only difficult, knowing conditions today, to appreciate the amount of time that had to be devoted to domestic tasks, but it is also highly dangerous to try to evaluate tasks' relative importance since some — waiting at the table, for instance — did not have the same connotation then as they do now.

Clearly the subject of domestic service is very complex. Trying to tackle it involves social, economic, legal, psychological, and every-day history. In fact, to paraphrase Guiral and Thuillier, it is a type of "crossroads" history.6 Obviously it has been impossible to answer all the questions raised during the course of this research. However, I have tried to assemble the essential elements that, from a restoration point of view, will help present as faithful an interpretation as possible of a historic house's past and the lives of all the people who dwelt in it.

PART ONE

1816 TO 1820

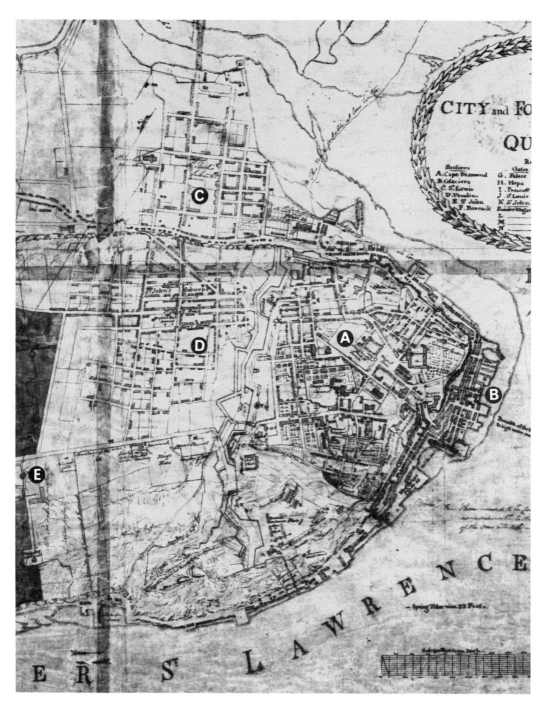

1 Quebec City in 1821.

A Upper Town   C Saint-Roch   E *Banlieue*
B Lower Town   D Upper Town *faubourgs*

INTRODUCTION

Arbitrarily choosing certain cities and periods was basically a way of being able to put a great variety of sources to use without taking a sampling as such. It also highlighted elements of domestic service that were constant or that changed over several decades.

Four cities first attracted my attention because their populations were decidedly larger than those of other Canadian cities in the first quarter of the century: Montreal (22 540 inhabitants in 1825),[1] Quebec City (18 626 in 1818),[2] Halifax (11 156 in 1816-17)[3] and St. John's, Newfoundland (10 000 in 1815).[4] However, as far as this research project is concerned, the value of the statistics available for the four cities varied greatly and documentation became the determining factor. A real series of hiring contracts, wills, and statements of goods and chattels[5] — documents essential to any study dealing with domestics — were only found in the Archives nationales du Québec. I therefore chose to focus on Montreal and Quebec City (see Figs. 1 and 2). In addition, they were the two largest cities at that time and the only ones that would reflect ethnic differences regarding service, if any existed, since both had fairly large English-speaking populations side by side with the French.[6]

A decision then had to be made on which period was reasonably representative of the early part of the century and 1816 to 1820 was selected. The Quebec City census taken in 1818 was to some extent responsible for this decision because it was the only one giving the occupations of all household workers, even though that of the head of the family was generally considered sufficient for census purposes at that time. The choice proved to be well-founded. The very first years of the century, which would have carried too much over from the 18th century, were thus avoided, as were the war years of 1812-14, which must have disrupted daily life. The 1820s marked the beginning of a highly eventful period politically, economically, socially, and culturally. For instance, 1822 witnessed the failure of the first plans for the union of the two Canadas, with all its attendant controversy,[7] and political agitation in Montreal and Quebec City in those years finally resulted in both cities gaining elected municipal administrations in the early 1830s.[8] On the economic side, large-scale construction projects were beginning to be undertaken — the Lachine Canal between 1821 and 1825, the Quebec City fortifications between 1820 and 1830[9] — and these must surely have offered many openings to a male labour force that until then had perhaps had to be content with going into

2 Montreal in 1825.

service. It was also the time when the urban middle class gained importance: in Montreal, for instance, it took over the development of the city and inaugurated the Committee of Trade in 1822.[10] On the social and cultural levels veritable upheavals were under way too. After 1820, massive immigration from the British Isles had an impact on society to an extent still not fully evaluated,[11] and domestic service was one of the areas most affected by the influx of abundant, cheap labour. The beginning of the decade also saw a flowering of literary pursuits: the inauguration of the Fabre Library in Montreal in 1823, the founding of the Literary and Historical Society of Quebec in 1824, the opening of the Theatre Royal in Montreal, and the publication of Michel Bibaud's *La Bibliothèque canadienne* in 1825. This was also the period when acts were passed creating schools that were under the control of the parish (1824) and schools that were under the control of the legislative assembly (1829), as well as when several classical colleges were founded: Sainte Thérèse and Chambly in 1826, Sainte Anne de la Pocatière in 1829.[12] These great events certainly affected domestic service as schooling became increasingly accessible. All in all, it was a hectic period and it is difficult to observe clearly what daily life must have been then. By comparison, the years 1816 to 20 appear relatively "ordinary"[13] and therefore better suited to a study of the "ordinary" lives of domestic servants — a moment to be seized considering that, just ten years later, it was gone forever under the invading floods of immigrants.

THE PEOPLE INVOLVED — AT THE BEGINNING OF THE CENTURY

The first problem encountered when trying to determine who was who in domestic service is one of vocabulary. Several French terms describe the various categories and the terms most frequently found in the documents consulted are *domestique* (domestic), *engagé* (hired hand), *fille* (girl), *garçon* (boy), *servante* (female servant), and *serviteur* (manservant).[1] These were used more or less interchangeably although there was a definite preference for the first term and the last two terms.

In English documents, however, usually only "servant" and "domestic servant" were used, although "menial servant" or "indoor servant" were occasionally found. The *Oxford English Dictionary* (1970) shades meanings very little: it defines a "domestic" as "a household servant or attendant," "boy" as "a servant," "girl" as a "maid-servant," and "servant" as "a person of either sex who is in the service of a master or mistress."

Reverting to French usage — since part of the documents consulted was in that language — it appears that the term "domestic" became narrower during the 19th century, whereas "hired hand" gained a very wide meaning. "Girl" and "female servant" remained more or less synonymous, as did "boy," "manservant," and "domestic." However, "female servant" came to be increasingly associated with household and menial work, whereas "boy" lost the connotation it had of being "the only servant and not wearing livery." Finally, "manservant" remained virtually the same and only Larousse distinguishes between this term and "domestic."

The documents consulted follow this usage to a great degree, even if in Canada one usually spoke of a domestic or servant, and the words could be used interchangeably within the same document. Only the provincial statutes are exceptions and there one can read "if he is a domestic or a servant."[2] In the same way, "boys" were not "the only servant"; in the Quebec City census, for example, they were almost always found in families where there was more than one domestic.[3] As for girls and female servants, it was impossible to determine whether or not they were at the very bottom of the scale. It would be reasonable to assume that a lone female servant in a household would have had to do all the work; however, a woman identified as the lone female servant may simply have been the lone live-in servant; she may not necessarily have been the only servant in a household. For example, rather than give his resident female servant the heavy work,

15

George Pozer, a merchant in Quebec City, employed a woman for the household chores and a handyman, neither of whom lived in his house. The servant residing in Pozer's house, therefore, perhaps only had light duties; indeed, her standing in the household is evident in her refusal to allow the other two servants to eat at her table.[4] This might have been the case in several other instances. Finally, "hired hand" was the term given the widest meaning in the documents consulted since it encompassed all the other terms and could also mean a labourer or journeyman.[5]

The term "lackey" was never encountered and "valet"[6] occurred only once in the documents consulted. The dictionaries define "lackey" as one who followed his master and wore his livery; because all evidence points to the fact that Canadians usually did not wear livery,[7] it is logical that "lackey" should not be found. "Valet," found just once in the census, referred to a 60-year-old manservant; this would be in line with the notation in Bescherelle's dictionary (1858) that the word had "already taken on an unfavourable meaning and is often replaced by domestic or manservant."[8] Therefore, in view of all the above, I have limited my usage to "domestic" and "servant" (male or female), alone or together, and the terms are used interchangeably.

Domestic Servants

The majority of the information on those engaged in domestic service came from two types of document: censuses and hiring contracts. Although there are limitations inherent in both, there are also interesting overlaps and each clarifies the other to some degree.

Two censuses are available for the first 25 years of the century: one taken in Quebec City in 1818,[9] the other in Montreal in 1825.[10] However, only Curé Signay's 1818 Quebec City census provides the names, ages, and addresses of servants as well as the names, ages, and occupations of their masters. Jacques Viger's 1825 Montreal census enumerated people by age group and civil status, giving no indication of whether or not the household had servants. However, I was able to use the conclusions reached by researchers investigating 19th-century Montreal society[11] after they analyzed Viger's data.

First, a few words on the method used by the parish priest, Curé Signay, in Quebec City. The census was taken by district: Saint-Roch, the *banlieue* (outskirts), the *faubourgs* (suburbs) of the Upper Town, the Lower Town, and the Upper Town itself. The priest visited each house and took a census of each Catholic household, indicating whether the master was an owner or tenant and noting the master's name, age, and occupation, his wife's name and age, and the names and ages of apprentices, clerks, hired hands, children, and any other relatives living in the household; he also included the names and ages of domestics — although sometimes leaving the latter at "3 domestics" — together with the names and ages of any other non-family residents included in the household. However, none of this information was given for Protestant families except when Catholics were living with them. Very often he would just write "a Protestant family," or perhaps "Smith, William, 6 children, 13 Protestants." Finally, he indicated the number of Catholics, communicants, and Protestants in every household.

It was very evident right from the beginning that handling such data would not be easy. On the one hand, there was no information on the Protestant households, and on the other, the occupations of the very high number of non-family residents listed with the families were given in only 40 per cent of cases. Given these problems, I decided to consider all categories likely to refer to people in service, including unidentified non-family residents. Only apprentices and clerks specifically identified as such were omitted. Even though they very often performed many servants' duties in households and stores, they were nonetheless considered as having separate status.[12] On the other hand, in order to respect Signay's somewhat vague vocabulary insofar as possible, I have referred to the categories overall as "domestic help" rather than "domestic servants." Moreover, in order to rectify, even to a minor degree, the absence of information on Protestant families, I added a "possibilities" category covering all households that most probably included servants. In most instances these were families known through earlier research;[13] in other cases they were families included in the census in the same way as William Smith's, mentioned above. Families were allocated the average number of domestics for their area of town (Table 7) although in the case of some men of importance, the resulting average is far below what their social standing would have allowed. Military personnel are a case in point. Even though we know from newspapers of the period that officers arriving with their families often brought three servants[14] with them, only 2.1 were allocated (the average for the Upper Town) to Major Cortlandt and two (the average for the *banlieue)* to Colonel Harvey, whose household nevertheless contained 16 people.

Hiring contracts were examined for Montreal and Quebec City from 1816 to 1820, and only those covering the hiring of menservants, female servants, or domestics were taken into account — 196 out of approximately 1500.[15] These documents confirmed that the decision to use all Signay's categories had been correct. Comparison of the names of 60 servants contracted in Quebec City between 1816 and 1818 with the names from the census verified that some servants had been included in the census without mention of their status. Of the 60 servants who contracted out in Quebec City between 1816 and 1818,

12 were named in the census: seven had been included after their employers' families but not identified as servants, two were shown as hired hands, another was under the "boy" category, and the remaining two were included with their own families rather than with their masters' households.

At first glance, a ratio of 12:60 for the two documents may seem small. But the contracts drawn up in 1816 and 1817 for 18 of the 23 adults were for periods of a year or less and their employment must already have ended when the census was taken. Too, the parties to 19 of the 60 contracts were English-speaking, and since the priest gave no details about Protestant families, it is possible these domestics were in the service of such families and consequently untraceable. Also, five contracts dating from the autumn of 1818 could have been finalized after the census. In other words, only six contracts out of 60 cannot be accounted for, and it is conceivable that some omissions crept into Signay's records.

Who were the domestic servants at the beginning of the 19th century? To come to grips with this question, all the information gleaned from the census and the hiring contracts was tabulated in the hope that, upon comparing the tables, various trends would emerge. Obviously the tables can only serve as guides and are subject to all the weaknesses inherent in the source documents. The 1818 census had to be considered separately from the hiring contracts because neither the census nor the contracts were organized in a way that facilitated grouping the data they contain.

Table 1

Domestic Help in Quebec City, 1818

| | Total Help | Domestic Help of Known Age and Sex | | | | | |
		Total	Men	Women	Average Age Men	Average Age Women	Average Age M and W
Servants	220	27	10	17	27.5	36.2	32.8
Hired hands	183	168	81	87	22.8	24.9	23.9
Non-identified help	783	710	367	343	21.4	24.4	22.7
Possibilities (Protestant families)	169						
Total	1355	905	458	447			
Average					21.7	24.9	23.3
Percentage	100	68.8	50.6	49.4			

Joseph Signay, *Recensement de la ville de Québec en 1818*, preface by H. Provost (Quebec: Société historique de Québec, 1976).

A few comments are in order concerning Table 1. Sixty-seven boys and 65 girls were under 16 years of age (average 12.4), whereas 24 men and 53 women were over 40 (average 51.4 years). If percentages were based only on the total of the known domestic help — those whose names and ages were known — domestics under 16 would account for 14.5 per cent and those over 40 for 8.5 per cent, whereas the figures would be 11.1 per cent and 5.6 per cent if they were taken on the overall total.[16]

Generally speaking, domestic help appears to have been fairly young — 23.3 years old on average — and divided equally between men and women, 50.6 per cent and 49.4 per cent respectively. But does this reflect the true state of affairs? Viger's 1825 Montreal census shows that the proportion was closer to one-third versus two-thirds in favour of the women,[17] but some women might have been included in more than one place due to their great mobility. And this same mobility might equally well have induced Signay in Quebec City to omit women from his census — which would explain why we only have the names of 27 domestic servants out of 220, most of the others, perhaps women, being shown as "x domestics." That those identified as domestics were generally much older than the others could also be due to the same reason — the priest only included those who had been or were to be with the family for a long time. Along the same lines, the number of male servants in Quebec City might have been inflated by the unidentified help category, which could have included a certain number of apprentices and clerks. John Hare, who has worked for a considerable time on Quebec City, observed that the city's age-pyramid at the beginning of the century was completely different from that for the rest of Lower Canada for women between 18 and 25 years of age due to obvious over-representation.[18] This factor might perhaps have been due to the presence of numerous female servants who seem to have been overlooked in the priest's census. It is also possible that the seven-year gap separating the two censuses is very significant, and that the 1820s coincided with an increase in the number of women entering domestic service, a fact observed elsewhere since the turn of the century.[19]

The contracts also confirm the fact that a number of female domestics had been omitted from the documentation. Out of a total of 196 hirings for the two cities, only 21 cover women; ten of those women were hired together with their husbands, and four others had just arrived from Europe (Table 2).

Table 2

Domestic Servants Hired Under Contract, 1816-1820

	Total	Men	Women	Same Town	Other Town	Rural	Europe
					Origin		
Montreal							
Children	66	25	41	57	0	7	2
Adults	43	37	6	32	0	3	8
Total	109	62	47	89	0	10	10
Quebec City							
Children	46	20	26	34	3	8	1
Adults	41	26	15	26	1	1	13
Total	87	46	41	60	4	9	14
General							
Children	112	45	67	91	3	15	3
Adults	84	63	21	58	1	4	21
Total	196	108	88	149	4	19	24
Percentage	100	55	45	76	2	10	12

ANQ-M and ANQ-Q (see "Abbreviations Used"), notaries' records and hiring contracts, 1816-20.

The average age of children hired under contract was between 11 and 12 years, and 24 were aged nine or under; however, most children (14) were hired at 12, 13, and 14 years of age. Given these facts and taking into account the few adult women (21) hired under contract, the most interesting aspects of Table 2 are the details of origin, whether the servant came from the same city as his master, from the countryside, or from Europe. The table shows that 76 per cent of our 196 domestics came from the same city as their masters, and moreover, that they were often hired in the part of town in which they lived, in contrast to what was occurring at that time in France and England where, according to various authors, servants usually came from the countryside.[20]

Death records in Montreal for the period 1816-20 support these data since they also show that 76 per cent of domestic servants came from the city.[21] It may therefore be assumed that servants here did not suffer the same dislocation observed elsewhere, and that since children in service were not far from their families, contact could be maintained. It is possible that at the beginning of the century a good number of domestics in Canada were city dwellers who did not have any of the difficulties country people experienced when they came to search for work in town.

Generally speaking, servants' social origins were fairly humble. According to the contracts, 91 of 196 domestics (nearly half) came from labourers' families and 40 (20 per cent) from those of tradesmen. In six cases children under the guardianship of their uncles were put into service; three of the children came from professional families and the others from merchant families. For the remainder, or about a third of domestics, there are no details. It also seems, based on the contracts, that young children were only put into service when their families could not provide for them. For the majority of domestics, young people in their early twenties, entering service was probably the only way to accumulate a small nest-egg before getting married, and some of them also contributed to the upkeep of their families. As far as the older servants are concerned, they would probably have left

Table 3

Servants' Ability to Sign Based on
Contracts, 1816–1820

	Contracts	Signatures	Signatures (%)
Montreal			
Children	66	32	48.5
Adults	43	12	27.9
Total	109	44	40.4
Quebec City			
Children	46	23	50.0
Adults	41	15	36.6
Total	87	38	43.8
General			
Children	112	55	49.1
Adults	84	27	32.1
Total	196	82	41.8

ANQ-M and ANQ-Q, notaries' records and hiring contracts, 1816-20.

service if they could have found another means of earning their living. All in all, it is impossible to know whether the details on social origins found in the contracts reflect the true situation or whether they are greatly understated.

A similar problem occurs with servants' ability to sign their names. The contracts are the only means of knowing this, and on that basis, 42 per cent of domestics — or parents — knew how to sign (Table 3). Taking the two cities separately, a higher percentage of people in Quebec City were able to sign than in Montreal, 43 per cent versus 40 per cent. The general total, however, requires some clarification because percentages do not take ethnic differences into account and these were very clear cut. The contract was drawn up in the language of the domestic servant who, de facto, was nearly always hired by a master speaking the same language. In Montreal, for example, 51 of the 59 contracts drawn up in French covered Franco-phones and 49 of the 50 contracts drawn up in English were entered

Table 4

Masters' Occupations in Quebec City and Montreal, 1816-1820

	Based on Census		Based on Contracts	
	Masters	%	Masters	%
Commerce	134	21.5	34	21.3
Transport	47	7.5	3	1.9
Manufacturing	99	15.8	17	10.6
Construction	83	13.3	4	2.5
Professionals	39	6.2	25	15.6
Services	8	1.3	10	6.2
Civil servants	20	3.2	9	5.6
Agriculture	8	1.3	5	3.1
Various "bourgeois"	9	1.4	23	14.4
Various "workers"	31	5.0	-	-
Unknown	147	23.5	30	18.8
Total	625	100.0	160	100.0

Joseph Signay, *Recensement de la ville de Québec en 1818*, preface by H. Provost (Quebec: Société historique de Québec, 1976); ANQ-M and ANQ-Q, notaries' records and hiring contracts, 1816-20.

into by two Anglophones. The remaining nine were drawn up in the domestic's language. Judging by the appearance of the names, it seems that 77 per cent of Anglophone parents signed as against 23 per cent of Francophones. In Quebec City the ratio was 64 per cent to 42 per cent. The difference is even more marked for adults: 50 per cent of Anglophone Montrealers signed compared with five per cent of Francophones, whereas in Quebec City the ratio was 35 per cent to 21 per cent. If it is true that 42 per cent of domestics or their parents knew how to sign, the signing group comprised almost three Anglophones for every Francophone.

Masters

The 1818 census and the contracts provide a number of details on whom domestic servants worked for and where they were likely to be found in the cities. It was possible to group masters according to occupation, age, and household. When drawing up tables covering occupations, I referred to the work of the team of historians studying Montreal and used the same categories as they did in their analysis of professional structures found in the city in 1825[22] (Table 4). Our Quebec City parish priest, whose census shows that 625 households had domestic help of some kind, only specified the head of the household's occupation in 75 per cent of cases and only rarely gave details about the heads of Protestant families. In an attempt to determine the relative importance of the occupations according to both the census and the contracts, their respective percentages have been compared in Table 4.

Comparing the two types of document brings various interesting features to light. The first is the number of people involved in commerce (which, of necessity must be interpreted fairly broadly and must be understood to include wholesalers, merchants, small shop-keepers, etc.). The second feature concerns the professional and various middle-class families that appeared proportionally far more frequently in the contracts than in the census. Does this mean that, due to their profession or standing in the community, they were more likely to enter into contracts, or was it simply that they clearly had more servants than other families, all things being equal? The reverse question could be asked concerning the transport, manufacturing, and construction trades, which appeared far less frequently in the contracts. The distribution of different types of domestic help in Quebec City in 1818 according to their masters' professions (Table 5) clearly indicates that professionals and middle-class families employed a good proportion of the servants identified as such. Although they repre-

Table 5

Average Distribution of Domestic Help Based on
Masters' Occupations, Quebec City, 1818

	Servants	Hired Hands	Unidentified Help	Total Help
Commerce	28.2	29.3	22.2	23.7
Transportation	0.5	4.1	7.2	5.5
Manufacturing	2.0	19.3	19.1	17.9
Construction	-	6.4	11.9	9.9
Professionals	15.8	6.4	5.3	6.7
Services	0.5	2.9	1.9	1.7
Civil servants	17.3	-	3.1	4.6
Agriculture	-	3.5	1.6	1.4
Various "bourgeois"	12.9	-	1.6	3.0
Various "workers"	0.5	1.2	4.0	2.7
Unknown	22.3	26.9	22.1	22.9
Total	100.0	100.0	100.0	100.0

Joseph Signay, *Recensement de la ville de Québec en 1818,* preface by H. Provost (Quebec: Société historique de Québec, 1976).

sented 6.2 and 1.4 per cent of masters (Table 4), they actually accounted for more than a quarter of those the curé identified as servants; that is, 15.8 per cent and 12.9 per cent respectively. In addition, while 3.6 per cent of masters came from the tradesmen category (transport, manufacturing, and construction; Table 4), they only employed 2.5 per cent of the census-identified servants overall (Table 5). However, if domestic help is considered as a whole (Table 4), the distribution seems to correspond fairly closely to that of masters in the 1818 census (Table 5). It is impossible to judge whether certain people were more likely to want the guarantees inherent in a contract than others because only the 196 contracts covering urban domestics have been analyzed.

The census also provides interesting information on masters. We know their ages, the number of people in their households, the extent of the domestic help employed, and whether they were owners or tenants of the houses in which they lived. However, this last element is not really very significant because a master could easily rent one

Table 6

Households with Servants, Quebec City, 1818

	Average No. Domestic Help	Average Age Master	Percent. Masters/ Owners	Percent. Masters/ Tenants	People in House
Domestics	2.1	50.9	62.6	37.4	4.5
Hired hands	1.6	42.9	68.9	31.1	5.2
Unidentified help	1.6	41.6	61.5	38.5	4.8
Total:					
Average	1.8	42.2			4.8
Percentage			62.0	38.0	

Joseph Signay, *Recensement de la ville de Québec en 1818*, preface by H. Provost (Quebec: Société historique de Québec, 1976).

house and own several others, or alternatively, prefer to rent because it would be impracticable to do otherwise, as in the case of military personnel who usually had no idea how long their postings might be. These various elements are compiled in Table 6 (the average number of people per household does not include the average number of domestics in column 1).

Study of the data seems to show that families with domestic help of some sort were fairly well established. As a general rule, such a master owned his house, was in his early forties, and counted five or so people in his household. Only the masters of "domestics" did not conform to these guidelines for they were much older than the average. This, however, comes back to the specific use of the term "domestics" and the possibility that Signay only used this term in his census for those who had been or would be with a family for a long time. Families that had been established for some time could no doubt employ domestic help on a permanent basis, or alternatively, the master's advanced age led him to ensure he was continuously served by one or several domestics.

Distribution by district is also most interesting (see Table 7). One of the first observations was the concentration of domestic help in the oldest parts of the city — the Upper and Lower Towns. In fact, 62 per cent of domestic help worked in areas containing approximately 41 per cent of the city's population.[23] Indeed, 85 per cent of "domestics" (186 out of 220) lived in these two areas, 65 per cent of them in the Upper Town. This must have affected these servants'

Table 7

Domestic Help by District, Quebec City, 1818

	St-Roch	Banlieue	Faubourgs Upper Town	Lower Town	Upper Town	Total
Domestics	6	23	5	43	143	220
Hired hands	48	30	17	35	53	183
Unidentified help	130	28	161	180	284	783
Total	184	81	183	258	480	1186
Percentage of domestic help	15.5	6.8	15.4	21.8	40.5	100.0
Average no. per household	1.6	2.0	1.4	1.7	2.1	1.8
Percentage of population	28.0	6.3	24.1	19.7	21.9	100.0

Joseph Signay, *Recensement de la ville de Québec en 1818*, preface by H. Provost Quebec: Société historique de Québec, 1976).

social lives when the small area covered by the Upper Town and the numerous daily errands each performed are taken into account (see Fig. 1).

Another point worthy of note is the average number of servants per household. The average was 1.8 servants per household, which is the same as the figure for England and very close to the figure for France (1.5) around the middle of the century.[24] Along the same lines, of the 34 cases that Judge Sewell reported in accounts of trials he had heard in Quebec City between 1808 and 1820 — that is, in the 34 houses where crimes took place — 61 servants were mentioned, either as the accused or as witnesses, which also results in a figure of 1.8 servants per household.[25] However, only 20 or so households were found with five or more servants, which means that a good many households had only one live-in servant. The census shows this to be true in about 60 per cent of cases. The same phenomenon was observed almost everywhere[26] and these single domestic servants were usually women; only when a family had the wherewithal to hire several domestics did anyone think of hiring a man.[27]

The remaining factor is the number of heads of households who could consider hiring domestics. In Quebec City the figure was one in five. This is the average obtained if the minimum 84 households likely to have had domestic help are added to the 625 heads of household that did have such help, Signay having canvassed 3730 households in all. This figure is corroborated by Luce Vermette's analysis of *donations inter vivos* recorded in the Quebec City and Montreal areas between 1800 and 1820: one donor in six specified, in a notarized document, that the recipient of the gift would guarantee him the services of a domestic whenever requested.[28] This figure is comparable to that observed elsewhere: for example, McBride estimated that in France one family in six had domestics at that time.[29] The 20-per-cent figure for Quebec City therefore seems very plausible for the beginning of the 19th century, especially when one considers that the city was then the seat of government and therefore was home to a good number of family heads in important positions. It was also the headquarters of the British army and consequently most of the senior officers in the country were stationed there.

This study therefore deals with two very distinct social groups. On the one hand we have the domestic servants, almost entirely young men and women from generally humble backgrounds. For most of them this type of work was only the transition from childhood to adult life, and they are estimated to have accounted for approximately eight per cent of the population — this is the figure for both Montreal (based on Viger's statistics of 8.6 per cent) and Quebec City (Signay's data, 8.2 per cent).[30] On the other hand we have the masters, a minority of families (one out of five), but among the most affluent people and almost all belonging to the professional or business classes.

What was the relationship between these two groups? What rules governed them? What impact did such coexistence have on them and, in a ripple effect, on the society of the day? These questions formed the basis of this study.

DOMESTIC SERVICE

Domestic service may be one of our oldest institutions but that does not prevent it from being one of the least known. Servants have never attracted attention and have always been considered "part of the furniture," or by the very nature of their calling, inferior beings not worthy of interest. This, at least, is the attitude many authors reported in studies on slavery, service, or minorities.[1] Our contemporary perception of service no doubt also plays a large role in this lack of appreciation.[2] How, for example, can we conceive the amount of time required to brush and clean clothes at a time when washing clothes took several days and only happened a few times a year? Or how can we have any idea of the time required each day to run errands in an era without modern conveniences? And how can we judge the individual importance of each of these tasks and the places they occupied in the servants' world? This poses a real problem that may well remain unresolved due to the limited sources available and our distorted perception. On this point Philippe Ariès' excellent book mentions that it was the son of the family who waited at the table and that it was not sufficient "if one wished to appear well brought up to know one's table manners, as it is today: one also had to know how to wait at the table."[3] Despite all these restrictions, a good deal of information on domestic service was documented and it has been possible to gather data on hiring domestic servants, types and lengths of service, the rights and duties involved, and the resulting advantages and disadvantages.

Hiring

How did one find "a situation" at the beginning of the 19th century? How did one find a domestic servant? It seems fairly certain that the most popular method was by word of mouth. In towns with several thousand inhabitants, where the wealthiest mainly lived in the centre of the town, it must have been just as easy to know who required servants as to know which servants were about to leave whose employ. The market square played a vital role, since everyone met everyone else there and employment could thus be solicited or offered (see Figs. 3 and 8). There do not seem to have been hiring fairs in

3 Quebec City marketplace, 1829.

Montreal and Quebec City as there were in France and England, nor such events as auctioning the poor, which occurred in New Brunswick in that period.

Most of the time domestic servants applied for employment in person. Sometimes they offered their services to a previous employer, a relative, or someone already employing a relative (11 per cent of domestic help in Quebec City in 1818 was related).[4] Occasionally some would stop off at a house to ask for food or to warm themselves and would never leave again, as happened in the Roquebrune family.[5]

Masters sometimes made arrangements for people to come from the Old Country. Enquiries were also made of the religious orders who looked after orphans, for orphans were usually put into service once they reached adolescence. Servants could also be enticed away from neighbours by cunning or promises. And both parties had recourse to advertisements in the newspapers[6] and the hiring or placement agencies that appeared in Quebec City in 1818 and in Montreal two years later.

I was able to trace some 200 newspaper advertisements for domestic positions: 44 per cent were placed by the servants themselves and 56 per cent were placed by families seeking help. Did demand then exceed supply? Some people thought so. Dalhousie, for instance, wrote in his journal in 1819, "they suffer inconvenience from want of servants."[7] In addition, it seems unlikely that people would try to poach other people's servants if they had been in good supply. However, the higher number of masters' requests might simply mean that, since they were better educated, employers were more likely to resort to advertisements than servants were. Advertisements provide a wealth of information because, although they often went no further than offering or seeking a position of "manservant" or "female servant," in most cases (69 per cent of those seeking, 58 per cent of those offering) the type of employment was specified (see Fig. 4). For women, the position of cook most commonly recurred, whereas for men the most common position was that of a groom who could also wait at the table. Interestingly, 35 per cent of the offers were for men and 65 per cent for women — ratios reminiscent of the one-third/two-thirds mentioned in the preceding chapter. Nearly all the advertisements mentioned references: on the one hand, that they could be provided, and on the other, that no one would be considered without them. After hiring and employment agencies opened in the two cities, far fewer advertisements appeared, no doubt because the placement service was used with increasing frequency. Its purpose was to provide information, judging by the following example that appeared in the *Montreal Herald* on 4 March 1820:

> A Register is opened by Mr. Gilchrist at the Montreal Repository, St. Antoine Street, in which will be enrolled the names of all persons in want of employment as Household Servants, Labourers and Tradesmen and all who may be desirous to engage servants of any description are requested to apply to Mr. Gilchrist who will furnish them with every information in his power with respect to the character and qualification of such [sic] apply to him in order to obtain employment.[8]

Servants had no training as such, simply experience acquired during previous employment. Schools in which they were taught how to take care of household matters were still far in the future.

Types and Length of Service

An easy answer to the question of what domestic work entailed would be "Everything." The domestic had to "serve his said master

La Gazette de Québec/
The Quebec Gazette

1 May 1817
Small family in the Upper Town requires a maidservant to perform Cooking and other Household chores. References required. Apply through the Publisher of this newspaper. [Translation]

30 October 1817
Temperate middle-aged Manservant wanted. Must be accustomed to serving a small family, waiting at the table, and performing regular chores; will have a Garden to maintain and cow to tend. A certificate from his previous Employer attesting to his good character over twelvemonths must be produced. Apply at this Printing house (preference will be given to a Canadien). [Translation]

24 February 1820
Wants a situation — A Young Man, a Native of England, would wish to engage either as in or outdoor Servant with a Single Gentleman or in a Family. Can produce a good character from his last place. Apply at this office.

La Gazette de Montréal/
The Montreal Gazette

12 September 1816
Manservant wanted, capable of waiting at the Table and caring for a pair of horses. Apply at this Printing house. [Translation]

The Quebec Mercury

24 June 1817
A Female Servant wants a Situation
A Middle Age Woman just arrived from Dublin where she served in some of the most respectable families wants an eligible Service — she is capable of acting as a cook, housekeeper, house maid, laundry maid or dairy maid, is perfectly conversant with milk and butter, the latter she can make in a superior stile, she has no objection to Town or Country.

26 January 1819
Situation Wanted
A Young Woman wishing to engage herself with any respectable family as Cook or House Maid, she can produce certificates of recommendation.

The Montreal Herald

23 March 1816
Situation Wanted
A man and his wife, one as a Groom or house servant, the other as a cook. Satisfactory recommendations can be produced. Apply to Mr. Robert McNabb recollet suburb or to the printer.

29 November 1817
Wanted in a small family where only one servant is kept a steady woman who understands PLAIN COOKING And can produce a good character from her last place. Enquire at this office.

4 Typical domestic servant job advertisements in Quebec City and Montreal newspapers between 1816 and 1820.

diligently and faithfully, keep his secrets and lawful commands" (see standard contract, Appendix A). For women servants who worked alone, and this was the case in about 60 per cent of families, this meant the upkeep of the house, responsibility for the kitchen, and looking after the kitchen garden and sometimes the children too. In houses with two or three servants, work became a question of specialty or sex. There was usually a cook, a female servant who did the housework, and a manservant who drove the carriage, looked after the outside work (wood, animals, kitchen garden), and also handled the task of waiting at the table. In households with many servants, in addition to the male or female staff serving the master, mistress, and children, a housekeeper or head servant was usually responsible for managing household affairs and supervising the lower echelons.

Few documents give any details of the work of the different servants, most likely because everyone knew what was expected of them. Even the hiring contracts, which by their very nature should have defined such duties, contain no information except very occasionally. In such cases we find that the person had to "wait on the table, polish the knives, forks, shoes ... tend the horses, cows, drive the carriages, saw wood, run errands...." Or they had to cart manure in summer and snow in winter. One small girl had to look after her mistress's linen and another had to "help her mistress with routine household duties thrice weekly."[9] Domestics working for artisans sometimes had to sell wares in the streets of the city and suburbs.[10] As valuable as this information is, it gives no idea of all the work a servant was required to perform in those days. For instance, there is no mention of fires to light and stoke; water, wood, and garbage to be carried; floors to be scrubbed; washing and ironing to be done. The sources have not a single word to say on this subject.

More information is available on the duration of the contracts signed. As a general rule, a servant hired out by the month and changed employment frequently. All authors have noted this fact: servants remained in the same position rarely longer than a month, "they are dismissed just as easily as they give notice," or they remained in one place just long enough to get used to it.[11] Certainly the documents bear out such statements, and in the regulations for the Montreal police in 1817 one can read: "all domestic servants ... hired for a month or a shorter or longer period...."[12] Trial reports include the evidence of more than one servant along the lines of "in the month of July I was in service with...."[13] In this respect the report of Susannah Davis's trial (see Appendix B) is most revealing. If we exclude the four years spent with her first employer when she was scarcely adolescent, in just under three years — when she was 15, 16, and 17 — this young woman served in nine houses, averaging slightly more than three months in each position. One can learn the employers' points of view from an amusing account of the tribulations

Table 8

Average Duration (in Years) of Contracts, Executed 1816-1820

	Men	Women	Average
Montreal			
Children	5.3	7.3	6.5
Adults	1.5	0.8	1.2
Quebec City			
Children	7.2	9.0	8.2
Adults	1.3	1.7	1.4
Total			
Children	6.1	7.9	7.2
Adults	1.4	1.4	1.4

ANQ-M and ANQ-Q, notaries' records and hiring contracts, 1816-20.

suffered by a Mrs. Packard, an American, when hiring domestic servants.[14] Much to-ing and fro-ing took place in the lives of Susannah Davis and Mrs. Packard, and this seems to be one of the main features of domestic service at that time.

Contracts, however, were exceptions to the rule, which was no doubt precisely why they existed. They were drawn up so that both parties would be sure the employment would last longer than a few months. In fact, adults who contracted out their services did so for slightly more than a year, whereas children were hired for seven years on average (Table 8).

It also seems clear that the terms of the contracts were respected. Of the 196 analyzed, only 22 were terminated early — which agrees with the ratio Hardy and Ruddel noted for artisans.[15] In our documents only two reasons for cancelling a contract are given: marriage and desertion.[16] When it was cancelled gives us no further information since it could occur from several days to five years after the contract was signed.

On the other hand, in his study of Montreal apprentices, Audet found several reasons for contract cancellations. Eighty-five out of 114 contracts were terminated without reasons being given, but 12 were ended because parents bought back their children's time; five because of illness, accident, or insanity; four because of disagreements; three because the apprentice had damaged the master's property; two because the apprentice had requested his release; one because he was absent without permission; one because he was returning to Quebec City; and one because he could fend for himself.[17] In many cases Hardy and Ruddel also had difficulty determining the exact causes of cancellations; however, they found some instances of mistreatment, accidents, or dissatisfaction either on the master's or the apprentice's part.[18] Such reasons would equally apply to domestic servants. Perhaps to avoid such problems, people preferred to hire by the month on the basis of verbal agreements.

Rights and Duties

Hiring contracts provide the greatest source of information on servants' rights and duties. However, the part of the form that refers to their duties was designed to be so general and all-encompassing that it totally lacks precision. Thus, a domestic servant should be loyal, diligent, hard-working, and obedient; he should not absent himself without permission nor cause harm to his master nor allow it to be caused; in addition he should refrain from drinking and gambling. Some contracts hold valuable information such as the stipulation that the servant must accompany the family if it moved; sometimes "within this province" was stated, sometimes "in Upper Canada," and one contract even specifies "in whatever country [the masters] may go and decide to fix their residence."[19] Several masters took care to include this clause because they were forbidden by law to take a servant outside the district in which he or she had been employed unless they had a previous agreement to that effect.

Other contracts give information on the days and hours of work. In one case a young boy was required to work six days a week from five in the morning to six at night. In another, a girl of 14 was to work until nine at night in the winter and seven in the summer. And in yet a third case the domestic had to serve "by day and by night at such hours as shall be directed and made known to him."[20] Do such clauses give an idea of a servant's normal working hours, or are they rather the exceptions? The second possibility seems more likely. In fact, it seems rather unusual that, on the one hand, a servant's work would finish as early as six or seven and that, on the other, it would be as demanding as in the third example. In general, servants were most likely on call 15 hours or so a day, as was the case elsewhere.

Some contracts also contain negative clauses that are very revealing. For example, servants were not entitled to marry before

35

Table 9

Master's Obligations to Servant Based on Contracts, 1816-1820

	Total number of contracts	Act as parents	Regard to sex/age	Lodge	Feed	Clothe	Wash	Mend	Upkeep	Heat and light	Religious observ.	1st Communion	Tend if sick	Teach to read	Teach to write
Montreal															
Children	66	11	8	66	66	59	34	15	27	-	23	17	26	19	17
Adults	43	-	-	37	37	3	8	2	-	7	1	-	1	-	-
Total	109	11	8	103	103	62	42	17	27	7	24	17	27	19	17
Quebec City															
Children	46	13	7	46	46	41	8	5	24	-	21	14	8	5	4
Adults	41	-	-	36	33	2	2	2	-	7	-	-	1	-	-
Total	87	13	7	82	79	43	10	7	24	7	21	14	9	5	4
Total															
Children	112	24	15	112	112	100	42	20	51	-	44	31	34	24	21
Adults	84	-	-	73	70	5	10	4	-	14	1	-	2	-	-
Total	196			185	182	105	52	24			45		36		
Percentage		21	13	94	93	54	27	12	46	17	23	28	18	21	19

ANQ-M and ANQ-Q, notaries' records and hiring contracts, 1816-20.

the end of their contracts, nor could they go out without permission or have visitors "neither in the house nor in the stable."[21] A servant's duties seem to have been onerous and restrictive, demanding total and absolute availability.

And what could the servant expect in return? The contracts are far more explicit in this area (Table 9). Certain clauses, concerning board and lodging for example, were included in nearly every contract. They were included in all children's contracts and were found in 87 per cent (lodging) and 83 per cent (board) respectively of adult contracts (73 and 70 contracts out of 84). Another striking point is that all the other clauses, except for those covering heating, lighting, washing, and mending, almost exclusively concerned children. For instance, a clothing clause was included in 89 per cent of the children's contracts (100 out of 112) compared with six per cent of adult contracts (five out of 84). Such provision was always qualified by something like "appropriate for a servant" or "in keeping with his condition," but such expressions were very common at the time.

In addition, only in childrens' contracts were masters requested to act as responsible parents and have regard to their servants' age or sex or both. Twenty-eight per cent of children's contracts specify that the child should take first communion, 21 per cent that the child

36

Table 10

Methods of Paying Servants, 1816-1820

	Total No. of Contracts	Payment In				Payment By/On			
		Money	Goods	Money & Gds	Total	Month	Year	Departure	Total
Montreal									
Children	66	16	9	4	29	6	6	17	29
Adults	43	39	0	3	42	27	15	0	42
Total	109	55	9	7	71	33	21	17	71
Quebec City									
Children	46	11	2	0	13	3	6	4	13
Adults	41	38	0	0	38	11	26	1	38
Total	87	49	2	0	51	14	32	5	51
General									
Children	112	27	11	4	42	9	12	21	42
Adults	84	77	0	3	80	38	41	1	80
Total	196	104	11	7	122	47	53	22	122

ANQ-M and ANQ-Q, notaries' records and hiring contracts, 1816-20.

should learn to read, and 19 per cent that the child should learn to write. And sometimes contracts also stipulate that the child should be "maintained"; that is, a master was not only to provide the child's basic clothes, but also see to shoes, caps, and bonnets.

Were so many of these provisions omitted from adult contracts on purpose or were such matters covered by convention or tacit agreement so that the majority of the contracting parties did not feel it necessary for such provisions to be written into the contract? For example, that the master had to provide heat and light for the servants was only specified in a few cases. Does it therefore follow that the vast majority of servants did without both or was it a matter of accepted usage? In the same vein, what of the clause covering care in case of illness?[22] Since such care is indicated in only 18 per cent of cases, should we assume that the majority of servants were dismissed if they fell ill? As people were usually very specific about money matters and expenses in those days, one is more inclined to think that masters had certain customary obligations towards their servants that were known to everybody, and so there was no great concern about them always appearing in the written agreements. However, if such were not the case, analysis of the contracts seems to show that servants did not hope for much from their masters because the latter's obligations almost exclusively concerned food and lodging, even if "maintenance" was also included for children. This last item was usually replaced by a monthly or yearly wage in adults' contracts. However, this does not mean that children were never paid: a few were paid in money or goods, often when their contracts came to an end (Table 10).

Table 10 shows that 44 per cent of children were paid in Montreal (29 out of 66) and 28 per cent in Quebec City (13 out of 46), and half of the children received these payments upon leaving their employment. The amount was usually around £15 for boys and £10 for girls. When payment was in goods, it nearly always involved new Sunday clothing (ten out of 11 cases); in three instances a second outfit was included for weekdays. The eleventh contract stipulates that payment consisted of 50 acres that the master would give the hired child's father straight away.[23]

As far as adults were concerned, payment of wages appears to have been generally accepted because they were paid in 95 per cent of cases (80 out of 84). In half of these, payment was monthly. When the salary was an annual one, it was sometimes paid as and when the servant had need of it, or alternatively, in four equal instalments. In Table 11, wages are expressed as current pounds sterling — some were paid in pounds sterling, others in French *livres* or Spanish piasters — and expressed as rates per annum. In addition, I have divided the adults into four types: single men, single women, men and women hired as a couple — there were seven in Quebec City and three in Montreal — and finally, men who did double duty, such as gardener-cum-servant, coachman- or cook-cum-servant. Not surprisingly, the wage paid a couple was less than that paid a single man who filled two positions: couples often had a young child who was also given bed and board.

Whether these wages were acceptable for the time is difficult to say, but the impression is that they were fairly good. Women's wages fit in very well with the norm for England around 1825;[24] men's wages compare rather favourably with those of other workers since, according to the *Gazette du Québec* published on 31 December 1818, the wage for a boy working in a hospital was £25 per year (there is no indication whether board and lodging were included). Likewise, at the Forges du Saint-Maurice a labourer earned £42 per year in 1818 and also had to provide for his family.[25] All things considered, servants in Montreal and Quebec City — at least the men — had no reason to complain about their wages when they were compared to other workers' or labourers' wages at the time.

Nothing is specified in the contracts about servants' days off except in the case of James McCanna, a gardener-cum-servant in 1820, who was to remain at the house every other Sunday in order to perform work that might be required of him, meaning he had alternate Sundays off.[26] It seems unlikely that this was a common arrangement

38

Table 11

Servants' Average Annual Salaries,*
1816-1820

	Montreal	Quebec City	Range
Single men	20.5	19.6	12.5 - 30
Single women	9.5	9.4	4.5 - 18
Couples	38.0	38.0	23.0 - 45
Men with dual duties	39.4	39.4	31.0 - 66

* In current pounds (Halifax rate).
ANQ-M and ANQ-Q, notaries' records and hiring contracts, 1816-20.

because pains had been taken to specifically include it in the contract. Servants no doubt had an hour or two on Sunday mornings and holidays to attend divine service, but not all may have been entitled to this. Some might also have had a few hours free during an afternoon once a week or once every two weeks, but no documents mention this.

Advantages and Disadvantages

When one considers the multitude of tasks awaiting a servant, the constant attendance demanded, and the insecurity inherent in the position as well as the loneliness the majority most likely experienced and the little liberty they enjoyed, one can wonder why they would hire out as servants, or alternatively, put their own children into service. Advantages had to outweigh disadvantages.

One advantage was that domestic service represented a type of social assistance or security. At the beginning of the 19th century, poverty was the lot of many. Indeed, it was not unusual to read in the newspapers of a family found dead from hunger and cold in the hovel that was their home.[27] It is therefore easy to understand why being in service was desirable: board, lodging, and upkeep were assured. More than one child's contract, in fact, states that the family could not provide for his or her needs, especially when the mother was alone. Sending a child into domestic service meant sending it into security and ensuring its survival. Many also must have found being in service beneficial since masters were nearly always professional men or merchants. For example, a youngster aged 15 was employed for five years by a merchant who undertook to teach him to read and write "until he be able to take down the auction accounts and keep records of them, in which case he will be relieved of servant's duties and henceforth only be employed in the store running errands, keeping and recording accounts."[28] He was perhaps not the only one to be so fortunate. The same considerations applied to older servants, usually widows or widowers. Being in service afforded them the protection and means of survival that their families could not provide.

The majority of servants, usually young people, enjoyed an additional advantage: since board and lodging were assured, it was easier for them to save towards the time when they could set up on their own than it was for labourers or other workers their age who had to provide for all their wants as well as adjust to fluctuating prices and seasonal unemployment. British and French studies have shown that servants often lived better and more comfortably than working-men or labourers.[29] Being in service also placed servants in contact with different lifestyles from the kind of life they already knew, lifestyles to which many aspired. McBride estimated that about one-third of domestic servants rose in the social scale after having been in service.[30]

Finally, it is also very likely that life was changed and improved in many families because of the large number of women who learned how to tend house while in service. Becoming a domestic servant, therefore, could also have been perceived as a good apprenticeship for the future. We will never know whether entering service was a matter of choice or necessity for the majority, but the fact remains that some must have benefited from the advantages it offered at that time.

EVERYDAY LIFE

Being interested in the everyday life of domestic servants means having to accept that, at times, a wealth of documentation will not be available. Few people were concerned with noting down minor, everyday events or describing those near to them. What is more, those who did were usually foreigners or visitors, alert to differences or peculiarities rather than similarities and commonplace occurrences. Therefore, despite a concerted effort to explore all likely avenues, much of the information was gathered piecemeal, and even though it gave me clues and sometimes was even highly revealing, it nevertheless represents isolated instances from which generalities cannot be drawn without risking the distortion of conditions actually existing in those days.

I examined accounts of travels by the dozen, together with a good number of personal diaries, all in vain. Servants were barely mentioned. Furthermore, it was not even possible to determine whether Canadians had any particular attitude towards service and servants since virtually no literature (novels, tales, short stories, plays) that could truly be identified with Lower Canada existed in 1820. Certainly journalism was in full flourish, but newspapers had nothing to say about servants either except for regulations affecting them and offers of or requests for employment.

Pictorial records were also most disappointing. Although artists of the time (for example, James Cockburn) delighted in outside scenes, very few were interested in interiors and none concerned themselves with servants. However, some information could be gleaned from the documentation available and contemporary writers. The following details are those I consider most meaningful: the daily round, bed and board, and mores, pastimes, and crimes.

The Daily Round

All sources indicate that domestic servants were on call 15 or 16 hours a day. These were more or less the same hours as those apprentices worked at the time and slightly longer than those of journeymen, who usually hired themselves out for 12 hours a day rather than 15.[1] Ten-hour days and several hours off per week were far away at the end of the century.

It seems clear that servants got up around five or six in the morning and went to bed around nine or ten at night. That is what servants stated when they were questioned during trials presided over by Judge Sewell in Quebec City between 1808 and 1820.[2] They went to bed at the same time as the family, but rose slightly earlier.

There is no mention of the order in which the multiple household tasks were tackled, and authors who have reported timetables, such as Guiral and Thuillier or Pamela Horn,[3] have based the timetables on statements made after 1860, which might not have been valid for the early part of the century. However, we can imagine the sequence of the day's work. Early in the morning, whether there was one servant or several, fires would have had to be lit, the family breakfast prepared, clothes and shoes brushed, and errands run. The rest of the morning must have been spent cleaning the bedrooms, carrying wood and water there, disposing of rubbish, and then preparing the midday meal. When the servants ate breakfast is not known, but they had their midday meal at one o'clock, or at least that was true for the large staff in Bishop Mountain's establishment.[4] In his studies of apprentices, Audet stated that they were granted 45 minutes and one hour respectively for breakfast and their midday meal;[5] this may also have held true for the servants too. Once dishes were washed and put away, utensils cleaned and polished, and the kitchen put in order, a great deal of household work doubtlessly remained to be done: dusting and sweeping the living rooms, staircases, passages, and corridors; cleaning lamps; polishing silverware; etc. Then the evening meal had to be prepared, and it seems that once this meal was ended and, of course, the dishes washed and put away and the kitchen tidied, the servants had some time to themselves, even though they had to be ready if one of the master's family called.

We might wonder whether the day of a single servant was more exacting and crowded than the day of one of several servants in a house, or alternatively, whether a master with several servants was more demanding than one who employed only a maid-of-all-work. The documents give no hint as to this, but my impression is that the difference lay not only in the number of tasks to be performed, but also in the loneliness and weariness, which might have made a maid-of-all-work's lot far harder and more difficult to bear than if she could have shared it with someone.

Bed and Board

The important point concerning bed and board is that the servants' world — except, obviously, for those who worked out of doors — was bounded by the kitchen. They worked there for the best part of the day, ate there, relaxed there during the evening once work was done, and very often slept there or nearby.[6] In houses with large staffs (about four per cent according to the Quebec City census in 1818) the servants had a common room — the "servants' hall" — where they took their meals and spent the evening, but this room was also close by the kitchen. Kitchens were relatively well equipped, but lighting and ventilation could leave something to be desired.

Only 14 of the hundred or so turn-of-the-century house plans consulted give details of kitchens and servants' quarters. Lists of goods and chattels were not more forthcoming (ten out of 320). In the 24 houses for which this information was given, the kitchen was in the basement in two-thirds of the cases, generally at the back of the house, and was usually fairly large (20 by 22 feet, for example). Sometimes an inside stairway led to the kitchen or garden. The servants' room was right next to the kitchen and often opened off it. The servants' room would generally be very small — one measured only six by seven and a half feet. If by chance the room was large, it was used by two, three, or even four female servants.[7] When the servants were of opposite sexes, the man usually had the larger room. For instance, one basement room for a female servant measured eight and one-half feet by 15 feet, while the man's was 15 by 17. In that instance the former's room opened off the kitchen whereas the man's was separated from it by a large hallway[8] (see Fig. 5). And the smaller room must have been shared by more than one female servant, unlike the man's.

The rooms contained rudimentary furniture: a bed — sometimes several — and a few chairs.[9] Occasionally it also served as a storage room (see Fig. 6).

We do not know whether children shared the adults' rooms. Only Mrs. Packard mentioned that.[10] One document mentions a young maidservant of 14 or 15 who had to share the bed of one of the daughters of the house (who was ten or 11) near the kitchen hearth,[11] but that is the only such arrangement mentioned.

Details vary widely concerning couples serving in the same house. Some hiring contracts specify that the couple would have a small house adjoining the master's house and have use of the kitchen garden.[12] On the other hand, some couples did not even share the same room in their masters' houses: this meant that husband and wife slept separately since the wife would be with the female servants (see Fig. 6).[13] It is hard to say whether this was the exception or the rule.

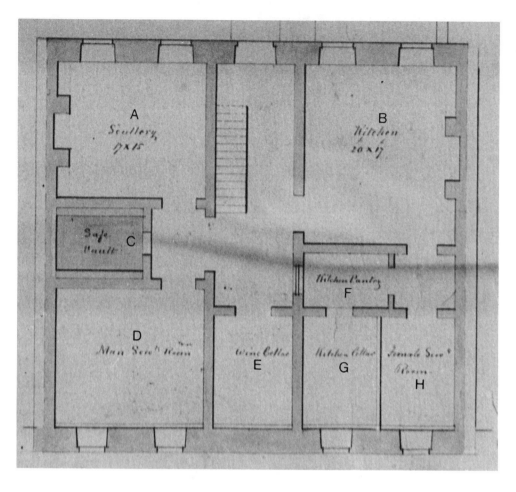

5 Servants' basement quarters, early 19th century.

A Scullery   E Wine cellar
B Kitchen   F Kitchen pantry
C Vault   G Kitchen cellar
D Manservant's room   H Female servants' room

Judge De Bonne Property Inventory

In the room where the maidservants sleep behind the kitchen

One small mirror appraised forty *sols* .... -/1/8
Item, one cot, one straw mattress, one small overlay mattress,
     one small bolster, one pillow, and one old blanket, the
     whole appraised three shillings .... -/3/-
Item, one old cot, one straw mattress, one feather bed covered
     with ticking, ditto one bolster, two pillows, one pair of
     homespun sheets, one white wool blanket, and one ditto
     homespun, the whole appraised thirty shillings 1/10/-

[Entered in the margin beside the last item is: "Marguerite
Giroux, wife of the cook André Dorion, claims this bed upon
which she sleeps as having been promised to her by Mr. De-
bonne."]

F. Coulson Property Inventory

In the Servants' Bedroom

One cot appraised one shilling .... -/1/-
Item   one bolster and one feather bed appraised together two
      pounds 2/-/-
Item   two blankets appraised together two and one-half shil-
      lings .... -/2/6
Item   one chair appraised two shillings .... -/2/-
Item   one bird-cage lot appraised two and one-half shil-
      lings .... -/2/6
Item   sixty dozen empty bottles appraised two *sous* each 3/-/-
Item   ten new empty casks appraised twenty shillings in total
      .... 1/-/-
Item   one lot of baskets, old chairs, the whole appraised ten
      shillings .... -/10/-

Property Inventory of the Late Sara Bruner and Moses Knapp

In the Servant's bedroom

One bunk bed with its contents appraised one pound 1/-/-
Three chairs appraised five shillings each .... -/15/-

6 Inventories of furnishings in servants' quarters in Montreal and
Quebec City between 1816 and 1820.

Nor is there ready information on how servants were fed, whether they had enough to eat, and whether their diet was a healthy one. The problem most likely did not arise in wealthy families; for instance, Bishop Mountain's servants sometimes invited the washer-woman's husband to eat with them,[14] which would mean there was more than enough in that particular household. But how was it in families who only had a maid-of-all-work? It has been estimated that a servant's food cost twice as much as her wages,[15] so were corners ever cut in terms of quantity or quality? No Canadian documents mention such matters and European researchers have strongly opposing views. Some consider that servants were reasonably well fed, and others that the food was no doubt acceptable since it had become more varied and balanced at the beginning of the century. On the other hand, some report that feeding servants cost a great deal and a number of families were somewhat reluctant to set aside sufficient amounts for them. Yet still others mention the servants' numerous complaints that some masters measured milk with eye-droppers and cut portions of meat better fit for cats than servants.[16]

Since there are no complaints or comments, should one assume that in Canada servants' food was generally good and sufficient? If we can rely on the *donations inter vivos* made in the Quebec City and Montreal areas, Canadians generally ate rather well,[17] but the ser-vants' situation must wait for clarification in future studies.

Clothing is another aspect on which little information is avail-able. Masters had to ensure children were clothed "in keeping with their condition," but no contract states what that entailed. A dozen or so contracts mention that the child should receive new clothing upon leaving, but those clothes were nearly always for Sunday wear. More-over, few specifics are mentioned: "a new and decent suit of clothes, from head to foot, and six shirts of linen or cotton"[18] is one state-ment. Masters also had to see that the clothing was cared for, and contracts often stipulate that the servant would be "washed and mend-ed," but nothing was said concerning children's hygiene and cleanli-ness. Did the same situation exist here as in France at that time when "being clean" simply meant "having clean clothes?"[19] In addition to material well-being, masters also had to see to children's spiritual and intellectual well-being (Table 9) and in certain cases, to teach them a trade.[20]

Information on adult clothing is also scanty. Some writers have stated that Canadians refused to wear livery.[21] Does this mean that domestic servants arriving from England wore it if they belonged to a house that could afford to deck out its servants in livery? Towards the end of the century a Quebec play entitled *En livrée* ridiculed a French-Canadian family that wanted its servant to wear livery,[22] which would mean that some livery was worn, but the period referred to followed large-scale immigration from the British Isles and nothing indicates

7 Dinner in an eighteenth-century Canadian manor house. (Philippe Aubert de Gaspé, *Les anciens Canadiens* [Montreal: Fides, 1971; reprint of 1864 ed.].)

whether such customs were current at the beginning of the century. Some desertion notices do give a little information on men's clothing:

> Patrick Bogan, native of Ireland, about 6 feet tall,
> black hair, strong and well-built, at the time of his
> desertion thought to have been wearing a blue
> waistcoat, tobacco coloured or blue greatcoat, light or
> blue breeches and a nankeen or yellow jacket.[23]

Even less information is available on women's clothing. It seems they did not dress in any specific way. In England at that time there was no special costume for women servants; they generally dressed, it was said, like ordinary folk.[24] Pictorial records do not provide the information hoped for: only one illustration was found as far as Canada was concerned, in a book by Philippe Aubert de Gaspé and in which the servant is wearing a shift, skirt, bodice, and neckerchief, but the subject was clearly a servant of the 18th century (Fig. 7).

How servants dressed in early 19th-century Canada seems to divide into three possibilities. First of all, the fact that some might have been dressed in the style of years gone by and thus closely resemble the servant in Figure 7 should not be dismissed. On the other hand, it is just as likely that they sought to wear clothes that were in fashion at the time or worn by the working class. Since nearly all women servants lived in the centre of town and were often sent on errands, they could also go into the shops themselves and be completely up to date on current styles. Some might have tried to imitate their mistresses and sought more luxurious clothing;[25] the documents mention one servant who had stolen a black veil and another who was looking for a seamstress to make a silk dress for her.[26] These are telling examples.

When all is said and done, we have no information on whether domestic servants were lodged, fed, dressed, and kept in satisfactory manners. We do not even know what their criteria or requirements were in these areas. Did they consider their rooms to be comfortable, or at least acceptable? Were they better off in service than living with their parents? Was this even a consideration, since they changed places four or five times a year? Comfort must obviously have been directly related to one's standing in the domestic hierarchy,[27] and it would be reasonable to assume that someone who had been in service with a family for some years would certainly enjoy decent food and lodging, otherwise he or she would have looked for another position. And if we consider that the majority of the children were sent into service because their families could not provide for them, we can conclude that conditions had to be better in their masters' homes than in their parents'.

Mores, Pastimes, and Crimes

Writers who have studied 19th-century domestic service have often devoted much attention to the mores of the times. However, to some extent it was impossible to use their observations because in several instances they considered the century as a whole. Furthermore, their sources were nearly all Victorian, even from the end of the century, yet the resulting portrayal of servant life has been applied uniformly throughout the 1800s. This does not mean that the portrait is completely false; in fact it strongly resembles that depicted by authors writing about previous centuries, and the basics will be summarized here.

According to the majority of authors, it seems that the way of life and conditions were hard for servants. They toiled long hours in grinding work; they suffered either from loneliness because they were the sole servant or from lack of privacy imposed by cramped, shared quarters; many were at their employers' mercy, victims of changes of mood, false accusations, mistreatment, and even assault. And they lived without a shred of security, never knowing whether they would be summarily dismissed nor whether they would be cared for if they became seriously ill or suffered an accident.

All this seems to have resulted in the propensity for crime being higher among servants than among other social groups. They acquired the reputation of being more immoral than others: reports gave them high rates of theft, drunkenness, prostitution, and infanticide.[28] In large towns in France, for instance, half the prostitutes had apparently been servants.[29] Several 19th-century writers made it their duty to warn readers against the dangers to which children could be vulnerable if they associated with servants or were exposed to their presence. Servants were strangers in the midst of a family, to be distrusted and held at a distance.[30]

A somewhat different image of the domestic servant is found in Canadian documents. If some considered that servants' reputations for immorality sprang from high crime rates, servants in Canada at the beginning of the 19th century do not appear to have been much more immoral than anyone else. In fact, according to Judge Sewell's trial notes, 20 out of 272 cases involved servants (7.3 per cent), a figure that more or less corresponds to the percentage of servants in Quebec City and Montreal at that time. Likewise, the register for the Quebec prison from 1816 to 1820 numbered 1642 entries, 89 of which were identified as offences committed by domestic servants. In fact, only 84 servants were involved — three were mentioned twice and one three times — representing 5.4 per cent of offences committed. I have sometimes assumed that someone in service was involved because the offence in question was desertion; the number of domestics involved in actual "crimes" might therefore have been even lower.

On the other hand, although some consider that the harshness of servants' lives was due to the harshness of their working conditions, none of the documents studied mention this. Evidence given during trials, for example, showed no animosity towards the work itself, the masters, or other people in the household, yet any such feelings could have easily been expressed since by the time the servant gave evidence it was two, three, or four months after the affair in question, and the servant had nearly always found another position by then. This may have been one of the reasons why servants changed employers so often, but while departures were common, servants sometimes returned to previous positions. In addition, the hours worked, which seem so long to us now, were perhaps not seen in the same light at that period, when long hours of work were common.[31]

8 Marketplace, Upper Town, Quebec City.

Our servants appear to have been very ordinary folk, people who, when they could, enjoyed the same pleasures as everyone else: visits to neighbours, evening card parties, evenings around the kitchen fire, and occasional dances.[32] They also must have enjoyed needlework of some description or even reading, for those who were able.

Furthermore, like everyone else, servants were subject to the laws of church and state, and insofar as servants were concerned, these laws were even stricter for them than for the general populace. The state often passed legislation concerning domestics, and one notice in the provincial statutes forbade innkeepers and proprietors of gaming houses to admit servants on penalty of fines or withdrawal of their licences.[33] Some of these regulations, which also applied to apprentices and labourers, were published in newspapers of the time, such as the *Montreal Herald* (21 June 1817) and *La Gazette de Québec* (20 July 1818) (see Appendix C).

Admittedly, servants did commit offences and there were undoubtedly good grounds for preventing their entry to gaming and drinking houses. However, nothing indicates that they committed more crimes than other people of their age who were not in service. The age factor is very important, and several authors have recently been studying the problem of crime among young people at the beginning of the 19th century.[34] The average age of the 84 servants listed in the prison register between 1816 and 1820 was 19. No one was under 17 and only one over 21. And this in its own way is logical. It is difficult to imagine a child servant committing some grave offence,[35] just as the problem most likely never occurred with older adults who had been in service in the same household for several years. If their behaviour had been rather on the shady side, they would most certainly have been discharged long ago. There is no reason to think that their way of life was anything but completely acceptable, and in some cases, exemplary, as Madame Casgrain attested concerning Léocadie Anctil.[36] In only one case was an older servant accused of a crime: he was 59 years old and had deserted his master, threatened to set fire to the house, and spent money entrusted to him.[37] Interestingly, he was only sentenced for having deserted.

It is the young servants who appear in trial and prison records. In the 20 trials involving domestic servants presided over by Judge Sewell, 16 servants were charged with theft (seven were found guilty),[38] one with assaulting his mistress with intent to rape (guilty), one with murder (acquitted), and two mothers were accused of murdering their illegitimate children (acquitted of murder but guilty of having concealed their pregnancies and the children's deaths).

The same kind of compilation could not be made of crimes mentioned in the register of the Quebec jail because 20 or so cases carry two or three indictments. However, taken in order of importance, desertion was the most frequent offence (see Table 12).

Table 12

Crimes Committed by Servants According to the Register of the Quebec Gaol, 1816-1820

	No. of Occurrences
Desertion	38
Absence without leave	18
Poor conduct	14
Disturbance, nuisance and damage	12
Refusal to perform duties	6
Theft	6
Assault	5
Insolence	4
Threats	4
Drunkenness	3
Fraud	1
Prostitution	1
Fighting with fellow servant	1
Introducing prostitute into master's house	1
Total	114

ANQ-Q, Register of the Quebec Gaol, Vol. 6, 1816-20.

If desertion and absence without leave are eliminated, both of them being directly related to the fact that the offender was a servant, those in service appear to have been no more immoral than anyone else. Seventy-eight of the offences recorded in the register were committed by men, compared with 11 committed by women. In the Sewell trials the 20 accusations were divided equally between the sexes. How, then, could the very few women (11 in one instance, ten in the other) convicted of crimes in Quebec City between 1816 and 1820 be deemed to prove that there was a high crime rate among servants when there were more than 600 female servants in Quebec City in 1818 alone? Clearly the Sewell trials and the prison register do not take into account all the crimes that occurred. To begin with, Sewell only gave details of 60 per cent of the trials he heard between

9 Montreal prison, 1837.

1816 and 1820, and a comparison of both sets of records provides further proof: whereas 80 per cent of Sewell's trials dealt with theft, only six cases of theft are to be found in the prison register. It also seems that masters were more likely to bring their servants before the court for desertion than for any other offence. The small number of women involved would indicate that they were less likely to desert, perhaps because they were far more mobile than the men.

If masters only considered taking action in cases of absence or desertion, did they knowingly shut their eyes to the lax morals said to be rife among servants? Very little is said about sexual morals in the documents I consulted. The register of the Quebec prison reported 76 cases of vagrancy and prostitution involving 60 women and 16 men, but the present or previous occupations of the accused are not given. I therefore compared that list of names with those names of servants mentioned in the 1818 Quebec City census and the 1816-20 employment contracts. Only two men and one woman were in service. It was impossible to estimate how many of the others had been in service at

53

some time; that would have required examining all trial records for several decades, no easy task since people's occupations were rarely given, and in addition, some records are completely unobtainable, such as those for Montreal. Judge Sewell's records do contain a few blots on servants' sexual escutcheons: Susannah Davis, for instance, was said to have been rather free with her favours (see Appendix B); other documents mention a girl accused of prostitution and a housekeeper who bore three of her master's children.[39]

But what about the majority of servants? Speculation on the subject could continue for some time without a satisfactory answer being found. However, if any credence can be given to the impression provided by the documentation for 1816 to 1820 as a whole, normality seems more plausible than marginality. We can also wonder whether servants' reputations were not more — or at least equally — products of their youth than their occupation.

Matters were perhaps different in the second half of the century when longer hours were worked as families dined at eight rather than six o'clock, with a consequent reduction in the time available for servants' rest or amusement; when servants perhaps worked harder because the standards of cleanliness had altered with the introduction of running water in houses. At the beginning of the century no such considerations disturbed servants' workdays, and it seems that they were little different from their peers who also worked for their living.

SOCIAL RELATIONSHIPS

Perceptions of Service and Types of Servants

If one concept ran throughout the centuries, it was that service was as much a part of the natural order of things as night following day. It had existed from the beginning of time. Many hoped to take advantage of its existence, since to have servants conferred a certain distinction and confirmed membership in a specific level of society. Another concept, just as widespread and just as constant, was that standards of service were constantly deteriorating, and as was only too obvious, had been far better a generation ago. Formulated in the 16th century, this reproach could apply equally well to the 12th or 19th centuries: "These days servants push their spirit of independence and insolence to such lengths that they refuse to obey not only their masters but also public authority."[1]

Each succeeding generation considered itself less well served than were its parents or grandparents, and employers concluded that servants were more inclined to undesirable activities than the servants they had known during childhood. Their opinion was often all the more firmly held because the servants they remembered from childhood had often been in the family's service for several years, loved children, and had formed lasting attachments with them. The attitude must also have been shared by the newly rich who, never having had servants during childhood, formed idealistic concepts of what domestic service represented.

Was this point of view at the roots of the poor reputation attributed to those in service and of the distrust with which they were regarded? In the Sewell trials, for example, 80 per cent of the cases involving servants concerned theft and more than half of these ended in acquittals. When something disappeared, was the immediate reaction that it had been stolen by a servant? Yet servants entered in the register of the Quebec jail were there mainly because of desertion or absence without leave; might they have been acquitted on a variety of other scores?

Furthermore, did this undesirable reputation apply to all servants? In analyzing the documents, I found three types of domestic. First, child servants: they might have been placed with a family from their earliest years, say when they were aged two or three, but usually they were anywhere from 12, 13, to 14 years old. Children were sent into service because they were orphans or their families could not provide for them. We do not know whether they were well-treated; none of the documents give any information, for or against. Generally speaking, it seems that child servants lived better than if they had stayed with their own families, but any comfort they enjoyed was due to effort or merit, and in some instances it is highly likely that their comfort was gained at high cost.

Widows and widowers formed the second category of servants, together with single men or women past their first youth who had been in service with a family for a good number of years. They were considered the embodiment of the ideal servant — faithful and discreet; friend, confidant, and even accomplice — and it was often they who were depicted in literary works of the period. Together these first two categories represented one third of all servants; those under 16 years of age accounting for around 14 per cent, those over 25 for some 20 per cent.

The third type — servants aged between 16 and 25 — made up the remaining two-thirds of the servant population. Young and extremely mobile, they were perceived as unruly and profiteering, and if certain plays are to be believed, they were skillful, cunning, prying, and even tyrannical. Servants' reputations for immorality and a penchant for crime came from this group.

Despite these more or less clear-cut categories, we still cannot speak of a "typical servant" because the documents have revealed many different sorts. One made advances to her master and then accused him of rape (Appendix B); one assiduously pursued his mistress and even tried to rape her. On the other hand, one sought employment with her masters to be nearer the church and gained their complete confidence; yet another had a son studying law and a daughter who was a nun at the Hôtel-Dieu. One washerwoman was so traumatized by the fact that a bag of her master's washing had been stolen from her that she lost her mind (according to her husband).[2] And then there was the Pointe-aux-Trembles servant who had plenty of pluck:

> We hear that a Woman, lately at Service at Point aux Trembles, near Montreal, being desirous to quit her Place, demanded her Wages, but having no written Agreement with her Master, a Neighbour was call'd to witness the paying her [sic] the Sum due, after receiving of which she set out to seek another Residence, and passing thro' a Wood was met by the same Man who had been Witness to her receiving the Money, who, presenting two charg'd Pistols to her, demanded her to give him her Cash, or then he would murder her, whereupon she took the Money out of her Pocket, and threw it in the Snow on one Side of the Road, desiring him to take it rather than her Life; he being over

desirous for the Prize, inadvertently laid down his Pistols in the Road, which the woman immediately seiz'd, and Shot him dead on the Spot, but did not re-take her money 'til she had alarm'd the nearest Neighbours to the Place where the Scene was transacted.[3]

These examples give an idea of the diversity found in the servant population and also of the differences that existed in the relationships servants had with their fellows.

Master/Servant Relationships

Anyone seeking to know the types or qualities of relationships that existed between masters and servants can find a little of everything in the documentation. There are examples of kindness, benevolence, and recognition on the master's side, and faithfulness, deference, and devotion on the servant's. On the other hand, indifference and maliciousness, even outright hostility, also existed on both sides.

On the credit side, a Mrs. King loaned money to her maidservant so that she might purchase a veil she liked; a Mr. Farran paid his female servant a higher wage than had been agreed upon and did not hector her one day when she was ill and unable to finish her work; and when his female servant told him there was no wood for the next day, a Mr. Organ told her to go to bed for he would cut enough wood for the morning's needs. Some servants did not hesitate to pursue a thief stealing their master's money, and others made a point of telling their mistresses whenever anything out of the ordinary occurred, no matter how trivial.[4]

But the prime evidence of good relations between master and servant is found in wills. Out of nearly 1000 wills studied for Montreal and Quebec City, 15 contained bequests to one or several servants. In most cases, for 20 of the 23 servants who inherited, sums of money were involved, and in five cases the bequests took the form of annuities. The remaining three received goods or the usufruct of certain goods.

In some families the practice seems to have been to leave something to all the servants in the household. Charlotte Guilman, the Widow McGill, bequeathed £100 to her companion, £50 each to the two menservants, £10 each to the four female servants, and £10 to an elderly servant, entrusting him to her son, who was to take him as his own servant until the old man died.[5] Others only left bequests to specific servants. For example, Anne Tarrieu de la Naudière, the Widow Baby, left an annual pension of £18 to a female servant who had been in her service for 20 years[6] but nothing to the three others who were in the house in 1818[7] according to the priest's census. These three were young women, aged 19, 22, and 25, who had no doubt been with the family only a short time.

From the wills it appears that bequests were made as tokens of appreciation for past services, like care given during an illness.[8] It also seems that bequests were related to the servant's position in the domestic hierarchy or the number of years the servant had spent with the family. There is some indication that when all the servants received them, bequests were more or less equivalent to a year's salary. Historians who have studied wills made in France also noted this, even though some pointed out that such bequests were often simply payment of outstanding debts; that is, payment of wages that were several years in arrears.[9] Whether this was the case with servants in Quebec City and Montreal is unknown because the wills give no hint as to whether it was a bona fide gift or a settlement of outstanding debts. On the other hand, a Quebec City merchant's will made no secret of the fact that the housekeeper receiving a handsome bequest was also the mother of his three natural children.[10]

Although several documents bear witness to good relationships existing between master and servant, the silence of the great majority of documents could be put down to indifference: servants were paid little attention and received little mention. In any case, it was not the custom to maintain close relationships with people of inferior classes. This is very clear in the documents studied and substantiated by this extract from Lady Sherbrooke's journal:

> One of the Helpers in the Stables was found dead in the stable this morning the coroners' Inquest sat on the Body and brought in their verdict died from the excessive use of spirituous liquors — A showery day I did not go out....[11]

Was Lady Sherbrooke this resigned in the face of death or indifferent to a servant's fate? Researchers examining families' account books have noted that reference is usually made to the "second servant" or the "third servant" rather than to "Angela" or "Margaret."[12] And more than one author has observed that a master sometimes changed his servant's name because he preferred another.[13] Further evidence of disinterest was the custom, which dated from the French régime, of transferring a contracted servant to another master during the period of the contract, maybe to repay a debt or a favour.[14] And finally, the ease and frequency with which servants changed their places of employment — or were turned out — is a resounding example of the vast indifference that characterized many master/servant relationships.

Prison records and trial notes contain several examples of maliciousness or hostility.[15] On the one hand, servants were accused of misconduct, insubordination, insolence, or absence without leave.

58

Some assaulted their masters, others threatened them, and one tried to rape his mistress. On the other hand, masters mistreated their servants (one cause for terminating a contract and no doubt also for desertion), others were demanding beyond all reason (for example, service to be provided both by day and night), many abused their position and sexually assaulted their servants.[16] Some were obnoxious: one female servant, given the choice of going to prison or returning to her master's house, chose prison.[17]

Several authors who studied master/servant relationships generally concluded that the relationship, initially paternalistic, gradually evolved into an increasingly contractual arrangement. Some state that this change took place towards the middle of the 18th century and lasted into the first decades of the 19th, and others that contractual arrangements of this type became common in England sooner than in France.[18]

Did the paternalistic or the contractual relationship predominate in Canada? At first glance, it cannot be denied that paternalism could have been part of the relationship between master and servant child. Several contracts stipulate that the master was to act as a responsible parent and have regard to the child's age and sex (see Part I, "Domestic Service," Table 9). Upon occasion it was also specified that he should correct the child if need be and chastise it if necessary, but always as its own parents would. For instance, a clause in a young girl's contract (her mother was a servant) states that her mistress was to see to her morals and conduct, and treat her humanely, but correct her like a true mother, kindly and humanely, for the faults into which she might fall.[19] When children remained in service for long periods, this relationship — when it existed — probably continued until the child came of age and left domestic work.

Likewise, as far as older servants who had been with a family for a good number of years were concerned, strong bonds of affection must have developed. But was this regard still tinged with paternalism? Philippe Aubert de Gaspé's *Mémoires* assert that this was so,[20] but can we believe this elderly gentleman who warmly defended the seigneurial tradition in which he lived? Evidence of affection, or at least a master's feeling of responsibility for his servant, exists in documents such as wills, but we do not know whether this was a question of paternalism or a laudable desire for fair treatment. Yet other sources indicate that a great deal more respect was involved than paternalism: "Your father thought so highly of [the Casgrain family's female servant] that he used to say her presence alone brought order."[21]

There may well have been a certain amount of paternalism towards servants, young or old, who had been in a household for an extended period of time. However, it is difficult to believe that a master could establish a paternalistic relationship — in the best sense of the word — with a 20-year-old male or female servant who would only be staying two or three months, perhaps even less, in his house. And the question is even more pertinent in households where the staff was so large that it was supervised by a head servant. No doubt, as far as most such servants were concerned — and they constituted the large majority of those in service — the master/servant relationship was more or less contractual. A verbal agreement covered one or two months' employment and the servant left at the end of the agreed period. There is very little question here of the condescension or submission that would be appropriate in the case of children, nor of the marks of mutual respect as one would expect in the cases of older family servants. One has the impression with respect to the young, highly mobile elements that the desire, on both sides, was to keep each other at a proper distance. A master could always brandish the need for good references as his weapon because they would be requested before the servant's departure and were often vital in finding another situation;[22] a servant could gossip (a means of expression used by those in subordinate positions), with all the attendant problems that gossip could cause in a tight little society.[23] In addition, the scarcity of servants might also have provided servants with a bargaining tool that would contribute to a fair balance being maintained between parties. All might have been different had supply exceeded demand, but at the beginning of the 19th century this was not the situation.

Servant/Peer Relationships

There is little information on how servants behaved towards their fellows serving in the same house. Again a little of everything appears in the documents, but nothing allows us to generalize or state that one specific attitude predominated.

Many servants were doubtless on fairly good terms with each other, terms that were enhanced by several circumstances: they ate together most of the time, played cards together, sat around the kitchen hearth in the evening, and sometimes two or three shared the same room; some were even related.[24] Their common lot no doubt created a feeling of solidarity, especially felt and expressed when the family was absent. In fact, during the family's absence, parties were sometimes held and servant neighbours and friends invited over.[25] This practice is portrayed in several plays.[26]

On the other hand, servants did not hesitate to denounce a fellow servant for theft if only to clear themselves and avoid accusation. Chests belonging to other servants were searched if the latter were under suspicion of some kind, and when relationships deteriorated,

60

blows could be exchanged.[27]   How did servants deal with problems of age (their attitude towards both children and old-timers), rank (towards both subordinates and superiors), sex, language, or religion? Did they abuse their positions, show rivalry or jealousy? When there was more than one servant in a household, did they form friendships, or at the very least, manage to come to terms with living side by side with strangers, even sharing the same room? We simply do not know. Nevertheless, one cannot help but wonder whether they would have stayed longer in one place if they had had friends there. But these may be non-issues because at that time the ability to get on with other people was most likely far less important than the close relationships considered vital in today's world.

Discussing relationships between servants and their families is difficult. Absolutely no information is available on this point. Those who came from the town in which they were working must occasionally have visited their families, but whether masters permitted the other servants to do likewise for a few days is not known because no such clauses appear in the contracts. In addition, travelling was a complex undertaking. Nor do we know how many servants still had parents to visit; some studies on New France have estimated that 50 per cent of children had lost one parent, usually the father, by the time they reached 20, and that between 20 and 25 the figure rose to 60 per cent.[28] If these percentages were still valid at the beginning of the 19th century, they must have been even higher for the servant community because many of its members were in service precisely because their family could not provide for them, the death of a parent, especially a father, being a strong reason for a family's reduced circumstances.   Only four cases were found where parents are mentioned: once at the termination of a contract, twice when contracts were signed, and once more in a case Judge Sewell heard.[29]

Details concerning servants' neighbours are no more abundant. Some servants received visits from neighbouring servants, and others visited neighbours in the evening.[30] As for the rest, one can only found speculations on certain basic facts: towns were not very spread out and houses were close to each other; servants often ran errands, sometimes going to market; they did not stay long in one place, and lived at a time when there was far greater social contact in the street than nowadays (see Figs. 1 and 2). In fact, there is every indication that servants living at the beginning of the 19th century had far closer — perhaps even more important — relationships with their neighbours than with their own families.

PART TWO

1871 TO 1875

INTRODUCTION

When choosing a period typifying the second half of the century, I had to include 1871 since the census carried out that year was the first census that could be considered uniform across Canada. Since the census offered a possibility of comparing various Canadian cities with each other, it also seemed important that all the regions of the Canada of those days be involved and therefore cities in Ontario and the Maritimes were added to those of the Province of Quebec. I chose the largest city in each of the new regions — Toronto and Halifax.

Placing these cities within the context of the time will be helpful. With the rise in industrialization and the immense progress realized in transportation technology, the 1850s and 1860s had generally been good years as far as the world economy was concerned.[1] The outlook for the seventies was prosperous. However, the situation deteriorated after 1873 and some sectors of the economy remained in precarious states until 1896. Economic conditions in Canada were also affected by these long-lasting trends. The large-scale immigration of people from Ireland and Britain that had marked the thirties and forties slowed for several years due to the improved living conditions in Europe; in addition, the 1840s and 1860s saw massive construction work undertaken, such as canalization of the St. Lawrence and the building of the Grand Trunk Railway, as well as the birth of many private businesses, such as Redpath and Ogilvie in Montreal. However, Ontario was affected by the depression in 1873, Quebec in 1874, and Nova Scotia in 1876. The outpouring of emigrants from Canada to the United States during the last 30 years of the century bore witness to the extent of the crisis.[2]

The nation's situation was still good at the moment when, through the 1871 census, we open a window on the cities and the lives of urban domestic servants. Society reflected a period of prosperity, although the reflection darkens in the later years. Our view is, in any case, somewhat distorted due to the fact that the study encompasses only the four largest cities of the period, but fortunately their differences are such that they are nevertheless representative of urban society of the time (Figs. 10-13).

The cities differed first in population. In 1871 Montreal had 107 225 inhabitants; Quebec City, 59 699; Toronto, 56 092; and Halifax, 29 582.[3] In addition, two of them — Montreal and Toronto — had experienced strong demographic upswings, whereas the other two cities remained more or less stationary. Another factor was that

Quebec City and Montreal dated back to the 17th century, whereas Halifax was founded in the 18th century and Toronto just as the 19th century began. Finally, they represented three distinct geographic entities — Ontario, Quebec, and the Maritimes — and two separate linguistic communities — Anglophone and Francophone. All in all, they differed enough to show the tendencies that might have been characteristic of a given geographic area, the growth level of a given city, or perhaps a particular ethnic group. It seemed that through them we could gain a fairly accurate idea of what domestic service in Canada entailed at the beginning of the 1870s.

10 Toronto in 1875.

A St. James
B St. David
C St. Andrew
D St. Patrick
E St. George
F St. John
G St. Lawrence

11 Montreal in 1875. A: Saint-Antoine district.

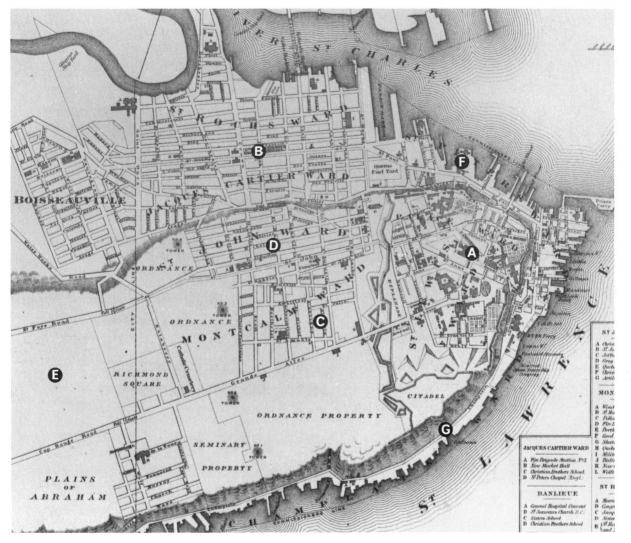

12 Quebec City in 1875.

A Palais/St-Louis
B St-Roch/Jacques Cartier
C Montcalm
D St-Jean

E *Banlieue*
F St-Pierre
G Champlain

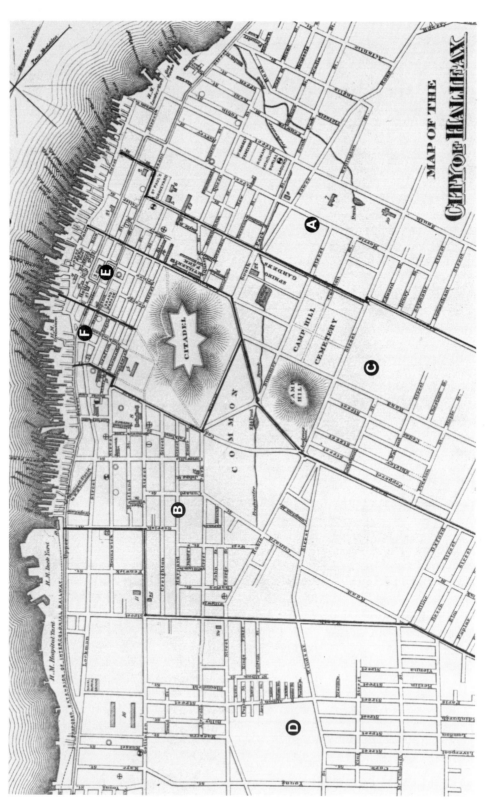

13 Halifax in 1875.

A Ward 1   C Ward 2   E Ward 3
B Ward 5   D Ward 6   F Ward 4

THE PEOPLE INVOLVED — IN 1871

The 1871 census[1] was the major source of data; however, this document, like so many others, has certain drawbacks, and it was impossible to eliminate all the errors inherent in it, errors that arise mainly from the fact that the enumerators were many and differed with respect to environment, language, concerns, and perceptions.

One of the first problems is terminology. Though the enumerators generally used *serviteur, servante,* and *servant,* some preferred *domestique.*[2] Likewise, although some had taken the trouble to specify a servant's functions (coachman, cook, groom, lady's maid), by far the majority contented themselves with more general terms,[3] thus inadvertently depriving us of very useful information as well as the possibility of listing all the various types of servants in the country.

Other problems, such as omissions and errors, can be detected here and throughout the census, which means that great caution should be exercised in interpreting the data. For example, "servant" was used to describe a two-year-old baby (I have not included such cases). Three people aged 20, 28, and 32 were included when a family of seven was enumerated; there was no indication of the trio's occupations and they seemingly had no connection with the family, but were listed where servants generally appeared. Finally, Hannah Walker, a Presbyterian servant, was stated to be of French origin[4] (see Fig. 14), an anomaly if there ever was one. I therefore restricted the study to those people specifically designated as domestics and accepted the information given for them even if it seemed to be somewhat doubtful at times.

While these problems may have been minor, the situation is very different for the occupations of the various heads of households and the manner in which they were classified. For example, although at first glance "merchant" seems to be straightforward, such is not the case because there were proportionately far more of them in Halifax than elsewhere. According to the published census, they represented 6.4 per cent of occupations versus approximately five per cent for Toronto and Quebec City.[5] Was this is a true reflection of the situation or did the word have a more general meaning in Halifax compared with the other cities? Classifying occupations is, in fact, a major concern for census users and several of them have drafted classification models for the period.[6] However, none of their models met my needs because I wanted to utilize the data already compiled for Quebec City[7] so that I could compare employers' occupations for

OLD REGULUS.—"*It is necessary, Bridget, that you should inform me of your age and origin that I may comply with the law in filling up the census.*

BRIDGET.—"*Is it me age ye're wantin' to know, sir? An' faith I've often heerd me mother say I was born the same day as Mrs. Maloney's Pat that killed hisself wid drink; but me origin, faith! yer honour, I'ven't the laste idea of me origin.*"

14 "Incidents of the Census," 1871.

the city over time. I therefore preferred to use the same general categories as before, classifying people as being in commerce, professionals, civil servants, of independent means, or working in manufacturing, transport, construction, or services. Those who did not fall into any of these categories or who had no stated occupation were covered under the heading "Others."

Finally, there is one last problem with the census: servants did not always live in their master's houses and it was live-in servants on which the study was to focus. I have therefore defined three categories of servant and compiled data on each category. The first category covers those who worked in hotels, hospitals, or religious communities; the second covers those who clearly did not live with the family employing them — for example, heads of households enumerated as domestic servants but living with their own families; and the final group comprises all those enumerated in association with a family other than their own and who were identified as servants. In my opinion only the latter were live-in servants and my statistics relate to this group, the other two groups being used only occasionally.

Domestic Servants

Domestic servants accounted for approximately five per cent of the population of the cities,[8] and 70 per cent of all servants were live-in servants. The latter figure is obviously an average because the number of live-in servants residing in cities (Halifax, 78 per cent; Quebec City, 69 per cent; Toronto, 60 per cent) fell from east to west in inverse proportion to the number of immigrants (Halifax, 8.4 per cent; Quebec City, 22.4 per cent; Toronto, 63.2 per cent). Thus the lower the number of immigrant servants living in a city, the higher the number of live-in servants in that city. The situation was somewhat different in the wealthiest sections of each city, where 90 per cent of servants lived in the houses in which they served.[9]

The number and proportion of servants also varied greatly from one area to another within a given city and did not always reflect the actual proportion of a city's total population that lived in that part of town (Table 13). For comparative purposes certain neighbouring areas of Quebec City were grouped together, such as Palais and Saint-Louis.[10] The districts are listed in Table 13 in decreasing order of the percentage of live-in servants who lived there.

Concentration in specific districts was less obvious in new cities such as Toronto than in older centres such as Quebec City and Halifax. Toronto had no district with a concentration of 41 per cent of servants as in Halifax, or 49 per cent as in Quebec City; on the other hand, no

Table 13

Ratio (%) of Live-In Servants to Urban Population, 1871

Toronto			Quebec City			Halifax		
District	Serv.	Pop.	District	Serv.	Pop.	District	Serv.	Pop.
St. James	30.3	17.4	Pa./St-L.	48.8	8.9	Ward 1	40.9	22.4
St. David	19.6	20.0	St-Roch	20.2	47.4	Ward 5-1	13.4	16.2
St. Andrew	14.4	15.9	Montcalm	10.0	13.0	Ward 2	12.8	11.2
St. Patrick	11.8	14.1	St-Jean	8.3	13.3	Ward 6	11.2	13.4
St. George	11.3	6.3	Banlieue	7.6	4.4	Ward 3	10.5	11.1
St. John	8.3	19.4	St-Pierre	4.4	6.2	Ward 5-2	9.4	17.8
St. Lawrence	4.3	6.9	Champlain	0.7	6.8	Ward 4	1.8	7.9

PAC, Census ... 1871.

Table 14

Live-In Servants, 1871

	Percent.		Av. Age		Percent. Widow-er	Wid-ow	Unable to Read	Write	Percent. Immigrants
	M	W	M	W					
Combined Districts									
Toronto	9.5	90.5	25.8	24.9	0.6	4.6	2.1	3.5	63.2
Quebec	12.0	88.0	27.9	26.9	2.9	2.5	11.0	16.7	22.4
Halifax	5.5	94.5	28.0	24.7	2.7	2.5	4.8	9.1	8.4
Wealthy Districts									
Toronto	3.9	96.1	22.6	24.0	0.0	3.2	0.8	1.3	56.4
Quebec	12.1	87.9	27.5	27.8	3.7	2.4	7.9	12.7	24.8
Halifax	4.3	95.7	28.4	25.1	0.0	1.5	4.2	9.0	8.7
Montreal	9.7	90.3	28.9	27.0	1.7	3.7	8.8	12.1	42.2

PAC, Census ... 1871.

part of Toronto was as poor as the Champlain district of Quebec City, for example. In Montreal, where industrialization was more rapid than elsewhere, the wealthy classes no longer lived in the centre of the city, which must have had a definite impact on live-in servants who became increasingly isolated as their well-off masters moved their households to the suburbs.

Data compiled on these live-in servants in the second half of the 19th century are given in Tables 14, 15, 16, and 18 for Toronto, Quebec City, and Halifax. Another series of tables, based on the same elements, covers the wealthy districts of these cities: St. James in Toronto, Palais/Saint-Louis in Quebec City, Ward 1 in Halifax, and Saint-Antoine in Montreal. It seemed worthwhile studying these individual districts because they contained the type of house or household that Environment Canada — Parks is normally called upon to restore and interpret. One additional point: there were 1712 live-in servants in Toronto, 1738 in Quebec City, 1355 in Halifax, and 1790 in the Saint-Antoine district of Montreal.

The servants were almost all single and there was only a low percentage of widows or widowers (Table 14). The great majority (90 per cent) of those in service were women,[11] which is an important change from the beginning of the century, when the ratio of men to women had been half and half in Quebec City in 1818 and one-third/two-thirds in Montreal in 1825.

There are other differences. At the beginning of the century only 42 per cent of servants or servants' parents were able to sign the 196 hiring contracts analyzed; in 1871, according to the census, very few servants could not read or write.[12] The average age also varied from one period to another: in 1871 it was 26, whereas in Quebec City in 1818 it had been 23 (see Table 1).

The question of age warranted more thorough examination. In 1871 more than 60 per cent of servants were under 25 years old — 67.3 per cent in Toronto, 61 per cent in Quebec City, 72.7 per cent in Halifax, and 58.1 per cent in the wealthy district of Montreal (Table 15). While the majority of servants were in the 16- to 25-year age group, generally speaking, those under 16 averaged 14 years of age, those over 40 averaged 48.1, and the remainder, 24. When comparing the total number of domestic servants by age group with the census data compiled for that age group, it appears that servants accounted for 0.5 to 0.6 per cent of the male population under 16 and two to four per cent of the female population. In the 16-39 age group the figure for males is between 1.0 and 1.5 per cent and from ten to 15 per cent for women, whereas servants over 40 years of age accounted for 0.4 per cent to 0.6 per cent of the men and 3.1 to 3.3 per cent of the women.

It would have been interesting to have compared these data with the situation in Europe and the United States at that time, but because

Table 15

Live-In Servants by Age Group, 1871

	Under 16	16-25	26-39	40 & Over
Combined Districts				
Toronto	7.3	60.0	22.5	10.2
Quebec	4.7	56.3	25.0	14.0
Halifax	5.7	67.0	19.3	8.0
Wealthy Districts				
Toronto	7.5	63.6	20.0	6.9
Quebec	2.9	56.0	26.3	14.8
Halifax	3.8	69.0	19.1	8.1
Montreal	4.2	53.9	29.6	12.3

PAC, Census ... 1871.

Table 16

Live-In Servants by Ethnic Group, 1871

	Engl.	Scot.	Irish	Fr. Cdn.	U.S.	Eur.	Other
Combined Districts							
Toronto	27.5	17.1	50.5	0.7	2.4	1.1	0.7
Quebec	5.2	2.4	32.8	58.8	0.5	0.3	
Halifax	25.5	24.5	38.5	2.0	0.3	4.9	4.3
Wealthy Districts							
Toronto	26.0	20.2	48.9	0.8	2.5	1.0	0.6
Quebec	6.4	2.3	38.2	52.5	0.5	0.1	
Halifax	20.8	28.7	41.5	1.4		4.7	2.9
Montreal	12.9	20.5	47.8	16.9	0.9	0.8	0.2

PAC, Census ... 1871.

the study is only concerned with live-in servants here, the results might have been distorted. However, these figures are very similar to contemporary figures reported for Europe and the United States.[13] And we can compare the 1871 age groups with those in Quebec City at the beginning of the century. In 1818, servants under 16 represented 14.5 per cent of all those in service; the 16 to 25 age group was 65 per cent; 26 to 39, 12 per cent; and those over 40 accounted for 8.5 per cent. In addition, those under 16 averaged 12.4 years of age whereas those over 40 averaged 51.4.[14]

Another difference: whereas in 1816-20, servants came from the surrounding areas,[15] in 1871 they were often immigrants or sons and daughters of immigrants, and among these there was a slight over-representation of Irish given their demographic presence in the cities as a whole.[16]

Data concerning ethnic origin appear in Tables 16 and 17. When comparing these two tables, readers should remember that almost all the servants shown under "Other" in Table 16 were black Americans, whom the enumerators always identified as "Africans" rather than Americans. In Table 17 "U.S." is not shown because the published census did not give data on Americans even if they had been identified when the census was taken.

That there were quite a few more Irish servants in Toronto, Quebec City, and Montreal than one would have thought given their demographic presence is evidence of the strong influx of Irish immigrants in the preceding decades. In addition, the further west one goes, the higher the Irish population in the cities. This, of course,

Table 17

Urban Population by Ethnic Group, 1871

	Engl.	Scot	Irish	Fr. Cdn.	Eur.	Other
Toronto	37.8	14.6	43.0	1.0	2.3	1.3
Quebec	6.7	3.1	20.7	68.5	0.9	0.1
Halifax	32.9	16.3	39.4	1.6	6.0	3.8
Montreal	12.0	9.2	23.7	53.0	1.8	0.3

Canada. Parliament, *Census of Canada/Recensement du Canada, 1870-71* (Ottawa: I.B. Taylor, 1873), Vol. 1, pp. 266-67, 288-89, 304-305, 326-27.

corresponds to the higher level of immigration in the west than the east (Table 14).

Although data on ethnic groups gives no indication of whether servants came from the country or the city, the age pyramids based on such data (J.-C. Robert's for Montreal, for example[17]) clearly show that there were many more women between 15 and 30 years of age than men at the time, meaning that many young women from the country or abroad were working in the cities. Further details are available from other documents. For instance, Montreal death records[18] show that in 1871, 43 per cent of servants appeared to come from the city, whereas in 1816-20 the same source shows a figure of 76 per cent (confirming the hiring contracts for the 1816-20 period; see Table 2). This can therefore be taken as an indication that far more people from rural areas worked in town in the later part of the century than at the beginning.[19]

The question of religious affiliation remains. Tables 18 and 19 seem to show too many Catholics and Presbyterians and too few Anglicans. Overall, however, servants' religious affiliations virtually followed the same curves as those for the population as a whole. For example, if figures for the Catholic and Anglican populations in the

Table 18

Religious Faith of Live-In Servants, 1871

	Cath-olic	Angli-can	Presby-terian	Meth-odist	Other
Combined Districts					
Toronto	31.3	26.9	17.6	15.2	9.0
Quebec	90.9	6.2	1.2	1.1	0.6
Halifax	44.6	19.9	18.8	6.0	10.7
Wealthy Districts					
Toronto	30.1	12.3	21.4	18.3	17.9
Quebec	89.9	6.8	1.7	1.4	0.2
Halifax	44.4	19.8	25.1	4.2	6.5
Montreal	58.5	16.2	16.6	5.3	3.4

PAC, Census ... 1871.

Table 19

Religious Faith of Urban Population, 1871

	Cath- olic	Angli- can	Presby- terian	Meth- odist	Other
Toronto	21.2	36.8	16.0	17.1	8.9
Quebec	87.7	6.8	2.7	1.3	1.5
Halifax	42.0	27.4	13.3	8.4	8.9
Montreal	72.7	10.8	8.5	4.2	3.8

Canada. Parliament, *Census of Canada/Recensement du Canada, 1870-71* (Ottawa: I.B. Taylor, 1873), Vol. 1, pp. 114-17, 158-61, 190-193, 234-37.

four towns are compared with those of servants of the same faiths living in those towns, the percentages are very similar: about 70 per cent of the urban population and of servants were Catholic, about 17 per cent were Anglican. In any case, except for Quebec City where almost 90 per cent of the population and servants were Catholic, religious faith did not seem to be a major consideration because servants worked for masters of the same faith in only 25 to 28 per cent of cases (25.5, 26.5, and 27.6 per cent for Toronto, Montreal, and Halifax respectively).

Despite all the detail contained in the tables, it is impossible to define the typical domestic servant in 1871 further than that she was a young, single woman in her early twenties who knew how to read and write. At the time, people seemed to delight in representing her as an Irish immigrant,[20] and here we stumble over one of the major stereotypes of the period; however, it cannot be applied to servants as a whole. Indeed, it is not the only stereotype that was current. Many thought for a long time — and still do — that very many households had servants, even whole staffs of servants. But for some time now several authors have been querying this belief[21] and our sources add further weight to the argument (see Fig. 15).

THE VICISSITUDES OF HIGH LIVING.

Mistress to Maid:—"You must go, Nancy. We cannot afford a servant any longer. I must hereafter do my own work. Now-a-days the girl who earns her wages is safer than the lady who rolls in wealth."

15 The lack of job security in service.

Masters

According to the 1871 census, only ten to 15 per cent of urban households were able to afford the services of one or several live-in servants, and these households were very unevenly divided throughout the various parts of the cities (Table 20; in Quebec in 1818 the proportion had been 20 per cent[22]). This means that servants were employed in one household out of seven in Halifax, in one out of nine in Toronto, and one out of ten in Quebec City. It could be said that these statistics are lower than those for some European countries and the United States, where it is estimated that one household in six had servants.[23] In fact, however, the situations were very similar since the statistical reports in those countries were based on the number of domestic servants per thousand households and on the assumption that they numbered 1.5 per household.[24] Had I taken the same course, I would have had one household out of five in Halifax, one out of six in Toronto, and one out of seven in Quebec City and Montreal. A minimum of five per cent would have been added to the number of households boasting a servant, and in Halifax, for example, the total of 903 households with servants would have risen to 1175 — an appreciable difference. While our figures do not cover servants who did not live in, we have no indication that non-resident servants only worked

Table 20

Percentage of Households with Live-In Servants by District, 1871

Toronto		Quebec		Halifax	
St. James	21.2	Palais/St-L.	51.2	Ward 1	28.0
St. George	17.7	Banlieue	10.3	Ward 2	15.5
St. David	11.5	Montcalm	8.9	Ward 3	14.7
St. Andrew	11.2	St-Pierre	7.4	Ward 5-1	14.4
St. Lawrence	7.9	St-Jean	7.1	Ward 6	13.1
St. Patrick	7.4	St-Roch	5.9	Ward 5-2	10.1
St. John	4.9	Champlain	1.1	Ward 4	4.0

PAC, Census ... 1871.

Table 21

Households by Number of Servants Employed, 1871

	One	Two	Three	Four	Five & Up
Combined Districts					
Toronto	72.5	18.4	6.0	1.8	1.3
Quebec	68.5	17.9	9.1	2.8	1.7
Halifax	65.8	23.5	7.9	1.5	1.3
Wealthy Districts					
Toronto	76.3	18.2	4.5	0.5	0.5
Quebec	51.1	26.1	15.9	4.5	2.4
Halifax	54.2	28.5	12.7	2.5	2.1
Montreal	51.9	27.3	13.2	5.6	2.0

PAC, Census ... 1871.

for families that employed non-resident servants exclusively. Resident and non-resident servants may well have worked side by side. The household of George Pozer, a Quebec City merchant in 1818, is a good example of this. In addition, non-resident servants could equally well have found temporary employment in the institutions that employed some 20 per cent of the servant population in 1871.

Households employing servants did not have great numbers of them. The 1871 census shows an average of 1.5 servants per household; the figure for Quebec City in 1818 is 1.8. However, in the wealthy sections of the 1871 cities the average (based on the census) generally ran around 1.7 to 1.8. Two out of three homes had only one servant and it was very rare that five or more servants worked in a home (Table 21). The situation in 1818 was similar: 60 per cent of families only had one servant; however, those families with five or more accounted for around four per cent.

Table 21 shows that 80 to 88 per cent of households had no more than two servants and only two to four per cent had four or more. When we consider that only ten to 15 per cent of homes had servants and that among these only two to four per cent had several, we are obviously a far cry from the picture of a 19th century peopled with servants. Of course in better areas of the cities the figures were somewhat higher. In Quebec City and Montreal it verged on seven per

Table 22

Households with Live-In Servants, 1871

	Percent. H'hold	Masters		Av. Age		Av. No. Children	Av. No. Persons per Household
		M	W	M	W		
Combined Districts							
Toronto	11.3	91.4	8.6	43.0	50.1	3.5	5.2
Quebec	9.7	90.3	9.7	43.2	52.4	3.6	4.9
Halifax	15.4	88.2	11.8	43.0	52.7	3.2	4.8
Wealthy Districts							
Toronto	21.2	89.1	10.9	42.1	51.4	3.4	5.1
Quebec	51.2	87.1	12.9	46.6	51.4	3.7	4.7
Halifax	28.0	89.2	10.8	46.1	58.3	3.3	4.9
Montreal	23.5	90.5	9.5	43.9	51.4	3.5	5.2

PAC, Census ... 1871.

cent, but even then it is very modest. Indeed, it is interesting to compare these statistics with those for Boston in 1845, which are very similar, when 67.2 per cent of Boston households had one servant, 22.3 per cent had two, 6.3 per cent had three, 2.8 per cent had four, and 1.4 per cent had five or more.[25] Or take the town of Versailles in 1872, when 80 per cent of domestics were employed in houses where they either served alone or with one other person.[26]

The type of household that employed servants differed little from one city, or even from one period, to another. For example, families averaged five members,[27] the head of the family was around 43 years of age (42.2 in 1818 Quebec City), and men were only hired when three other servants were already on staff. (When it did happen that a man was the lone servant, he would generally be working for a bachelor.) In addition, in both periods families in which the head was in commerce were the most common.

Some of the features in Table 22 deserve comment. Women employers, who only represented ten per cent of employers, were almost all widows (about 80 per cent of cases). Also, only families with children were considered when establishing the average number of children per household. Finally, additional persons were present in 20 to 30 per cent of households: parents-in-law, brothers and sisters, or even outsiders. As a general rule these households contained 1.5 to two such people, but these figures do not include their servants.

Table 23

Households with Live-In Servants
by Master's Occupation, 1871

	Com.	Prof.	Civil Serv.	Ind. Means	Mfg.	Trans.	Const.	Serv.	Other
Combined Districts									
Toronto	32.1	21.8	4.5	3.2	11.8	4.0	2.5	7.4	12.7
Quebec	31.4	13.8	6.2	2.7	14.2	4.4	1.7	8.3	17.3
Halifax	40.6	12.0	5.0	0.9	11.8	4.8	4.2	5.2	15.5
Wealthy Districts									
Toronto	39.9	20.2	5.5	0.7	8.6	1.3	1.8	6.6	15.4
Quebec	27.5	21.7	9.9	3.2	4.3	2.3	0.4	8.8	21.9
Halifax	44.6	14.2	9.0	2.4	8.4	0.6	1.9	3.4	15.5
Montreal	42.9	15.1	3.7	4.9	12.1	2.7	3.3	3.5	11.8

PAC, Census ... 1871.

Table 24

Urban Households by Master's Occupation, 1871

	Com.	Prof.	Civil Serv.	Ind. Means	Mfg.	Trans.	Const.	Serv.	Other
Toronto	16.8	6.1	1.2	1.3	23.8	4.6	10.1	16.3	19.8
Quebec	16.0	3.6	2.1	0.9	19.1	9.0	13.4	14.6	21.3
Halifax	17.3	4.0	1.9	0.4	19.1	8.1	9.0	11.5	28.7
Montreal	18.5	5.2	1.3	1.2	23.4	5.1	9.6	17.2	18.5

Canada. Parliament, *Census of Canada/Recensement du Canada, 1870-71* (Ottawa: I.B. Taylor, 1873), Vol. 2, pp. 262-71, 286-97, 310-21, 334-45.

The number of people in commerce, the professions, and the civil service plus those of independent means employing servants was two to three times higher than the relative importance of their particular occupation in the population as a whole, whereas the opposite was true for people in manufacturing, transportation, construction, and services (compare Tables 23 and 24). Thus, in Halifax, heads of households in commerce (17.3 per cent of the city's population) accounted for 40.6 per cent of those employing servants; professionals (four per cent of occupations) accounted for 12 per cent. The figures are 1.9 versus five per cent for civil servants and 0.4 versus 0.9 per cent for those of independent means. Those in manufacturing (19.1 per cent of the working population) only formed 11.8 per cent of masters. For those working in transportation the ratios are 8.1 to 4.8 per cent; construction, 9 to 4.2 per cent; and in the services, 11.5 versus 5.2 per cent. These imbalances are confirmed by the fact that the average number of servants per household could vary greatly depending on the master's profession (see Table 25).

How the percentage of employers' occupations would vary between decades in a given city was also studied, and data were compiled for Quebec City in 1818, 1842, and 1871. According to Table 26, those in manufacturing, construction, and transport were losing ground whereas professionals and people in commerce were gaining. In 1818 there were 1.8 domestics per family; this figure dropped to 1.6 in

Table 25

**Average Number of Servants per Family
by Master's Occupation, 1871**

	Com.	Prof.	Civil Serv.	Ind. Means	Mfg.	Trans.	Const.	Serv.	Other
Combined Districts									
Toronto	1.3	1.7	1.8	1.7	1.2	1.3	1.4	1.3	1.3
Quebec	1.6	1.9	1.8	1.9	1.1	1.3	1.4	1.5	1.3
Halifax	1.6	1.8	1.7	2.1	1.2	1.1	1.1	1.1	1.4
Wealthy Districts									
Toronto	1.2	1.6	1.5	1.0	1.3	1.6	1.3	1.1	1.3
Quebec	1.9	2.1	1.8	2.1	1.3	1.6	2.0	1.5	1.6
Halifax	1.8	2.1	1.8	2.1	1.1	1.0	1.3	1.0	1.5
Montreal	1.9	2.0	2.1	1.9	1.5	1.4	1.1	1.5	1.7

PAC, Census ... 1871.

Table 26

Masters' Occupations, Quebec City, 1818, 1842, and 1871

	Com.	Prof.	Civil Serv.	Ind. Means	Mfg.	Trans.	Const.	Serv.	Other
1818	21.5	6.2	3.2	1.4	15.8	7.5	13.3	1.3	29.8
1842	26.4	9.5	4.1	3.2	20.3	7.2	5.2	10.4	13.7
1871	31.4	13.8	6.2	2.7	14.2	4.4	1.7	8.3	17.3

Joseph Signay, *Recensement de la ville de Québec en 1818*, preface by H. Provost (Quebec: Société historique de Québec, 1976); 1842 Quebec City census data courtesy of Jean-Pierre Hardy; PAC, Census ... 1871.

Table 27

Distribution of Heads of Households Employing Several Servants by Master's Occupation, 1871

	Com.	Prof.	Civil Serv.	Ind. Means	Mfg.	Trans.	Const.	Serv.	Other
All households	33.9	16.1	5.2	3.3	12.5	4.3	2.6	7.1	15.0
Households with 4 or more servants	37.9	27.4	11.1	7.9	3.2	1.0	0.0	2.6	8.9

PAC, Census ... 1871.

1842 and 1.5 in 1871. These figures may be evidence of the city's decline between 1840 and 1870, but that does not seem to be the explanation because the 1818 census figures are far less accurate than those in 1871, and insofar as domestics were concerned, the situation was perhaps similar in the other cities.

To take a closer look at households with several servants, I studied homes employing at least four domestics. There were 190 such homes spread over the four cities: 38 in Toronto, 51 in Quebec City, 26 in Halifax, and 75 in the Saint-Antoine district of Montreal. As a general rule these households differed little from the remainder: masters averaged 49 years of age rather than 43 and had four children instead of three. The households had an average of 4.6 servants, with one man for three women. The men were the same age as menservants in general — which is normal because men usually only worked in houses with several servants — and the women were three years older than women in service as a whole. The heads of these families were mainly professionals, civil servants, in commerce, or of independent means (Table 27).

Only 22 of the 190 households had six servants or more: three were in Toronto, six in Quebec City, four in Halifax, and nine in the Saint-Antoine area of Montreal. Female servants in these cases were over 30 years of age, a good five years older than female servants generally, which clearly shows that one could only hope to work in one of the better houses if good experience had been gained elsewhere. However, the heads of these households were younger (46) than the average of those having more than four servants. There were ten merchants, six civil servants, five professionals, and the remaining employer was a widow of no stated occupation.

We have to conclude that in the four most populous cities of the country in 1871, few households could employ a staff of servants. Indeed, even households with one servant were exceptions since only ten to 15 per cent of city households employed any servants. Canada was no different in this respect from the United States, France, or England since virtually everywhere it seems that at best only one household out of six had one or more servants. And in the other countries, percentages have been based on the servant population as a whole and not solely on those who lived in their masters' homes.

This is a far cry from the generally accepted belief that many households in the last century had domestic servants, even large staffs of servants. Nevertheless, that picture has persisted, mainly in literature,[28] and is still alive and well, as evidenced by the November 1980 issue of *En route*: "Our Victorian ancestors took many of the things we consider luxuries for granted. Servants, large houses...."[29] No doubt the generations that passed on this impression to us liked to think, when struggling with the problems of everyday life, that their forefathers had lived in a golden age that could come again. They probably also held a faulty impression of the make-up of the "middle class" to which they considered they belonged, preferring to think that it included most average people rather than admitting that it actually only represented a very small part of the population.[30]

DOMESTIC SERVICE

It is difficult to discuss what domestic service in Canada involved and what working conditions were like in the second half of the 19th century since there are few typically Canadian sources to consult. Although numerous hiring contracts were available for studying domestic service at the beginning of the century, these contracts became somewhat rare after 1850 and only a few were found for 1871-75.[1] Even though various treatises on household management were published in the United States, France, and Great Britain[2] throughout the 19th century, not until the second half of the century did such works appear in Canada.[3]

That does not necessarily mean that service here differed from that in Europe or the United States. Everything leads us to believe that it was very similar, and it is easy to imagine the popular books by Beecher, Beeton, and Pariset being read and consulted here just as much as anywhere else. (This situation closely parallels the one that existed for literature for it seems the novelists read here were mainly European.[4]) Other sources, however, proved useful, such as house plans[5] or certain personal diaries[6] that give a glimpse of some of the details of recruiting or hiring servants, as well as the type of work required and the conditions that prevailed at the time.

Hiring

Several avenues were open, here as elsewhere, to someone searching for a situation or for a servant. Commercial placement agencies were virtually everywhere and some of them dealt almost entirely with placing domestic servants. They were already operating in Quebec City in 1818 and in Montreal in 1820, calling themselves "Registry Offices" or "Bureaux d'enregistrement."[7] In Europe and the United States, agencies usually required a registration fee, which was far lower for employees than for employers.[8] However, as far as the servants were concerned, the sum still verged on exploitation because it was frequently the equivalent of a day's wages[9] and carried no guarantee of obtaining employment. In addition, servants often had to register with several agencies because information was not always passed from one agency to another.[10]

Moreover, such agencies often had poor reputations. This complaint has been noted by all the European and American authors who have studied the subject.[11] A a study carried out in New York in the 1880s estimated that 75 per cent of placement agencies did not hesitate to send young women into houses of poor repute.[12] We have no information as to whether the same situation prevailed in commercial agencies in Canada; however, in line with what was being done elsewhere, Canadian religious orders and charitable associations set up houses that sheltered out-of-work servants and offered employment agency services.[13] These agencies-cum-shelters often offered their services to domestics free of charge, but did request contributions from employers.[14] The doubling of shelter and employment agency was fairly widespread, and this type of charity was particularly popular around the middle of the century.[15] Several examples appeared in Toronto after the House of Industry Act was voted in 1837, as well as in Montreal during the 1840s.[16] Such houses also existed in Halifax, as can be seen by the annual reports of the Home for Young Women Seeking Employment (see Appendix D).

These various organizations were not the only means of gaining employment to which masters and servants had recourse; advertisements offering or requesting employment could be placed in newspapers. There were three times more offers of employment than requests for it in the documents consulted for the end of the century.[17] However, this ratio very likely does not reflect the true state of affairs since financially it was far easier for employers to advertise than servants. Some authors consider that only the better-educated servants thought of using newspapers, and furthermore, the fact that they had to go to the newspaper offices in order to reply to an advertisement discouraged both servants and employers. Both sides were convinced that more often than not the position had already been filled or the servant hired by someone else.[18]

Word of mouth was also a means of finding openings or staff and some authors state that it was the most widely used.[19] In cities where the mass of servants was often concentrated in one particular district, it must have been easy to know that a good place, or alternatively a good servant, was available.[20] The fact that members of the same family often worked in the same house is eloquent proof of this, for it is not difficult to imagine that a servant would praise the skills of one of her relatives if her employer was seeking a new servant.[21] In the four cities studied, nine per cent of servants working in houses having more than one servant were related.[22]

When they were actually hired, servants had only the experience acquired during previous employment[23] or the basics learned during time spent in a charitable institution.[24] For this reason employers usually requested references on the servant's previous work and conduct.[25] This was an old and very widespread custom;[26] it was rec-

90

ommended in all the handbooks[27] and was common practice here in Canada.[28] The requirement did not suit all domestic servants, and according to Lady Dufferin, some character references could have been manufactured.[29] Furthermore, a good number of employers did not attach much importance to references, a fact the *Acadian Reporter* deplored in 1875 when a series of thefts occurred in Halifax:

> There are several females prowling about this community at the present time, in the disguise of female servants, whose ways are dark and who abound in vain tricks. They hire from place to place, apparently with no other object than that of robbing their employers which they generally succeed in doing very soon after they have become domiciled.... Meanwhile, housekeepers are very foolish to take domestic servants without receiving and verifying certificates or characters from previous employers or other responsible parties.[30]

Whatever the means of hiring, and girded with good references or not, it seems that generally women started as maids-of-all-work and only reached employment with the wealthier families after gaining several years' experience.[31] This therefore means that the nature of the work and the conditions under which it was done varied considerably from one place to another and that both must have improved appreciably as the servant moved upward in the hierarchy.

Types and Conditions of Work

I will not take time here to describe domestic servants' various duties in detail. In any case, there would be a good chance that some duty would be forgotten because it is difficult to believe that one person could accomplish all the work that had to be done in a day according to household management treatises and servants' handbooks (Appendix E). However, such tasks differed greatly depending on whether there was just one servant in a household or several. Thus, the single servant found herself responsible (as at the beginning of the century) for the cleaning, cooking, errands, kitchen garden, and sometimes children, too. On the other hand, when there were several servants, duties became more specialized. For example, a family who could employ two servants engaged a cook and a woman for the housework; the third servant could have been a groom who would also be responsible for outside work and waiting on the table; the fourth would be a companion or children's nurse. The fifth would be another female servant or else a young boy for the horses; and when peo-

Table 28

Distribution (%) of Servants Working Alone or with Others in a Household, 1871

	One	Two	Three	Four	Five & Up
Combined Districts					
Toronto	51.2	25.9	12.7	5.1	5.1
Quebec	45.1	23.6	18.0	7.4	5.9
Halifax	43.9	31.3	15.7	4.1	5.0
Wealthy Districts					
Toronto	58.2	27.7	10.4	1.6	2.1
Quebec	26.8	27.5	25.0	9.5	11.2
Halifax	31.6	33.2	22.2	5.8	7.2
Montreal	28.7	30.3	22.0	12.3	6.7

PAC, Census ... 1871.

ple had six or more, a female or male servant was added, generally maintaining a ratio of one man for three women.[32]

For the cities studied I considered how servants were divided amongst the households (Table 28). Obviously only a minority worked in houses with at least four servants — 11 per cent for the three cities as a whole and 14 per cent in the wealthy areas. Nearly 74 per cent worked alone or with one other servant — 46.7 per cent and 26.9 per cent respectively. In the better areas the percentage rose to 66 per cent, the ratios being 36.3 and 29.7. However, these were in relation to domestic servants as a whole and were found to be very different if men and women were considered separately, the former working mainly in houses where staffs of several servants were already in place (Table 29; the percentages have been rounded off).

Working conditions must also have varied greatly depending on the number of servants in a household. To have a good idea of what was involved, one would have to review each type of servant individually and the conditions applicable to their specific work. This extremely lengthy process does not really fall within the context of this study, and I have therefore preferred to deal with the majority of servants — those who were alone or with one other — shading the findings by referring to conditions that might have existed in the more

Table 29

Distribution (%) of Male and Female Servants
Working Alone or with Others, 1871

	One		Two		Three		Four		Five & Up	
	M	F	M	F	M	F	M	F	M	F
Combined Districts										
Toronto	21	54	26	26	22	12	15	4	16	4
Quebec	14	49	24	24	32	16	14	6	16	5
Halifax	12	46	27	31	36	15	5	4	20	4
Wealthy Districts										
Toronto	15	60	35	27	30	10	10	1	10	2
Quebec	8	29	19	29	38	23	17	9	18	10
Halifax	8	36	21	32	29	21	8	5	34	6
Montreal	5	31	16	32	38	20	24	11	17	6

PAC, Census ... 1871.

well-to-do houses. Only the conditions of work as such will be dealt with in this chapter.

Duties and Remuneration

The first thing that must be said is that domestic service was hard, exacting work. A female servant often had to lift heavy objects and move them from room to room, even from floor to floor. In Canada, house plans that have been studied show that the majority of houses had two or three floors, sometimes four or five, with a basement and attic in addition[33] (see Figs. 16 to 19 as examples). That means there were nearly a hundred steps to go up and down with objects often weighing 30 pounds, and using the narrow, steep, and uncarpeted back stairs.[34]

Another aspect of the hard work was the constant need to keep the house clean and in good order: carpets, furniture, fire dogs, fireplace grates, staircases, wooden and stone floors (see Appendix E). In addition, some of the work was done in the kitchen where the heat

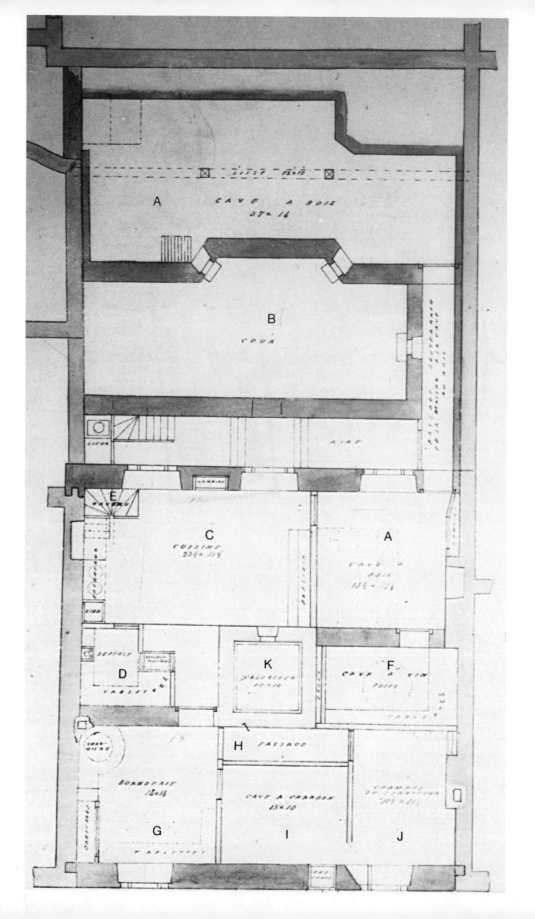

18 *Right:* second-floor plan, Cirice Têtu house, Quebec City, 1852.

A Storage	F Dressing room
B Hayloft	G Main stairs
C Courtyard below	H Bedroom
D Back stairs	I Drawing room
E Lavatory	J Boudoir

---

19 *Far right:* third-floor plan, Cirice Têtu house, Quebec City, 1852.

A Stable roof	F Anteroom
B Skylight	G Main stairs
C Courtyard below	H Vestibule
D Back stairs	I Bedroom
E W.C.	

---

16 *Far left:* basement plan, Cirice Têtu house, Quebec City, 1852.

A Wood cellar
B Unexcavated; court-
   yard above
C Kitchen
D Pantry
E Back stairs

F Wine cellar
G Laundry room
H Passage
I Coal cellar
J Manservant's room
K Furnace

---

17 *Left:* first-floor plan, Cirice Têtu house, Quebec City, 1852.

A Coach room
B Stalls
C Tack room
D Courtyard
E Back stairs
F Pantry
G Anteroom

H Main stairs
I Study
J Dining room
K Hall
L Vestibule
M Parlour

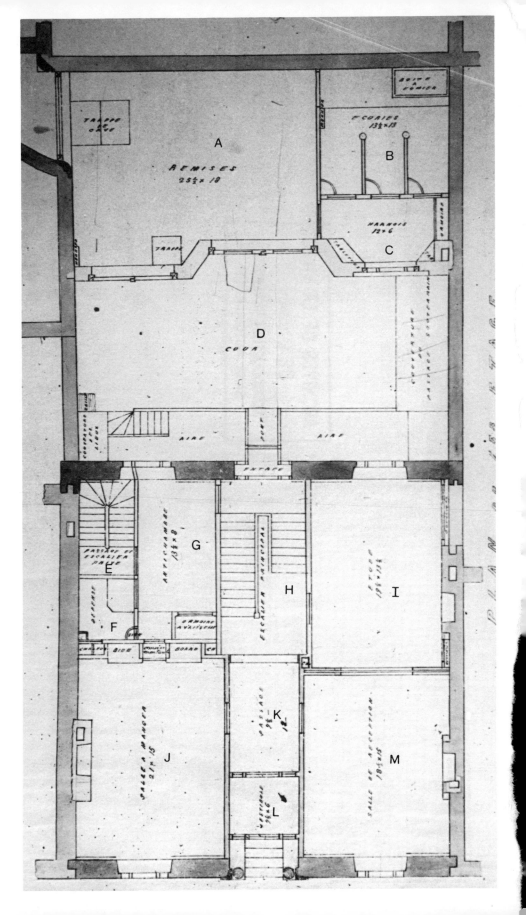

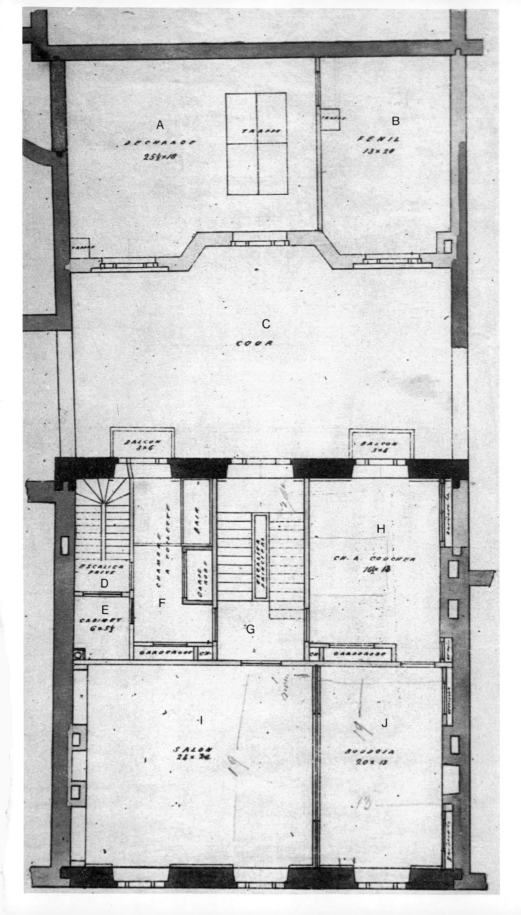

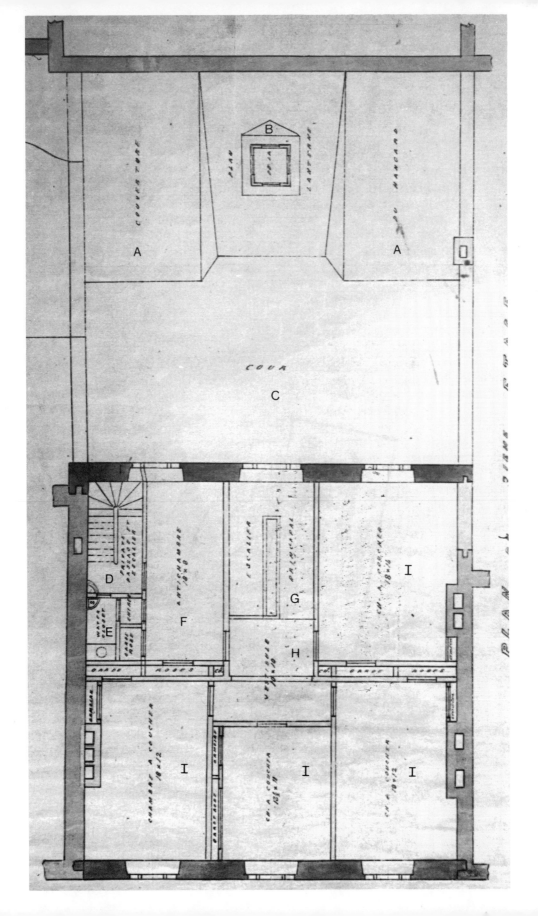

was stifling nearly all day long. These heavy and exacting duties were made all the more difficult because the servant was on call at all times, even when the normal day's work was ended.

Consequently, the workday was not only punishing, it also was long. It lasted 15 hours or so, sometimes up to 17 or 18 hours,[35] which everyone found normal:

> Ladies who rise at 11 o'clock and feel fatigued after
> their morning walk find it completely natural that
> their servant wake at 6 in the morning and work until
> 11 at night.[36]

Moreover, working hours in the latter half of the century were even longer than at the beginning of the century because polite society had acquired the habit of eating far later, around seven or eight o'clock.[37] Servants' days were therefore longer at the expense of the time previously available for rest and relaxation.[38] A day could even become as long as 18 hours because when the masters went out, servants had to await their return before going to bed (Fig. 20).

These difficult conditions meant that domestics tried to improve their lot by continually changing their place of employment. This was a constant complaint of employers at the time, and fairly often the servants left without notice or decided to leave at inconvenient moments.[39] All authors on the subject agree that servants' mobility was excessive. Europeans said that servants "remained in one place just long enough to get used to it,"[40] and American employers were at the placement offices three or four times a year.[41] It seems that the situation in Canada was similar. While we do not have documents such as household management manuals and servants' handbooks that make this as easy to observe as in the other countries, other documents contain information of interest.[42] For instance, a wage book belonging to Jules Quesnel of Quebec City shows that more than half the domestic servants in his employ did not stay a full year, the average being five months.[43] And the same situation existed in Toronto at the beginning of this century if we are to believe this old joke:

> A Magistrate remarked to a man brought before him
> for speeding.
> "The officer tells me that you were going forty miles
> an hour."
> "Yes Sir, your Honour," the culprit admitted, "I was. I
> had just received word from the Employment Office
> that they found a COOK who would agree to come to
> our house in the suburbs and stay at least a week."
> Fortunately the magistrate, too, lived in the suburbs.
> "Officer," he ordered, "Get my car for this man at
> once. It does at least sixty miles an hour easily."[44]

Obviously conditions in wealthier homes with several servants were easier. For example, the chambermaid who acted as lady's maid

20 Always the last to bed.

to her mistress did not have to make the physical effort required by the cook's help in the kitchen, and on her side, the latter did not have to clean the rooms — whereas a single servant had to take care of everything. Menservants' work in such houses was even less exacting because they represented an element of prestige for the household.[45] The caricatures of the time speak volumes on the subject, and it is not rare for them to show a maid hauling an enormous bucket of coal up a staircase followed by a manservant bearing a letter on a tray.[46]

Since conditions were better, domestics in well-to-do houses changed their positions less frequently than did other domestics. This is evident from personal diaries. It appears that in circles as wealthy as those of Lady Dufferin, Philippe Aubert de Gaspé, and Henriette Dessaulles, some servants remained with their employers for a long time. However, a uniform was generally required in these circles, a requirement that did not apply to the maid-of-all-work (compare Figs. 15 and 20). In any case, maids-of-all-work would not have had the means of paying for their uniforms, nor their masters the means of buying them uniforms.

Domestic servants were housed and fed in return for services rendered. This represented a major part of their remuneration since people at the time considered that servants' bed and board cost employers twice their wages.[47] In Canada a female servant received about five to six dollars a month[48] and a male servant could easily earn double that sum.[49] These figures were virtually the same as those in England, but below those of the United States.[50] At first glance such sums may appear paltry, but they were very close to wages for factory workers who, unlike servants, had to feed and house themselves.[51] Servants derived additional benefits from their employment: some received gifts at Christmastime, others received money from the merchants with whom they did business on their masters' behalf, and yet others sold kitchen scraps — fat or ashes[52] — to peddlers.

But they had little time off work. During the 1870s a servant could have an evening or half-day free once a week or every two weeks, but since she was required to finish most of her work before leaving, her time off only started after seven or eight hours of work.[53] It also seems that her time was not completely free, for some might have had to take children for a walk and others were deprived of their outings as punishment for some neglected task or disobedience, or because some urgent work — in the master's eyes — had to be carried out immediately.[54] Some employers also offered their domestics a week's annual holiday so that they could visit their families,[55] but in view of the very high mobility of the majority of them, it is debatable how many could have taken advantage of such offers.

If a servant was sick, she was generally cared for in her employers's home, but only in cases of very short illnesses.[56] A sick servant was simply dismissed from her employment.

100

THE PATENT GRIDIRON.

BIDDY.—"If ye plase, Ma'am, your new fanglings have dropped me mate in the fior! What'll I do?"

MISTRESS —"Well, Biddy, Professor Cook tells us that only the carbonaceous portion undergoes combustion, so I suppose you can quickly rescue the fibrinous residue!"

BIDDY.—"Faith, Ma'am, an' if it's this rat trap of a toasting fork ye mane, I wish it gone busted like the mate, shure I niver lost my stake thro' my fryin' pan that way."

21 The vicissitudes of a cook.

SCIENCE AT A DISCOUNT.

COOK.—" Please 'm, I've come down to give you notice once more, for the likes o' this I
never did see, nor will I staud. 'Ere's Miss Amelier a poking her glass thing-a-bob
inter my mince pies to try their tempers, and well I knows as it tries mine, a lettin'
down the 'eats aud coolin' the hoven. Has for Perfesser Cook, I'm tired o' 'earin'
of 'im, and I don't b'lieve there's no sich person as 'ud talk sich nonsense."

22 Harrassing the servants.

In well-to-do households, conditions were much better. Servants were generally better housed, fed, and cared for, and some positions carried with them wages far above average.[57] It was also easier to take time off because a servant could arrange for one of her fellows to cover for her so that she could leave early or return late. In addition, since servants in these houses were more likely to keep their positions, they no doubt also benefited from annual holidays to visit their families.

Many other aspects of working conditions deserve mention. The utensils used, for instance, have not been discussed because they are only mentioned in manuals on household management. Consequently we do not know whether they were adequate or whether there were enough of them, but one can frankly doubt that the majority of households had the ten different kinds of brushes that Isabella Beeton's *Book of Household Management* mentions as being virtually indispensable.[58] Likewise, I have not examined communication problems. Although servants were mainly hired to work in houses where the same language was spoken,[59] the masters' speech did not always resemble that of the servants, which must have caused problems on both sides (see Figs. 14, 21, and 22). Nor have I spoken of the loneliness and weariness that were to some extent inherent in a servant's work, especially in one-servant households (66 per cent). And I have not fully discussed the very temporary nature of service for the majority of domestics and the numerous difficulties that many consequently found in trying to improve their conditions of work. But be that as it may, many people entered domestic service and that it itself indicates that advantages were found in it.

Disadvantages and Advantages

There were many disadvantages to being in service (hard work, long hours, little rest or free time). Servants were consequently often liable to have accidents and contract sickness, some complained of poor digestion, and many suffered from anemia.[60] However, they could not afford to be ill because they were quickly sent packing if they could not carry out their duties. In addition, their work involved personal relationships in which they were, of necessity, the inferior,[61] and often over and above this, they were victims of their masters' various whims.[62] They felt poorly regarded, isolated, without roots or security.[63]

On the other hand, compared with other, poorer groups of the time, servants were well off. Their bed and board was assured; they suffered less from hunger and cold than the poor of the cities. In addition, since they received wages, they could save a little, which was not the case for their fellow workers.[64] Possible savings are, in fact, the advantage authors emphasize most. In Canada there were saving banks to which domestics could subscribe.[65] Those who worked for wealthy families also had the advantage of living surrounded by a certain degree of luxury, and some even had opportunities to travel. This, at least, was so for the servants of Lord and Lady Dufferin who accompanied the viceregal party across the country and to the United States.[66]

Did these advantages compensate for the many disadvantages of being in service? If we rely on the various statements concerning France, England, and the United States, the result is somewhat negative.[67] Regrettably, it is impossible to judge whether the same situation existed in Canada from the documentation available because Canada has nothing similar to statements made public in the other countries at the turn of the century[68] nor memoirs of servants of the time.[69] This silence could, of course, be interpreted in many ways, but all indications are that the working conditions of domestic servants in Canada closely resembled those in other countries.

EVERYDAY LIFE *ftnts p 197*

Servants' living conditions obviously more or less followed the same curves as those relating to their working conditions. "Living conditions" means, firstly, everything connected with bed and board — lodging, food and clothing; secondly, health and spare time; and finally, everything connected with mores and crimes. Certain factors had great impact on servants' living conditions — for example, the way in which they were perceived, employers' attitudes, family ties, or their relationships with their fellows. In view of their importance, these various aspects form a separate chapter ("Social Relationships").

Bed and Board

Feeding and lodging servants was a source of much concern at the time. Many denounced the poor conditions in which servants had to exist, considering them one of the main causes for servants' high mobility; others thought the conditions were suited to the station of people in service. Thus in the 1870s one could either become indignant at the idea that a maidservant often "must sleep in a comfortless garret; and that when a new domestic comes, perhaps a coarse and dirty foreigner, she must share her bed with her,"[1] or simply state, "It is generally thought that to warm their rooms is treating them with far too much consideration, and placing them beyond the sphere to which they belong."[2] These examples come from American documents, but equivalent ones can be found in British and French texts.

Authors today — American, British, or French — all agree that servants were generally poorly lodged.[3] Their rooms were small and dirty and provided no privacy or safety for the occupants. Rooms were poorly ventilated and ill-lit because the windows were small or merely skylights. Most rooms were also damp and badly heated, glacial in winter and tropical in summer. They were poorly furnished and decorated: there was normally an iron bedstead with a bad mattress, odd pieces of old furniture, and a small tarnished mirror. And, to top it all, rooms were normally in the most inaccessible parts of the houses: in France, in the garret; in Great Britain, in the basement (men) and the attic (women); in the United States, sometimes in the basement, above the kitchen, or in the attic.

Despite the statements made in home economic texts and house plans of the period on the importance of better lodgings for servants, nothing really changed. At the turn of the century the same kind of recommendation was being made in the same kind of book.[4]

Servants' bedrooms were not the only rooms that received bad press and bad reputations: people also became indignant about conditions in the kitchens. This was vitally important because the servants' world was precisely the kitchen.[5] That was where they passed the greater part of their working day, and where they ate and rested in the evening once work ended. But, although most kitchens were fairly spacious, lighting and ventilation were rarely adequate. In addition, since a good fire had to be kept going all the time, the heat was often stifling, even infernal. It also seems that furniture in it was sparse and uncomfortable and that it was frequently a most unattractive room since it was generally situated in the basement, at the back of the house. After the 1850s, house plans recommended that it should be moved up to the ground floor,[6] but not until the end of the century did this became a general custom, the changeover being far slower in the cities than in the countryside.[7] In the wealthiest houses, of course, lodgings were much better. Upper servants had their own rooms, and there was also a servants' hall where all servants could eat and relax[8] — this room was usually off the kitchen or nearby — but even there the situation could vary from one house to another.[9]

The Canadian situation corresponded closely to that elsewhere and we are fortunate to have many estate inventories and architectural plans that actually refer to the subject. Thus, among the more than 400 plans consulted,[10] about 50 were sufficiently detailed for the servants' quarters to be identified. In addition, some 40 of the 1260 inventories drawn up between 1871 and 1875[11] enable us to reconstruct how the quarters were furnished.

According to the plans, servants' rooms were usually small compared with other bedrooms in the house, and women's rooms normally housed more than one domestic. In fact, 63 per cent of female servants' rooms measured no more than 12 feet by 12 feet, and the majority of that 63 per cent were 8 feet by 10 feet. Data on 12 menservants' rooms and 43 female servants' rooms are given in Table 30. When room sizes were detailed, menservants' rooms were larger in every case but two, and men did not have to share their rooms, as was nearly always the case for women. When a manservant's room was smaller, it was only smaller by a few square feet (see Fig. 23).

The plans show that in two-thirds of the houses with both male and female servants, the servants' rooms were on the same floor, nearly always the basement (Fig. 23). Judging from post-1850 plans, it appears there was a tendency as the century progressed to move the servants' rooms towards the top of the house. At the beginning of the 19th century the majority were in the basement, near the kitchen,

106

Table 30

Size of Servants' Bedrooms Shown on House Plans, Second Half of the 19th Century

Measurements (Sq. Ft.)	Rooms	
	Male Servants	Female Servants
100 or less	3	16
101 to 150	3	11
151 to 199	3	6
200 and up	3	10
Total	12	43

House plans deposited in PAC, AO, ANQ-M, ANQ-Q, AVQ, and Toronto Metropolitan Public Library.

whereas in the second half of the century only 50 per cent were still located there. In Canada, however, the custom of lodging women in the attic does not seem to have taken hold[12] since only ten per cent of the rooms were located there according to the plans studied. The remaining 40 per cent were divided more or less equally between the ground floor and the bedroom floor (see Figs. 24 and 25 respectively). What did not change from one half of the century to the other was the proximity of the servants' rooms to the kitchen in two-thirds of cases, some being beside it and others just above (see Figs. 23, 24, and 26).

These data are essentially what could be extracted from the plans studied. However, I cannot state with certainty that the extracts represent servants' rooms in general for the second half of the 19th century because the plans mainly applied to new houses for the well-to-do. However, estate inventories seem to bear them out.[13] According to these, when domestics of both sexes were employed, their rooms were on the same level in two out of three houses (the basement in 50 per cent of cases), the remainder being spread over more than one floor. The inventories, which only cover 1871 to 1875, confirm the same upward movement because, taking the total number of rooms detailed, the proportion of basement rooms fell to 40 per cent in the 1870s, whereas those on the bedroom floor rose to around 35 per cent. The remainder were either on the ground floor (20 per cent or so) or in the attic.

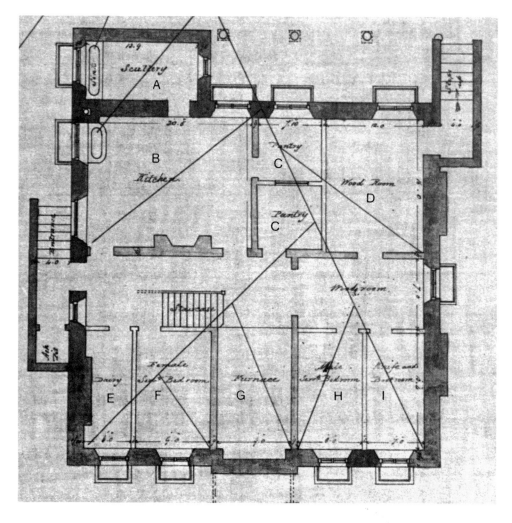

23 Basement plan, Egerton Ryerson house, Toronto, *circa* 1860.

A Scullery   F Female servants' bedroom
B Kitchen   G Furnace
C Pantry   H Male servant's bedroom
D Wood room   I Knife and boot room
E Dairy

Inventories also let us know how the rooms were furnished (see Fig. 28). The first thing one notices is that the furniture was very rudimentary, as was the case for American, British, and French servants' quarters. For example, of the 46 rooms for which a price was estimated, half were under ten dollars and only ten were worth more than 20 dollars. These sums are paltry considering that the furniture as a whole in some of the houses was valued at four or five thousand dollars.

The average room furnished for under ten dollars had an iron bedstead with mattress or paillasse, a small table, one or two chairs, a washstand, and a small mirror.[14] A well-furnished room, on the other hand (like those valued at over 20 dollars), could contain two beds with mattresses and blankets, a table, mirror, two chairs, dressing table, washstand, gas lamp, and a clock.[15]

However, a dozen or so inventories only stated "one Bed and Bedstead," so some rooms seem to have been below average. Likewise, although the inventories described 46 servants' rooms in all, one could only count 21 tables, 22 chairs, 36 washstands, and 24 small mirrors. And the totals of other objects mentioned are even lower: 15 dressing tables or chest of drawers, four gas lamps, three blinds, 23 pieces of worn carpet, and two clocks. Some inventories mention blankets, bedspreads, and pillows separately, but they were in the minority — only 11 inventories mention blankets, only seven mention bedspreads, and only 16 mention pillows. And out of all the rooms, only seven had more than one bed and only one had a stove.[16] The latter were all in very rich households employing staffs of servants.

In fact, in Canada as elsewhere, servants' furniture was very scanty and, most of the time, totally inadequate. The rooms also seem to have been unheated and unlit, and were generally innocent of any comfort or decoration. Apart from women employed in the houses of the very rich — and also those who worked alone, obviously — it seems to have been fairly common practice to have had to share one's bed.

At the end of the century a book on home economics published in Canada emphasized the importance of furnishing servants' rooms properly:

> It pays to make the servant's room as cozy and home-like as possible. A very little money and pain make all the difference between a dull, uninviting den and a dainty, pleasant chamber — curtains and carpets past their wear in the lower rooms, or if newly furnishing, why, cheap drugget and a bit of cheap muslin, make them home-like. A few cheap pictures, perhaps a shelf or a bright, innocent novel or two and last month's magazines. We know from our own experience how much we value our own special corner, which is ours alone.[17]

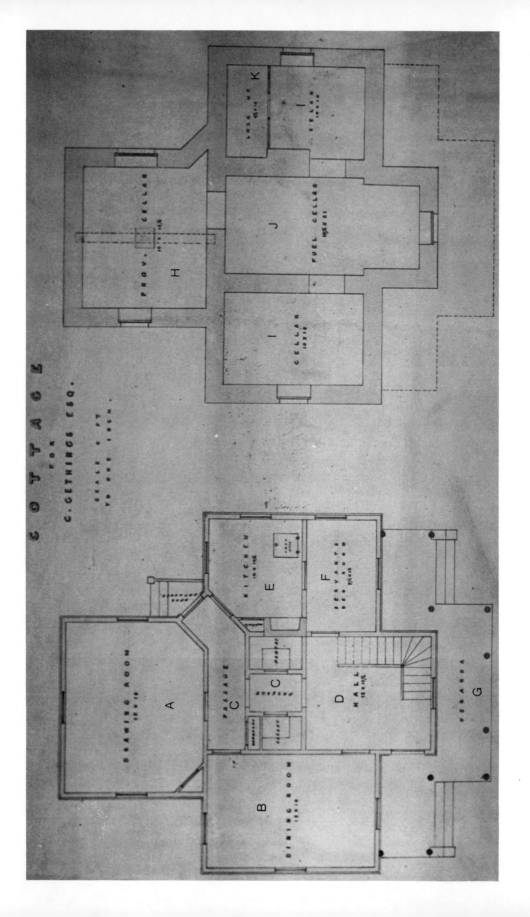

COTTAGE

FOR

C. GETHINGS ESQ.

SCALE 4 FT
TO ONE INCH.

A — DRAWING ROOM 19 x 18

B — DINING ROOM

C — PASSAGE

C — PANTRY

D — HALL 12 x 12½

E — KITCHEN 16 x 16

F — SERVANT'S BED ROOM 9¾ x 12

G — VERANDA

H — PROV. CELLAR

I — CELLAR

J — FUEL CELLAR

K — COAL UP.

I — CELLAR

24 and 25 Basement, ground-floor, and attic plans, C. Gethings cottage, Quebec City.

A Drawing room
B Dining room
C Passage
D Hall
E Kitchen
F Servants [sic] bedroom
G Verandah
H Provisions cellar

I Cellar
J Fuel cellar
K Lock-up
L Bedroom
M Wardrobe
N Lobby
O Gallery

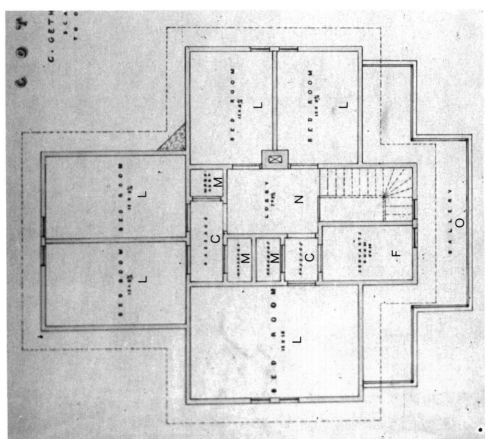

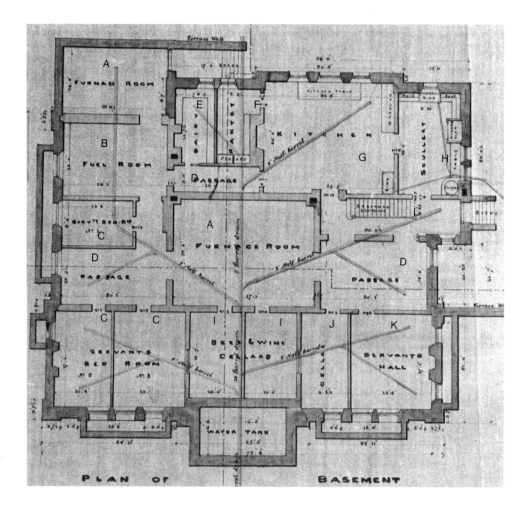

26 Basement plan, C.S. Gzowski residence, Toronto, 1855.

A Furnace room
B Fuel room
C Servants' bedrooms
D Passage
E Dairy
F Pantry

G Kitchen
H Scullery
I Beer and wine cellars
J Cellar
K Servants' hall
L Back stairs

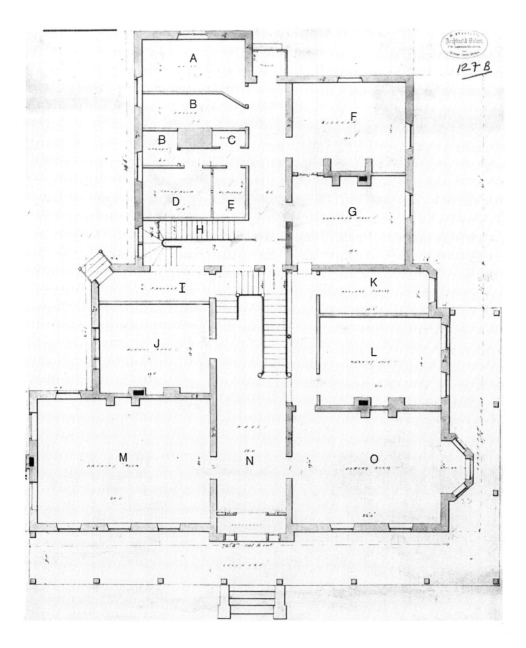

27 Ground-floor plan, J. Burstall residence, Quebec City, 1876.

A	Dairy	F	Kitchen	K	Butler's pantry
B	Larder	G	Servants' hall	L	Morning room
C	Glass	H	Back stairs	M	Drawing room
D	Storeroom	I	Passage	N	Hall
E	Kitchen pantry	J	Schoolroom	O	Dining room

Property Inventory of Louis Beaudry, Esq.

Servants' bedroom

One bed complete with bedding and cot, the whole valued	$ 5.00
One chest of drawers	2.00
One sofa	2.00
One small table	1.00

[The inventory notes that Mrs. Beaudry kept everything.]

Property Inventory of A.R. Sewell, Former Mayor of Quebec City

Servants room

Two single iron bedsteads valued two dollars each	$4.00
Two spring mattrasses [sic] two dollars and a half for the two	2.50
Two pillows valued one dollar	1.00
A towel horse valued twenty-five cents	0.25
A stove and pipes valued five dollars	5.00
A small table valued one dollar	1.00
Two small hair mattresses valued five dollars	5.00
Two pairs blankets valued one dollar and a half each pair	3.00
Two quilts valued one dollar each	2.00
A toilet glass valued one dollar	1.00
A washstand basin and jug valued one dollar and fifty cents	1.50
A scotch carpet valued four dollars	4.00
A large ___ box valued one dollar	1.00

28 Inventories of furnishings in servants' rooms in Montreal and Quebec City between 1871 and 1875.

In almost all the plans consulted the kitchen was fairly large — 300 square feet or more in many cases. Most were ill-lit, with few windows, and for that reason almost certainly poorly ventilated (see Figs. 16, 23, and 26). There was, however, a great improvement when kitchens were located on the ground floor (Figs. 24 and 27). Kitchen layout and equipment seem to have been fairly acceptable (see Fig. 16), and kitchens were relatively well equipped with utensils. As can be imagined, the heat must have been more overpowering there than anywhere else — Henriette Dessaulles wrote: "I feel sorry for the cooks, who spend their lives cooking themselves at the same time as our meals."[18]

We have less information on servants' living rooms. Only four per cent of plans mention them (Figs. 26 and 27 are examples), but the figure is significant because it more or less corresponds to the percentage of households employing four and more servants (see Table 21). Only one inventory describes such a room, the servants' room in the Montreal home of Sir William Logan. It appears to have been furnished with "one large sofa, two wood seat arm chairs, two plain wood seat arm chairs, one Pembroke table, one clothes basket and ironing blanket, one large water barrel and flower barrel," the whole valued at the sum of $9.75.[19]

Data are even harder to come by with respect to food and clothing. American, British, and French authors generally agree that servants ate well in the large houses but rather poorly in the more modest ones, where employing one or two servants could be a serious drain on the budget.[20] A number cite servants' complaints; others quote from household management manuals that seem to suggest that the servants took their meals after their employers in order to have the leftovers. And yet others mention that domestics were frequently accused of having stolen sweetmeats.[21] Some books on polite behaviour that appeared towards the end of the century emphasize that servants' food should be "wholesome and abundant."[22] This had not always been a matter for concern, for in the middle of the century the recommendation had been made that servants' midday meals should be taken while they "continued with their work, never being seated at the table."[23]

Clothing also depended on whether one was serving in a rich or modest home. In the former, men were required to wear livery, usually provided free[24] as had been the custom in the previous century. The women's situation was somewhat different since in the latter half of the century there was a growing insistence on a type of uniform — a light-coloured dress with cap and apron for the morning, and a dark dress in the afternoon — contrary to what had been the custom previously.[25] Some authors have remarked that the higher the family in the social scale, the greater the desire to have uniformed servants, even in the States, where livery had never been in style; in

115

She wore cotton combinations next to her skin, and over them she put on her corset. Then came long cotton knickers which buttoned at her waist and a kind of short vest called a spencer. Then came a flannel petticoat, and she had to wear thick black stockings that fastened to the legs of her corset. Her morning uniform was a blue cotton print frock, which came down to her ankles. She took it from its hook, behind a curtain that hung across one corner of her room and served as a wardrobe. She had to be very careful not to wake Rose Simmons, the house parlour-maid, who was asleep in the bed next to hers in their small, sparsely furnished attic bedroom.

She tied a white apron on over her dress, and put a heavy brown apron on over that. Then she had to put up her hair. This was difficult to do quickly. All servants had to wear their hair up, even if they were only twelve or thirteen.

29 Typical dress of a young female British domestic servant of Victorian times.

---

fact, some say that its popularity was renewed following the massive immigration of the 1840s and the arrival of an abundant force of servants on the work market.[26]

Being employed in a large house therefore meant that a man was clothed at his master's expense, whereas a woman's expenses increased. And it became even more costly as she progressed up the domestic scale because her work required that she be better dressed than the other female servants (compare Figs. 15 and 20). This was so for children's nurses, for example, and some authors have emphasized the considerable financial burden their position imposed[27] (Fig. 30).

In more modest houses servants were not required to wear uniforms other than the traditional caps and aprons (Fig. 31). Some servants were rather poorly dressed (Fig. 29), but many young ones desired the most luxurious clothing and hoped some day to to be able to buy it.[28] At the time — and often still today[29] — this attitude was considered to be copying one's betters, but it was also a question of circumstances: young housemaids did not have to provide their food or lodging so could upon occasion allow themselves the luxury of fine pieces of clothing. Indeed, some of them may have saved for no other reason than that.

30 A negligent nurserymaid.

The situation was no doubt similar in Canada. Some moneyed families required their servants to wear livery, like the one in Pamphile Lemay's comedy published at the end of the century.[30] Some servants of well-off families were very well dressed, as can be seen in the photo of Kate, the nurserymaid in the early 1860s, in Henriette Dessaulle's journal.[31] It also seems that Canadian servants emulated their European and American counterparts in fancying fine clothing even at the most menial level: Lady Dufferin noted in her diary on 23 September 1872, "I have been looking for a scullery maid ... one young lady in search of the place ... appeared in a smart hat and feathers."[32]

With respect to food we have very little real information that could allow us to judge its quality or quantity. In plays statements are made such as, "I really think we're going to have to eat the leftovers,"

117

31 At work in the kitchen.

which show that the situation was the same in Canada as elsewhere. We also know, because of *donations inter vivos* made between 1850 and 1870, that people ate really well in Canada, but that does not mean we can assume the same applied to domestic servants. According to a journalist of the time, servants in Canada were underpaid, overworked, and had hardly any free time in addition to being poorly lodged and poorly fed.[33]

Should we assume, then, that the great majority of domestic servants in urban areas in Canada lived under difficult conditions? And were they, in fact, difficult conditions for the period, taking into account the great poverty stalking the cities?[34] When all is said and done, there is every indication that servants were better lodged and fed in their masters' houses than in their families', at least as far as children were concerned since they were almost always placed in service by their family when it did not have the wherewithal to feed

118

and house them adequately. And many young adults must have found themselves in this situation, their wages very often going to help feed their families. As far as servants who only had to provide for their own needs were concerned, it is impossible to know whether they considered themselves better lodged and fed than they would have been at home. It is very possible, in fact, that for them food and lodging were not a question of quality and value but rather of security.[35]

Health and Pastimes

Data on health and pastimes are fragmentary in each country. Several authors have emphasized the danger to health and the risk of accidents occasioned by bad working conditions and poor food and lodging. Guiral and Thuillier, for example, listed the illnesses to which servants were prone: rheumatism, varicose veins, neuritis. They also highlighted the more insidious ravages of alcoholism, syphilis, and mental illnesses, and confirmed the high rate of mortality in young people "due to overwork, lack of rest and food."[36] McBride wrote of the widespread anemia and tuberculosis prevalent amongst servants. Showalter recounted that people at the time firmly believed that servants were the group most prone to mental illness.[37] Novels of the period perpetuated this idea, and Lamartine's *Geneviève* is a servant who should have been around 35 to 40 years old but whose age could not be discerned because her face was so worn by fatigue.[38]

Very little is known, too, about the hygiene of people in service. Most of them seem to have had washstands in their rooms, but it must have mainly served to splash their face and hands. In general, authors believe that in houses that did have baths, servants could not use them.[39] Did this pose any problems for servants? Unfortunately, research in this area still has too few facts on which to base a reply.

As far as servants' pastimes were concerned, authors generally agree that they liked to chat, walk and dance, and that they also enjoyed going to church, sewing, and reading.[40] Reformers and philanthropists of the time were most concerned about servants reading novels and preferred that they read recommended uplifting or moral texts.[41]

We shall never know how much time servants could spend on their pastimes in a day or a week. It undoubtedly varied a great deal depending on whether the servant was alone or not, the lone female servant certainly having less time and fewer means of amusing herself. It must also have depended on the masters' attitudes and how they treated their servants.

The situation in Canada was similar to that in other countries according to our somewhat meagre information. The Toronto census informs us of servants who suffered from lung, heart, and nervous diseases. Of the 27 servants who died in Toronto's St. David area in 1871, six suffered from consumption and two from pneumonia; three had heart trouble, two were debilitated, one was a hysteric, and one had an ulcer; ten died from typhus and two from unknown causes. Their average age was 35.[42]   Montreal death records reveal that servants there died at a very early age: between 1871 and 1875 their average age was 31 and three women died for every man, nearly half of them passing away in hospital, an eloquent reminder that being ill while in service was a cardinal sin.[43] It also seems clear that many domestics were committed. In the Toronto asylum, for example, 23 per cent of the inmates were servants,[44] an enormous number considering that they represented only five per cent of the urban population. Some must have been from surrounding areas and others were undoubtedly there because they had nowhere else to go, but the fact remains that they represented almost a quarter of the patients — a significant indication of the harsh life and working conditions many of them endured.

Pastimes of Canadian servants also seem to have been the same as the pastimes of servants elsewhere. They liked to talk, walk, and dance.[45] They read popular books and serials in the newspapers. In Doin's play *Le dîner interrompu,* Jocrisse reads *Le Juif errant, Les Predictions de Nostradamus, Le Parfait cuisinier,* and public newsheets.[46] They also liked to chat around the fire of an evening, invite others to their kitchen, go to church, and write to their families. Others liked story-telling: in the Dessaulles house Adèle, the cook, used to tell stories of werewolves and will-o'-the-wisps. And some of them, again like Adèle, might also have had pets as company.[47]

All these leisure occupations, one must admit, are harmless enough, and some domestics must have had very different pastimes — involving alcohol and vagrancy, to name only two of many. Such darker pastimes, which very often tended to swell to the proportions of offences punishable by law, are discussed below.

Mores and Crimes

Servants were often considered coarse and vulgar, and people delighted in saying that the crime rate amongst them was far greater than their number warranted. This is clearly shown by the literature of the time, and domestic science dissertations often begin with the recounting of a recent crime during which a servant apparently murdered his master,[48] or a daily newspaper would have a special column dealing with the servant crime rate.[49] However, as McBride pointed out, statistics for this crime rate were often based on the number of accusations, not the number of convictions, which were always substantially fewer.[50] Consequently it is difficult to judge servants' morals on the basis of sources in which so little trust can be placed. Nevertheless, authors who have studied such matters in the United States, France, and Great Britain have been able to discern certain trends that are worth mentioning.

Three kinds of crime seem to have been particularly prevalent among servants: theft, drunkenness, and prostitution. At that time some people appeared to consider that the need to steal was inherent in the profession, even that it was servants' outstanding legal infraction.[51] The kick-backs some domestics received from people in commerce were considered by some to be a more or less traditional form of theft.[52]

As far as drunkenness or alcoholism are concerned, authors mentioning these subjects spoke of them as vices more or less confined to cooks and menservants. They attributed the failing in cooks to the excessive heat in the kitchens and believed that as far as menservants were concerned, ease of access was the root of the problem since, very often, menservants were also responsible for the cellaring.[53]

Prostitution is the crime to which researchers have paid the most attention. It is generally accepted that female servants, more than any other group, were liable to take up prostitution at some time or another during their lives.[54] Some were victims of the machinations of employment agencies upon arriving in the city; others were raped by their masters or those near to them and dismissed when they became pregnant;[55] yet others had no other alternative if they had not worked for a long time, for an unemployed servant could spend up to four months' savings just to live for one week on her own.[56] It is estimated that half the prostitutes in every town had at some time been in service. An 1850 survey of 2000 New York prostitutes revealed that 933 of them had been servants.[57] Consequently servants constituted the majority of unwed mothers, and the opprobium so often attached to that state is well known.[58] In the second half of the century, 59 to 70 per cent of unwed mothers in London were servants whose children had been taken into the London Foundling Hospital.[59] In Paris at the end of the century at least half the unwed mothers had been servants.[60] An inevitable result was that the same people would also be involved in a high number of abortions, infanticides, and abandoned children.[61]

We cannot establish to what extent employed servants were involved in crime nor, more importantly, if such crimes were committed because they were servants. The great majority of servants were young, and it was generally urban young people who were under police scrutiny and the concern of charitable organizations. Some authors have studied delinquency during this period,[62] and it has to be admitted that domestics, like everyone else, were just as much people of their age as of their occupation.

Canadian sources follow the same lines as those of other countries. Here, as elsewhere, it was thought that servants were especially prone to crime, and following the example of European and American newspapers, *L'Evénement* of Quebec City had a special column dealing with servants' crimes.[63] Here, too, theft, drunkenness, and prostitution represented a good proportion of the crimes committed. In Halifax, for instance, the *Acadian Recorder* warned its readers in 1875 against false servants who stole from their masters,[64] and the *L'Evénement* crime column reveals that 60 per cent of servants' crimes consisted of drunkenness, the remainder being theft and a few minor infractions such as disobedience, swearing, and resisting arrest. In both newspapers isolated cases of infanticide and prostitution were reported.[65]

Among the legal sources consulted the greater part of the information on servant crimes came from committals to the Quebec City prison,[66] and these cover only the convictions, which represented about 68 per cent of the accusations brought.[67] During a five-year period from January 1871 to December 1875, 179 female and nine male servants were found guilty of 491 offences. Of these, 80 per cent of the convictions were for loose and disorderly conduct, seven per cent were for drunkenness, and six per cent for theft. Interestingly, the majority of these servants were not domiciled in Quebec City and a good many of them were considered pure vagabonds (Table 31). Although only seven per cent of convictions were for drunkenness, the committal orders specified that more than 60 per cent of the domestics imprisoned had overindulged.

Offences remained fairly steady over the five-year period. A servant seemed to average 2.6 offences over the five years, but in fact, 110 of them were only arrested once, 63 between two and five times, eight between six to ten times, four between 11 to 20 times, and three between 21 to 34 times.

It would have been interesting to go into far more detail on these servants' average age, which was ten years higher than the average for all servants in 1871. However, this calculation presents real problems since the servants were not always truthful about their ages. Sometimes there was a difference of eight to ten years between the age the servant gave on being arrested for the first offence and the age given at the second arrest. When this occurred (which was the case with almost half the domestics arrested more than once) I based my calculations on the age that recurred most often and then took an average as of the 1871 age. Ages varied between 15.5 and 83, and the servants were equally divided between age groups: 31 per cent were 25

122

Table 31

**Servants who Committed Crimes
in Quebec City, 1871-1875**

| | Men
9 | Women
179 |
|---|---|---|
| Ethnic origin | | |
| Irish | 5 | 93 |
| French Canadian | 1 | 76 |
| British | 1 | 8 |
| Scottish | 1 | 1 |
| Other | 1 | 1 |
| | | |
| Residence | | |
| Quebec City | 4 | 58 |
| Elsewhere | 2 | 44 |
| Vagabonds | 3 | 77 |
| | | |
| Temperate | 9 | 67 |
| Intemperate | 0 | 112 |
| | | |
| Average age | 31.9 | 35.2 |

ANQ-Q, Ministère de la Justice, Prison
de Québec, Mandats, Jan. 1871—Dec.
1875.

or under, another 31 per cent were 40 and over. If the average age of
servants convicted between 1871 and 1875 reflected their real age,
one could begin to ask whether being in service did not become more
dangerous the longer one remained in it!

Just to satisfy curiosity, I also researched the prostitutes. I
found that 231 of them committed 1000 crimes over the five-year
period. Their age — and the same problem recurs here — averaged
30.3 years, distributed in more or less the same fashion as the
servants: 32 per cent were 25 or under, 38 per cent between 26 and
39, 30 per cent were 40 and over, and the range was 15.5 to 60. This
list of prostitutes includes 20 per cent of the female servants who had

Table 32

**Number of Offences (%) Committed by Servants
and Prostitutes, Quebec City, 1871-1875**

	One	2-5	6-10	11-20	20-40
Servants	58.5	33.5	4.3	2.1	1.6
Prostitutes	46.3	31.2	10.4	8.6	3.5

ANQ-Q, Ministère de la Justice, Prison de Québec, Mandats, Jan. 1871–Dec. 1875.

committed crimes, and I discovered 36 women who belonged to both groups.

It appears that prostitutes were repeat offenders more often than servants were (Table 32). The five-year distribution was also different: there was a marked difference between 1871, when they numbered 117, and the following years, when they never exceeded 80. This is explained by the departure of the British garrison; the same phenomenon occurred in Montreal too, according to a statement based on the police chief's annual report.[68]

If we take the overall offences committed between 1871 and 1875, women were responsible for only 30 per cent of them; 58 per cent of the women were prostitutes and 28 per cent servants, the remaining 14 per cent having no stated occupation. We can conclude that servants, especially women, were perhaps more prone than other social groups to commit crimes, but that does not mean that the majority were of doubtful morals. The total of 46 servants convicted in 1871 — all women — compared with the total number of servants enumerated in Quebec City in 1871 (1925[69]) represents barely three per cent, and even if the 117 prostitutes were added to this, presuming that they had all been servants at one time, the total would only be nine per cent. No doubt the difficult conditions under which many lived induced them to seek better lives, but only a minority turned to reprehensible methods despite what their contemporaries might have thought.

SOCIAL RELATIONSHIPS

It is impossible to speak of the social relationships between servants and their masters, family, and colleagues in the latter half of the 19th century without first speaking of the perceptions and stereotypes that were common currency at the time regarding both domestic service as an institution and the servants themselves. Although relationships and perceptions are intimately linked whichever side may be involved, they have been examined individually in order to better understand them and bring out the essentials.

Perceptions of Service

In the second half of the 19th century it was commonly accepted that people were experiencing a period of poor-quality domestic service because, it was thought, in times gone by, service had been marked by faithfulness, perseverance, and devotion, and in addition had been the prerogative of a very large number of families.[1] This attitude closely resembles that of previous generations; all had considered themselves less well served than those who had preceded them.[2] A difference this time, though, is that such impressions were made public through various periodicals. People therefore came to believe that domestic service was indeed going through a period of unprecedented crisis and referred to it as one of the crucial problems of the century. And they thought that not only had service been better previously, but also that it was better elsewhere. Some French writers, for instance, believed that British servants were superior to their own,[3] whereas certain Americans maintained that French servants were the best.[4] The taste for things foreign, however, did not go further than that since, paradoxically, the "domestic service problem" was readily put down to the fact that the servants were often foreigners.[5]

These ideas mainly originated with the middle class that, as a general rule, had no family tradition of servants since it was renewed to a great extent with each successive generation.[6] The concept of domestic service consequently tended to become idealized, and people regretted a golden age that in fact had never existed. A veritable phobia existed about the "dangerous classes" from which servants came.[7]   Moreover, there was a growing tendency to believe that poverty was a self-inflicted evil and that the impoverished were themselves responsible for their condition.[8]   People not only considered that an increasing decline in domestic service was being inflicted on them, but also that those involved in it were frequently undesirables who deserved all the aversion with which they were regarded.

Perceptions of Servants

How servants were perceived in the 19th century will be only briefly touched on because several volumes could be filled on this aspect alone.   The perceptions of servants conveyed by various sources — novels, plays, books on household management, periodicals, magazines, private journals, and family correspondence — could all be analyzed, but that would go far beyond the scope of this project. Instead, I have taken a sampling from various works in each category, some of which have been analyzed in depth by present-day authors.[9] Certainly all the nuances inherent in a given source have not been captured; however, I have tried to demonstrate the major trends.

As far as these sources were concerned, writing about domestic servants meant referring to their behaviour and attitudes, and to the image people had of them.   These perceptions have been divided into three major categories: the criminal servant; the childish, insignificant servant; and finally, the good servant.

Frequent allusions were made to servants' so-called criminal and immoral behaviour — not hesitating to steal and taking pleasure in promiscuity, they were both corrupted and corrupters.   If their insolence, impertinence, arrogance, and untrustworthiness were not being denounced, then their clumsiness, negligence, or laziness were. They were thought to be unreliable, unstable, changeable, and above all, dangerous, especially insofar as children were concerned.[10] Several household management manuals emphasize this very point.[11]

Some writers, however, contented themselves with depicting servants as dirty and wretched; others, with some degree of compassion, maintained they were more naive innocents.[12]   And some — but very few — painted the trustworthy servant, faithful unto death, or the maidservant considered as friend and confidant, warm-hearted and comforting.[13]   Interestingly, people from very prosperous families were more indulgent towards their servants.   This was no doubt due to a longer and more pleasant experience of servants[14] and also a logical consequence of the fact that they were able to pay their servants better wages and provide them with better working conditions, and therefore have more stable, competent people in their service.

Rather a green 'un.

OLD GASTRONOMIC receives a present of a fine turtle.
IRISH SERVANT (*of an inquiring turn of mind.*) "*Now, Sur, might I be askin' ye whither that's a real turtle or a mock turtle?*"

32 Ridiculing an Irish servant.

Whatever the differences in how service was viewed, people at that time had two perceptions in common. The first was reflected in the custom of comparing servants to animals. Among the most popular descriptions were that of trustworthy, devoted servants being compared to dogs[15] and Irish servants being compared to monkeys.[16] The Irish were by far the most scorned ethnic group, at least in the United States and Great Britain. People delighted in caricaturing them as monkeys (see Figs. 14 and 32), some even firmly believing that their "inferiority" was a matter of race:

> Many members of the Victorian governing class be-
> lieved that Irish inferiority was a more or less per-
> manent state of affairs, the result of biological forces
> above and beyond the powers of enlightened English
> administrators to control or ameliorate. Irish inferior-
> ity was seen as a function of Irish ethnicity.[17]

The second perception people had in common was the conviction that servants belonged to a lower social class and had to be kept at a distance.[18] This attitude, inherited from previous centuries, was given substance in the second half of the 19th century by the installation of back stairs for the servants' use. After 1850, service stairs could be found almost anywhere, so intent were people on establishing a clear demarcation line between themselves and their domestic staff, protecting themselves from the latter's indiscreet eyes, and arranging matters so that the staff could work without being seen or heard.[19]

Such perceptions obviously affected what servants thought of themselves and their work. They very often had the impression that they were unimportant and performed work that was of little value. They would not openly admit to being servants, and some refused to be publicly rewarded for their services in order to avoid being identified as servants. A certain shame was felt in being a servant in the latter half of the 19th century, which became even more marked as servants became increasingly conscious of the fact that they were members of a specific class that many wished to keep at a distance. The title French servants chose for their newspaper at the end of the century, *L'Escalier de service* (The Back Stairs), is somewhat symptomatic of this.[20]

Servants had no higher regard for their masters. They generally considered their employers as being apart, "them" or "les autres," and if they were Francophone, often referred to their employers as "les singes" (monkeys) among themselves.[21] Such views were hardly con-ducive to smooth relation.

Were perceptions the same in Canada? Our literary sources are not as abundant and varied as those for Europe and the United States; however, foreign literature was very much in vogue here at that time, and consequently the same attitudes must have been current. Some documents lead one to believe that servants here, too, were considered criminal and dangerous, childish and careless, faithful and trustworthy.

The *Canadian Illustrated News*, for instance, advised its readers in 1878 to reflect on their fortunate circumstances and stop bewailing the difficulties of managing a household and the "perversity of servants,"[22] a sign that this was a topical subject in Canada. Abbé Mailloux's *Manuel des parents chrétiens* warned — in the 1850s — of the dangers servants, unless chosen with care, represented for children. And Testart de Montigny would write the selfsame thing 40 years later.[23] References to servants' negligence and incompetence can also be found.[24] Servants were treated with very little consideration. Joy Parr, who studied the fate of British children who came to work in Canada from the 1860s on, cited one example:

> When a prominent New Brunswick Liberal arrested for
> the rape of a girl aged 12 from the Middlemore home
> fled ... forfeiting his $1,000 bail, "the judge remarked
> that the girl was only low English and that it as not a
> very important matter."[25]

Evidence of trustworthy, devoted, warmhearted, comforting servants are more numerous, thanks to memoirs and personal diaries that have come down to us from well-known, very wealthy families such as the Aubert de Gaspés, Dufferins, Roquebrunes, and Dessaulles. The Canadian situation closely resembled that of other countries in this respect since here too the important families were considerate of their servants. They would say that their servants performed excellent work, and servants were remembered as people to whom one would go for comfort and even sometimes refuge in childhood. Eating in the kitchen could be a thoroughly enjoyed treat:[26]

> Each evening, I go to the kitchen towards five o'clock,
> when the stove is crackling and the lamp not yet lit
> and I have stories told to me of werewolves, witches
> throwing spells and will-o'-the-wisps. Adèle believes
> in all this nonsense and she recounts it with such
> liveliness and conviction that I am enthralled.[27]

In Canada, too, the Irish were ridiculed, given simian-like features, and their language and gaffes mocked, as *Canadian Illustrated News* caricatures demonstrate (Figs. 14, 21, 22, and 32). Here too servants were held at arm's length by means of the back stairs, as can easily be seen in house plans (Figs. 16-19, 23, 26, and 27).

However, we have no indication of what servants thought of themselves and their masters. Rosalie, a seamstress with the Dessaulles, said she was content with her lot, did her duty to the best of her ability, and was confident that God would do his duty towards her.[28] This is meagre in the extreme, and it is doubtful whether Rosalie was typical of the majority of servants. It seems that domestic service was not better esteemed here than elsewhere since there was a tendency to leave it to the immigrants.[29] As for the view Canadian servants took of their masters, that too was no doubt the same as in other countries, servants believing their masters to be as vexatious as they themselves were believed to be. It should not be in the least surprising that the relationship on both sides was difficult.

Master/Servant Relationships

It appears that some servants experienced stormy relationships, sometimes described as "war, revolution, and conspiracy." Others were the objects of disdain or indifference — a type of cold war, or "a permanent state of armed neutrality." A third group was fortunate enough to enjoy good relationships, although they were the exceptions.[30]

Stormy relationships were marked by maliciousness, abuse, pettiness, suspicion, and contempt on the side of the masters. Some, for instance, sexually abused their maidservants and then dismissed them if they became pregnant;[31] others beat their servants, punished them severely for the slightest escapade, or withheld their salaries if something was accidentally broken.[32] Physical health was not considered either: some masters forced their servants to care for people with infectious diseases and others skimped on food and lodging. Nor was servants' mental health a consideration: they were spied on, traps were laid for them, their rooms (which they were not allowed to decorate) were searched. Everything was kept under lock and key. Some masters even took the liberty of changing their servants' first names.[33] And all this was accompanied by the open mockery, demonstrated in numerous period caricatures, reserved for foreigners or people considered objects of curiosity.

If a state of cold war reigned, the relationship was not necessarily any better since it was still marked by suspicion, condescension, or at best, indifference. Therefore, even if there were no overtly hostile feelings towards servants, there was no hesitation in letting them live under lamentable conditions and giving them leftovers for food.[34] Every opportunity was taken to keep them at a distance and instill in them a due sense of "their place."[35] Some texts give very clear ideas of this, like this comment in a servants' handbook:

> Ladies have been educated in a very different manner.... It is not likely that you can have anything to say that will amuse or interest a lady. When she talks to you it is in kindness, and all the pleasure of the talk is on your side.[36]

And a child exclaimed in the Comtesse de Ségur's *Les deux nigauds:*

130

"Prudence is my nurse; I cannot be on social terms with her."[37] Attention should also be drawn to what seems the height of condescension. In some period novels, when a servant saved his master's life — often at the risk of his own — he received the ultimate reward: a handshake.[38]

Little in American, British, or French literature mentions good relationships between master and servant apart from novels and personal journals speaking of servants as faithful, trustworthy friends. These servants were no doubt treated with more regard and enjoyed more acceptable living and working conditions than their fellows. But, taking the available material as a whole, such relationships were rare.

Relationships being two-way streets, how did servants react to these various attitudes? It seems that maliciousness was often met with maliciousness and distrust with distrust. It is certainly not by pure chance that servants were accused of being insolent, impertinent, arrogant, and suspicious, which appeared to be their major characteristics.[39] And people in service had a sovereign remedy when illtreated: they changed employers. Some authors even maintain that quitting was the only way servants could show some independence and no doubt this is why they used it so often. If servant mobility was as great as people said it was at the time, the reason has to be that in the majority of cases, servant/master relationships were unpleasant.

Relationships were most likely the same in Canada, and one can imagine that they, too, were sometimes hostile or disdainful, sometimes understanding. Life for some servants was very difficult: a very large number of servants were committed to the Toronto asylum, and *L'Evénement* of Quebec City occasionally reported cases where a master was brought before the court for having beaten his servant.[40] Others must also have been treated with contempt since they were no better housed and fed here than elsewhere, and some must have suffered from the inconsiderate way in which they were treated. Various facts and anecdotes appearing in *L'Evénement* are good examples of the scant attention servants warranted in their masters' eyes. For instance, an employer and his servant were involved in a train accident. As soon as the master regained consciousness, he asked that his servant be brought to him since he wished the key to his trunk and this had been given to the servant. However, the unfortunate man was dead, having been cut in half in the accident. Upon learning this, the master, unmoved, requested that both halves of his servant be searched and the key found.[41] Whether this story was intended to be sarcastic or amusing, it nevertheless demonstrates the indifference inherent in certain master/servant relationships.

On the other hand, that Canadian servants too could have very good relationships with their employers is the impression gained from memoirs and private diaries.[42] And the available wills also contain evidence of some good feeling, even if bequests to servants were only made in one to three per cent of cases, depending on the city.[43]

Of the 3874 wills found for 1871-75 in the Toronto, Montreal, Quebec City, and Halifax archives, 50 or so mention bequests to one or more servants. Half of these involved a lump sum payment of some $250, others were only $40, while yet others went as high as $3000. The averages were $277 for Montreal, $275 for Quebec City, $241 for Halifax, and $62 for Toronto. The remainder of the bequests were equally divided between annuities and property. As a general rule, an annuity was for $60 per year (about one year's wages), except in Quebec City, where it averaged $116.[44] Those receiving property sometimes found themselves fairly well-off because they might inherit the usufruct of a furnished house for the rest of their days, and some were even named sole legatees.[45] Goods were mainly bequeathed in Montreal and Quebec City (12 of the 15 wills).

Servants who received something under a will had been in a family's service for a long time. Nearly all the wills specify that the bequest would only be made if the person were still in the family's service at the death of the testator, and annuities would only be paid as long as the legatee remained single.

Three servants' wills were also found, all from Montreal and all in favour of sole legatees. One servant left everything to her adopted daughter, another left everything to a male friend, and the third left everything to the person with whom she would be living at the time of her death provided that such person buried her, had a funeral mass sung for her, and had another mass sung on the first anniversary of her death.[46] This is eloquent proof of the solitary life generally awaiting those in domestic service.

That wills were made in favour of servants means that some masters and servants were on good terms. However, it is to be hoped that the number of cases was actually higher than it would appear, since the cases found only represent 1.3 per cent overall.[47] In addition, the value of these bequests should be clearly understood for in half the cases they often only represented one year's salary for servants who had given many years' service and who were perhaps no longer of an age to find other employment.[48] And in many families servants could have been better recompensed. For instance, in one household the servant was left $40, but Bishop Bourget received $20 000 for his charitable works and $25 000 was left to various other charities.[49] This is an extreme, but there were others, and it points to the fact that even where relationships were harmonious, servants still derived few benefits from them.

If all sources are taken into account — American, British, French, and Canadian — it has to be admitted that in the majority of cases, servant/master relationships were complex, based as they were on each perceiving the other as being from a different class, indeed a

132

different world. This is what historians have found; however, most have concluded that such relationships could be put down to paternalism.[50] This point of view can be justified, and there is no need to go any further than the etiquette books, servant handbooks, and household management treatises in order to realize that the portrait drawn there of a servant is that of an inferior being who needed to be supervised and controlled. In addition, it is easy to imagine that, as was found for the beginning of the century, cases existed where relationships were truly paternalistic — for instance, when a child was employed for several years or when servants remained with the same family for a long time. However, it is doubtful this was so for the majority of servants who constantly moved from one household to another and were hardly known to the employer. It seems that, from the outset, the terms "attitude" and "relationship" have been confused. Some masters may indeed have wanted to adopt a paternalistic attitude, but that in no way guaranteed a servant's response, which would have had to be subservient, obedient, grateful, or at least, deferential, all of which are essential in paternalistic relationships.[51] In the same way, the distrust between the lower classes and those who were better off may have been underestimated, a distrust that grew with the years since servants were increasingly regarded as strangers and made to feel so — witness the back stairs — a sentiment clearly borne out by the documents. Finally, the very temporary nature of service for the majority of those involved in it was a factor that did not encourage affection, obedience, or true respect, but rather mistrust, or at best, total indifference.

Servant/Peer Relationships

Servants' "peer relationships" encompass their relationships with their families, neighbours, and colleagues. Admittedly, very little information is available on servants' relationships with such people. It is therefore impossible to compare the Canadian situation with that in other countries; the most one can do is share the little information discovered.

We have only a smattering of information on servants' families. About 60 per cent of urban servants were far from their families in the second part of the 19th century, but many contributed to their families' upkeep, as was the custom of the time.[52] However, we do not know whether they could often visit their families, whether they had the means to do so, nor if they took the time or trouble to write frequently.[53] In households with two or more servants, a place could sometimes be found for another member of the family (for example, two sisters in the same house).[54] This could, of course, just mean that someone had a better chance of being employed if one of her relatives was already in service, but one could also believe that it was more a question of true family affection that helped ease the difficult conditions under which they lived and perhaps made the work more bearable because it was shared with someone close. Sibling bonds very possibly were stronger and kept up more than bonds with parents. Here again, the Canadian situation seems to have been very similar to that in Great Britain and France.[55]

No mention whatsoever of immediate neighbours or people in nearby areas appears in later documents. At the beginning of the century Judge Sewell's reports show that there was much visiting with neighbours; they would chat in the kitchen at night and return the visits. However, I cannot say whether this continued after 1850. Families dined later then and servants may not have had the time — nor permission — to enjoy such small outings. Indeed, in the last 30 years or so of the century there was a general trend towards stricter discipline at work,[56] and servants' employers would certainly have been no exceptions to the rule.

A little more attention has been paid to the question of servants' relationships with their fellows within the household although the resulting information usually reflects stereotyping. Several authors, for example, have emphasized the problems posed by the domestic hierarchy.[57] Servants who adopted disdainful attitudes towards their fellows were readily ridiculed, and this also applied to the way of speaking some of them affected. Employers delighted in stories like that of the servant who resigned his position because "the hother servants is so 'orrid vulgar, and hignorant."[58] Such caricatures were highly popular.

> Page Boy (to Jeames):
> "Where shall I put this 'ere dish of Ammonds?"
> Jeames (with dignity):
> "I'm surprised, Harthur, that at your hage you 'aven't
> learnt 'ow to pernounce the Har in Harmonds!"[59]

Indeed, some servants even reputedly adopted haughty attitudes towards their masters.

> Lady:
> "Resign your situation! Why, What's wrong now
> Thomas? Have they been wanting you to eat salt
> butter again?"
> Genteel Footman:
> "Oh no, thank you, Ma'am. But the fact is, Ma'am,
> that I have heard that Master were seen last week on
> the top of a homnibus and I couldn't after that remain
> any longer in the family!"[60]

Even if such attitudes were to be found, we must remember that only 25 per cent of servants worked in houses with staffs of three or more (Table 28), and of this number less than half had the better positions. However that may have been, to someone entering service as a maid-of-all-work, the presence of another servant more than likely would have been pleasant rather than unpleasant and there would have been a good relationship between the two. As the Beecher sisters put it, "Two [servants] keep peace with each other and their employer."[61] And other household management manuals state that the best way of keeping a servant was to have two.[62]

CONCLUSION

The question of domestic service could have been treated from several aspects: from those of legal or economic history, or from the more restricted ones of the history of workers, the family, women, adolescents, or even children. My standpoint was that of everyday history because my concern was the restoration and interpretation of the past in historical houses.

I have therefore not touched on many aspects that otherwise well deserve attention. For instance, it would have been interesting to study service as women's work, since the 50 per cent of the female workforce engaged in it in 1818 had become 90 per cent by 1871.[1] It would have been equally worthwhile to compare the view of women in general at the time with that of servants.[2] Did the idea that service had deteriorated in the second half of the century have anything to do with the fact that it was almost entirely women engaged in it?

Nor have I dealt with the different forms of pressure exerted on servants. Throughout the 19th century, religion was used as a means of ensuring servants' obedience and submission, as can be seen from the following extracts from manuals:

> A good servant is as estimable in the sight of God as a good master.
> Had God seen that it would have been better for your external good that you should be great and rich He would have made you so; but He gives to all the places and duties best fitted to them.
> Servants, be subject to your masters with all fear; not only to the good and gentle but also to the froward.
> For this is thankworthy, if a man for conscience toward God endure grave suffering wrongfully.[3]

Another worthwhile discussion would have been how domestic service was integrated into the political, economical, and social triumvirate of the time, and the impact of being in service on the servants themselves. These questions have all been hotly debated, and while most agree that domestic service had little impact on politics, opinions are sharply divided on the influence it exerted on the economy and social life. Some state that domestic service was an obsolete institution, a leftover from previous times.[4] Others see it more as an economic indicator, individuals' or families' prestige depending on the number of servants they employed, and the importance of an area in a town being judged by the number of servants

137

concentrated there.[5] Yet others lean more on the fact that domestic service was a factor in urbanization and modernization: it enabled social attitudes to be passed from the middle classes to the lower classes and urban values to be transmitted through the servants who returned to their rural homes once they married.[6] Much has been written recently on these theories of urbanization and modernization. Some have even queried the very meaning of the words and there is a growing tendency to rethink all the implications.[7] Opinions are also divided on the impact of domestic service on the servants themselves. Some state that servants benefited from their years in service, some domestics even to the point that they advanced in the social scale. Others maintain that the experience was degrading and negative.[8] I have not involved myself in these debates because my sources differ on these matters depending on which part of the century they cover. Indeed, they do not really address the question since they deal principally with houses and their occupants.

Nevertheless, some very interesting data were culled from these sources. The servants studied were those who lived in their master's homes and therefore this report covers only approximately 70 per cent of the domestic work force found in the large towns of Canada.[9] Servants differed little from one city to another — the majority were under 25 years of age and from fairly humble backgrounds — and they were very like their American, British, and French counterparts. As a general rule, each was the only servant in a household; two out of three houses only had one servant, and only a quarter of their number worked in households with at least three domestics.

Another constant feature was that households with servants were few: ten to 20 per cent of all households,[10] and only two to four per cent of these had four servants or more. It also seems that in more than one instance working and living conditions were poor: small, meagrely furnished rooms that were ill-heated and ill-lit; stiflingly hot kitchens situated in basements where the light was poor; 15- to 18-hour days spent in thankless work, carrying heavy loads and satisfying their masters' least whims. Servants were consequently highly mobile, always searching for a better place, the ideal place generally being found in one of the rare households that could afford three servants or more. In Canada as elsewhere, servants were viewed as being less adept than their predecessors, and the quality of service was considered to be in decline.

Although these factors are constant, differences did exist between countries, cities, and periods. For instance, although people everywhere complained about servants' great mobility, this seems less pronounced in Europe than in North America. However, this impression may be due to the fact that, unlike European studies but like American ones, I have only considered city dwellers. Thus, high mobility may have been an urban phenomenon rather than a rural one.

Cities, too, differed. For example, the servant population was far more evenly distributed in Toronto, which was a young city at the time, than in older cities, where concentration in particular areas was more marked. Thus in Montreal, which was industrialized more rapidly, servants had deserted the city centre in 1871, in contrast to Quebec City and Halifax, where the wealthier urban residents still lived in the heart of town. This development had a definite impact on domestics, who became far more isolated when the rich families left for the suburbs.

Servants themselves differed from one period to another. On average they were slightly younger at the beginning of the century, no doubt because the number of children was higher at that time. And servants in the latter half of the century were better educated than their predecessors. But the most obvious difference was that instead of 50 per cent of live-in servants being women as had been the case at the beginning of the century, 90 per cent of live-in servants were women at the end of the century. And these women, already outsiders because of their social station, became doubly so because very often they were immigrants.

Service as such also had its own particular features depending on the period, features that cannot be considered surprising given the different contexts of the two halves of the century. If I can rely on my strongest impressions felt throughout the project — a history of servants may perhaps always be "impressionistic" — I should emphasize the social functions filled by domestic service at the beginning of the century. Service at that time seems to have been a form of assistance that took care of orphans and children whose families could not fend for them. It was also a kind of education and apprenticeship for young people with little money and who did not have the advantage of schooling or a trade. It was also a means of support for old or impoverished folk whose families could not care for them. Some servants must have benefited from their situation, some maybe even exploited it. In addition, if servants did not find only drawbacks to their situation, masters did not find only advantages: they had introduced strangers into the family circle, strangers who had a certain influence over their children, who witnessed their quarrels and could also broadcast them.

In the second stage of the research the social function of domestic service became blurred — as of 1850, orphanages and almshouses for the aged began to be more common — and I became more and more preoccupied by the idea of co-existence within a confined space of representatives from classes at both ends of the social scale. It seemed, no doubt because of the abundance of material on household management, manuals for servants, and caricatures in newspapers, that a vast amount of time was spent defining the specific relationships, asserting the group to which one belonged, and

139

especially, establishing clear lines of demarcation (like back stairs and livery).

Consequently, and this difference appears the most important, domestic service seems harsher in the latter half of the century and servants seem to have been viewed less favourably. For example, works on household management dating from the beginning of the century recommend that servants should not be left in idleness, whereas later treatises recommend that their workload be lightened.[11] This says quite a lot on the amount of work that had come to be required of servants as the century progressed. In the same way, whereas people had busied themselves with reforming servants around 1840, around 1870 it was rather the reform of service as an institution that was considered.[12] Were individual servants considered less important than the institution? Master/servant relationships must have followed along the same lines, and perhaps we should not be surprised at the abundance in the second half of the century of books that set down rules so that life under a common roof should at least be bearable. Obviously there were good positions, good masters, and good servants in both periods, but they were in the minority. What is more, this minority was often made up of the wealthiest families employing several servants and living in fairly luxurious houses. Servants in those houses were not neophytes: the women were often three to five years older than the average servant. This is an important point because houses intended for historic restoration are usually those that were owned by this minority and have come down to us just because, generally speaking, they were in better condition than others and often belonged to prosperous families.

One problem consequently deserves consideration before the restoration of servants' quarters in a given house is undertaken. How can we draw attention to the shabby, negligent manner in which servants' quarters were generally furnished when the rooms to be displayed are not representative of servants' quarters in Canada because they are in houses much richer than the average? And consideration must also be given to placing these households in their proper social context so that the fact that families with, say, five servants represented only 3.5 families out of a thousand is not lost from sight.

If this study makes people aware of such facts and corrects some of the preconceptions that distort a true perspective of the period, it will have helped advance the knowledge and understanding of the 19th century in Canada.

APPENDIX A

EARLY 19TH-CENTURY HIRING CONTRACT*

ON THE   DAY OF   in the year
of our Lord one thousand eight hundred and   Before
the undersigned Notaries Public duly admitted and sworn for the
Province of Lower Canada, residing in the city of Quebec personally
came and appeared

[names, occupations, and places of residence of servant and master
listed here]

the said   in the presence of us the said Notaries
hath acknowledged and confessed to have voluntarily and of his own
free will and accord engaged himself and by these present doth engage
himself for and during and to the full end and term of
                    unto the said   who did and
hereby doth accept of the said   during all which
time the   doth hereby promise and engage to
serve his said master diligently and faithfully, to keep his secrets and
lawful commands everywhere readily obey, to do no damage to his said
master nor suffer nor see it done by others without telling or giving
notice thereof to his said master, not to waste his said master's goods
nor lend them unlawfully to any body, not to play at cards, dice or
other unlawful game whereby his said master may have damage, nor
haunt ale houses, taverns, or play houses, not to absent himself day or
night from his said Master's service without his leave, but in all things
behave and demean himself as a faithful   ought
to do, during the said term.

And the said   on his part

[the obligations of the master are listed here]

The whole to be executed under pain of all costs, losses, damages and
interests, FOR THUS, &c Promising, &c Obliging, &c Renouncing, &c,
Thus done and passed, at the aforesaid City of Quebec, in the Office
of   , one of us the said Notaries, the said
parties having to these presents, first duly read according to the law,
set and subscribed their names and signatures, together with us the
said Notaries in faith and testimony of the premises.

---

* Quebec (Province). Archives nationales du Québec, Quebec, greffe
de Jean Bélanger, acte no. 6193, 16 May 1816.

APPENDIX B

ACCOUNT OF THE TRIAL OF ALEXIS DE ROUSSELL
ACCUSED BY SUSANNAH ELIZA DAVIS OF RAPE, 1814*

7 May 1814.	Quebec. Oyer et terminer & Gen.[1] Gaol Delivery
Dominus Rex	Indictment for a Rape on Susannah Eliza Davis
vs	Tempus. 23rd February 1814 Locus. Parish of Beauport
Alexis de Roussell	Pro Rege The Attorney General
	Pro Def[te] Mr. Fletcher Mr. Vanfelson

Susannah Eliza Davis
-      I am 17, I have been in service in Quebec in several respectable houses — I know the [prisoner]. He lives at Beauport. Last winter in the month of January I entered his house while waiting for a place with Madame Duchesnay of Beauport — I asked for a bed and the next morning, I asked him if I could stay there until I find a place — I did not know him before, he is a married man, The wife of the P. was there — On Mardi Gras last Mad[e] Roussell departed for Quebec at two in the afternoon leaving in the house the P. myself and two small children of which the oldest is five — at eleven o'clock I went to bed. I put out the candle — and two hours after the P. came into the room where I was with a candle in his hand which he put on the table where he started to eat, He asked me to eat too but I did not want to.
       He came to my bed and said he wanted to lie down with me — I told him no — And thereupon I got up and went against the Table; He put out the Candle put his arms about me and threw me on his bed. I resisted. I started to cry out and he took me by the throat to stop me crying out. He also stopped me from getting up — the children were crying, He told them to be still and to stay in their beds — he said to me get up if you can — I continued to cry out and he asked me if I wanted to be heard by the neighbours — I cried out as loud as I could — The children were woken by my cries — There was no-one in the house except the P[r] myself and the Children that night — I was clothed — it was late when I went to bed and for that reason I had thrown myself on my Bed in my clothes being tired

[here Susannah recounts the rape]

At six and 1/4 in the morning I rose The church Bell had rung
shortly before — I wanted to depart and he told me stay and I will give
you money and goods — He said the same to me in the night. I went
out straightway, and, I was to Madame Filion's the neighbour of the
Pris^r — Mad^e Filion her daughter and some of her children were there.
Three young people came in — and after Mr. Filion — Before the
arrival of Mr. Filion I told Madame Filion and her daughter all that
happened in the night all that I have stated here — I went immediately
after to the Justice of the peace at Beauport, as Mad^e Filion had
indicated — His Lady wife told me he was ill and that if I had business
of importance I would have to go into town — Thereupon I returned to
Mad^e Filion who said to me because he is ill take your business to town
— I returned to the town and I went to Mad^e Bowen's and Mad^e Gaspé's
and the next day, the second day of Lent Thursday, I went to make my
complaint at the office of Mr. de Cuthbert.

My Father is a soldier with the Veterans and he is at St. Joseph
— Six years ago I entered Mad^e Trenk's employ My [father] had put me
in her hands to be as her child — I had always known them for people
of good character. I do not know exactly but I think I stayed there 4
years I left because I was too badly treated Mad^e Trenk beat me I then
stayed with Mr. Derouin the innkeeper five months or 6 months — I
then returned to Mad^e Trenk — I do not remember the reason Why I
left Mr. Derouin's — I do not know the exact time I stayed with Mad^e
Trenk where I had removed — then I stayed with Mad^e Parent 18
months and I left there for no reason — then I stayed with Mad^e
Cugnet 8 months — I left there because I was too fearful in the house
as they left me often quite alone — after I stayed at Judge Bowen's,
leaving Mr. Bowen's last Summer I do not know where I removed to. —
I was then after some days at Mad^e Gaspé's — I do not recall where I
stayed during the Time between the Day on Which I left Mad^e Bowen
and the day I entered Mad^e Gaspé's house — I stayed with Mad^e Bowen
one month and a half and with Mad^e Gaspé one month — and I left
because I was not able to do the work — I did not leave Mr. Gaspé's
because I often went out without permission — although I did go out
sometimes without permission — I stayed at Madame Drolet's then
Until I was to go to Beauport to hire out to Mad^e Duchesnay — Mad^e
Duchesnay refused to engage me because she had engaged an other,
and I was not able to do her Work — I saw Mad^e Duchesnay herself —
then I was at the Pris^r's it was not yet 4 o'clock in the afternoon — I
asked for a bed I did not ask to warm myself for the love of God — Mr.
de Roussel Mad^e de Roussel their two children and a little girl were at
the house I saw no others   There was maybe someone in the Shop but I
did not see them — The next day I asked permission to remain there
until I could find a place.

At the Pris^r's I told all that had happened at Mad^e Duchesnay — I said that Mad^e D. had not wanted to let me warm myself she told me to leave straightway to arrive in town before it was late — during the time I remained with the P^r he took no liberties with me and I took none with him — Mad^e de Roussel left for the town at quarter to three on mardi gras — she did not tell me she was going to town, I learnt it from the Pris^r at ten in the evening for the first time — There were young people on mardi gras, who were eating drinking and singing — I did not know them — I left them when I went to bed — I think they departed at midnight all the family slept in the same room ordinarily — I slept that night in my clothes — Rousselle came in with a Candle, he started to eat at the table and offered me something to eat — I was not asleep when he entered, he woke me when he opened the door — He said foolish words like you will bed with me, I will not sleep if you do not bed with me; I arose — He put out the candle — He put his arms about me He threw me on the bed — I had my back towards him then it was he who turned me around — I said I was afraid, but this was after he took me by the throat, I do not know if I saw someone in the Room but it seemed I saw someone "I said to him leave me" to go to my bed, I see someone "are you not ashamed" — I also cried out "ah my God what is there" I did not ask him to cover my head — I have said since "That I had seen a Ghost — that it was a man without a Head with great horns" When I told him there was someone, the P^r said to me it was not true — He asked me what I had seen — He did not say if you are afraid go and sleep at some Neighbour's house — Between the moment he threw me on the bed and the time he took pleasure of my body it was a half hour — When he took pleasure of me he did not use any violence, but he still prevented me from leaving his bed — I did not sleep all night — I do not know if he slept or not, but always when I tried to leave his bed he was awakened and stopped me — He rose first — a little before six o'clock — He left me in the bed but I got up right after — When he was up he said "go then now in your bed" — I said, no, I do not want to, I am going — I know Jean Valle — I got up immediately after the P^r got up — I do not know if there was anyone in the P^r's Shop while I was in his bed. The P^r put out the candle — I asked why he did so He was not undressed — He said to me therefore do you want a candle I replied no I do not need one I can easily go to bed without a candle He blew out the candle — while he was still holding it. In the P^r's house the first room is a shop, on the right is the room where this all took place and two closets, on the Left the taproom — None of the Young People who were in the house took liberties with me — none kissed me. The house is surrounded by other houses but they are further away than from here to the wall — I did not take Pleasure with the Young People who were in the house and they did not take pleasure of me And the P^r did not tell me to go into the taproom — I did not say to any one at all that I was expecting money from this case against the Pr Nor any other advantage — nor any like thing.

Rosalie Filion
- I know the P^r He is our Neighbour at Beauport there are thirty or forty feet between the two houses — I know Susannah Eliza Davis by sight — On Ash Wednesday she came to our house between 6 and 7 in the morning and told us that on the Tuesday night previous she went to bed at the P^r's — that after the P^r came against her bed and passed his hand over her face and said very low are you asleep — She replied no — that she said take your hand away from there it does not belong to you that she rose and leant against a table — that the P^r blew the candle out put his arms around her and carried her to his bed and that he had taken her by force and that if he had not taken her life it was because he could not — that she had seen against her bed a great man or a Great black woman with horns that a woman came in in the morning and that she departed — she also said she wanted to catch her — that he did not want to give her her clothing and thereupon she asked if there was a Magistrate in the village and I indicated Mr. De Salaberry saying go away and make him give you back your clothes —

[A witness — name illegible]
- The P^r's house is on the great [illegible] at Beauport. Henry Vallé lives beside opposite are the Pepin and Lesperance houses and on the other side is our house. When Susan Davis was at our house her complaint was of her clothes which the P^r refused to give her.

Ross Cuthbert
- Susan Eliza Davis lodged her complaint with me on the day after Ash Wednesday.

Defence

Pierre Langevin
- I am a Carpenter in Beauport I have known the P^r for 3 or 4 years — I know Susannah Eliza Davis. She stayed at the P^r's house last winter around the Time just before Lent — I was at the P^r's when she came for the 1st time — She asked permission to warm herself coming from the Town — they gave her to eat and she asked to sleep there — She remained a fortnight — I was working then at the house and I saw her daily — *She seemed to me to take many liberties with the P^r I saw her jump on his Back and take the pipe from his mouth,* but it was only once. It was not the P^r who started that foolery — yet his wife was there.

146

Jean Vallé

-      I know the P. and Susan E. Davis. I saw her at the P^r's I never saw the P^r. take Liberties with this girl but a Sunday I was at the P^r's waiting for Vespers in the time before Lent. *I saw her take the pipe from the P^r's mouth and Throw it in the stove.* She slept two nights at our house after the matter with the Prisoner —

Charles Giroux

-      I know the P^r and Susan Davis. I saw her in the days before Lent at the P^r's house That day she seemed very free — *She had her arm around him* and he wanted her to go away but she did not want to leave him Joseph Bellanger was with me. she seemed with him as if she had always stayed with him.

August Deguise

-      I know the P^r. and I know Susan Davis. she lived at the house of the P^r for a fortnight before Mardi Gras — I saw her — she seemed to me too free for a modest girl — one night I saw Susan Davis with her arms crossed on the P^r's shoulders. The P^r seemed to pinch her legs and she cried Mad^e De Roussell he is pinching my legs Mad^e De R. replied get away from there then but she stayed there —

Marguerite Vallé

-      I saw Susan Davis — She told me since the matter of Mr. Roussel that she was going to have a coat and a hat that Mr. Cuthbert had told her that she was going to have ten *louis* if De Roussel was shown [guilty] and that she would give me a piaster — she spoke at that time of this trial against the P^r — and told me she was going to appear as a witness against the P^r and that she must speak her best.

Marie Louise Parens

-      I know the P^r and I know Susan Davis by sight — It's since she left the P^r's house that I have seen her. She told me that she had a case against the P^r that there were ten *louis* at court marked for her — that she was going to prosecute the P^r. for having forced her that if she did not sue him people would say she had consented, but by prosecuting people could not say it and that as well there were ten *louis* for her that if she lost her honour she would still have the money — She told me she did not intend to prosecute the P^r but that the neighbour had counselled her to do so because she was young — and she did not know how to go about it. —

Elizabeth Gilley

-      I saw Susan Davis twice in Lent — two days after the matter in question she told me she was very pleased it had happened because she would gain some money. I do not know the P^r.

Christine Faillon

- I saw Susan Davis — and I have seen the P^r since before the matter in question I saw Susan Davis she spoke to me on the matter — she told me that there was another girl he had done the same thing to and he had given some money and she was going to gain from him too

Jeanet Deguise — contradiction

- I know the P^r and Susan Davis because I saw her Mardi gras last I saw her that day towards seven o'clock at the Prisonner's — she asked me where Md^e De Roussell was — The P^r was there and replied "you know well that my wife is in town" — she made no reply.

Michel Marcoux — militia captain

- I know the P^r — three or four years I have always known him for an honest man.

Claude Denechaud Esqr

- I know the P^r He stayed with me as a servant for 12 to 15 months — I have always known Him for an honest man, sober, and for a man of good morals —

Charge. The case is completely proved if you believe the prosecutrix — against her credibility are the following Facts — Proofs of wanton conduct before the fact with the P^r from which consent may be presumed — Doubtful whether she complained of having her goods retained by the Pris^r or of the rape when she went to Filions — Contradictions in her Testimony 1st as to her knowledge of Mad^e de Roussel being in town on the mardi gras — 2^d as to her expectation of reward or benefit to accrue from the P^r conviction — And her saying that she did not know where she went when she left Mr Bowen *last summer.* — If she forgets a fact so recent she may forget others; if she conceals it she may conceal other facts.

Verdict. *Not guilty* —

---

* Canada. Public Archives, MG23, GII, 10, Vol. 12, pp. 6117-6128 (translation).

APPENDIX C

REGULATIONS CONCERNING APPRENTICES, SERVANTS, AND JOURNEYMEN, 1818*

The following Regulations were originally framed under the Provincial Statute 42nd. Geo. III. entitled "An Act to empower the Justices of the Peace to make for a limited time Rules and Regulations for the Government of Apprentices and others;" and are now in force, in virtue of divers Acts made to continue the Act aforesaid.

As these Rules have been acted upon for several years with success, and since from their very general provisions, they may be applied with more exactness to the peculiar circumstances of every case than if they were more detailed, no alterations have been made. They furnish a remedy for every possible complaint that can be brought against Servants, Apprentices and Journeymen.

It is ordered,

1.   That if any indented or articled Apprentice, Servant or Journeyman, who may be bound by act of Indenture, or other written contract, for a longer time than one month, or by verbal agreement for one month, or any shorter period; shall be guilty of any miscarriage or ill behavior, refractory conduct, idleness, absence without leave or desertion, dissipating Master, Mistress or Employer's effects, and of any unlawful act or acts that may affect the interest, or disturb the domestic arrangements of such Master, Mistress or Employer; such Apprentice, Servant or Journeyman may, upon complaint and due proof thereof made by such Master, Mistress or Employer before the Justices of the Peace in their weekly or special sittings be by such Justices sentenced to be committed to the House of Correction, and there to remain at hard labour for any time according to the circumstances of each and every offence, not exceeding two months: or may, by such Justices be sentenced to pay for each and every offence, a fine not exceeding ten pounds current money of this province.

2.   That if any such Apprentice, Servant or Journeyman, bound and engaged as aforesaid, has any just cause of complaint against his or her Master or Employer, for any misusage, defect of sufficient and wholesome provisions, or for cruelty or other ill treatment, such Master or Mistress or Employer shall be summoned before such Justices, and if the complaint shall appear to

149

be well founded, the said Justices may inflict a penalty not exceeding ten pounds current money of this Province upon such Master or Mistress or Employer.

3. That on complaint made by any Master, Mistress or Employer, against his, her or their Apprentice, Servant or Journeyman; or by any Apprentice, Servant or Journeyman against his, her or their Master, Mistress or Employer, of continued misusage, and repeated violations of the ordinary and established duties of each to the other: the said Justices in their said Weekly or Special Sessions, may on due proof of such complaint, annul the agreements or contracts whether verbal or written, by which such Master, Mistress or Employer, and such Apprentice, Servant or Journeyman may be bound each to the other.

4. That in cases where any such Apprentice, Servant or Journeyman, so bound as aforesaid, shall absent himself, or herself without leave, or shall altogether desert the service of such Master or Mistress or Employer; such Apprentice, Servant or Journeyman shall be proceeded against by warrant under the hand and seal of any one Justice of the Peace.

5. That whatever time may have been lost by such absence or desertion of such Apprentice, Servant or Journeyman, shall, on due proof, be adjudged to be made good to such Master, Mistress or Employer.

6. That any person who shall knowingly harbour or conceal any such Apprentice, Servant or Journeyman, engaged as aforesaid, who may have deserted from his or her Master or Mistress or Employer, shall forfeit and pay a fine not exceeding ten pounds currency.

7. That no such Master or Mistress shall take and carry out of the District of Quebec, any such Apprentice or Servant so engaged as aforesaid, without the consent of such Apprentice or Servant, or his or her Parents or Guardian if a minor, except such as may be bound to the Sea Service.

8. That if any person or persons shall knowingly entice, by any means whatever, any such Apprentice, Servant or Journeyman so engaged as aforesaid, to depart from the service of his or her Master or Mistress or Employer, and that in consequence such Apprentice, Servant or Journeyman shall depart from such service, any person or persons so offending, shall be liable to a penalty not exceeding Ten Pounds current money of this Province, or be committed to the House of Correction for any time not exceeding two months.

9. That no person residing within the walls of the upper Town, or any part of the lower Town to the line of St. Roc Suburbs, shall hire or take into his or her service any Journeyman, Apprentice or Servant who has already resided within those limits, who shall

not have produced a discharge and character from his or her last Master, Mistress or Employer, under a penalty of Five Pounds; and any such Master, Mistress or Employer refusing to give such discharge and character when legally due, shall incur the same penalty.

10. That in all verbal agreements between Masters, Mistresses, Journeymen and Servants by the month, or any shorter period, notice of the intention of either party not to continue the agreement beyond its termination, shall be given to the other at latest, before the expiration of one half of such month or shorter period; otherwise the agreement shall be held to have been continued, till the expiration of a period equal to one half of the time of the original agreement, from the date of such notice; the whole under a penalty of Five Pounds, or commitment to the house of correction for any time not exceeding two months.

(Certified)   GREEN & VALLE,
                                              Clerks of the Peace,

PROVINCE OF LOWER CANADA,
District of Quebec,
IN THE KING'S BENCH,
June 17th. 1818.
No 838. J. SEWELL,
The Honbls. O. PERRAULT. Present.
E. BOWEN,

The Court having inspected and revised the Rules and Regulations of Police for the City of Quebec as altered and amended by the Justices of the District of Quebec, in a General Quarter Session of the Peace, held on Wednesday the 29th Day of April last past; doth confirm the same.

By the court
PERRAULT & ROSS, P.B.R.

---

* *Gazette de Québec*, 20 July 1818.

APPENDIX D

RULES OF THE HOME FOR YOUNG WOMEN SEEKING
EMPLOYMENT, HALIFAX, 1870*

1. Candidates for admission must be able to give references as to good moral character by written documents from their clergymen, or some well known respectable lady or gentleman with whom they have lived. The Matron is authorized to receive applicants without certificates for a single day, then refer such cases to the President or the Lady Visitors for the month.

2. Before admission, the Rules of the Institution will be read to each candidate, who must promise to obey them on being received.

3. All the inmates must attend family worship morning and evening, except in cases of illness or absolute necessity. Absence must be sanctioned by the Matron.

4. Cleanliness and neatness of appearance, propriety in conversation, and a hearty co-operation in promoting the order and arrangements of the house are expected from all the inmates. They are expected to do their own washing and keep their own rooms in order.

5. The inmates must inform the Matron before going out, and must always be home at half-past nine, or at the latest, ten o'clock at night.

6. The Sabbath must be strictly observed in accordance with the Divine command, "Remember the Sabbath day to keep it holy." It is expected that the inmates will either attend religious services in the Home, or at their own place of worship.

7. Any inmate wilfully violating these rules will expose herself to dismissal.

8. Bibles will be provided for the bed-rooms, and it is hoped and expected that each inmate will read a portion from the sacred

Book, and in prayer daily ask the blessing of God, without which they cannot expect prosperity.

9. The internal management of the Home shall be in the hands of a committee of ladies from the different churches, who shall meet once a month at the Home to advise with and instruct the Matron.

10. Two of the committee shall once a week meet the inmates of the Home, and as many of the girls living at service in the city as can be spared and are disposed to attend, and give them such instruction, advice and admonition as shall be deemed suitable and necessary, — the meeting always to be opened with prayer. Once a month a clergyman of one of the evangelical denominations shall be invited to attend these meetings to give a short address and tender such advice as he may think proper.

11. The Matron is authorized to collect the Board, $1.50 per week, or 25 cents daily, for any shorter time than a week, so as to admit of no arrears accumulating.

---

* "Report on the Home for Young Women Seeking Employment, Halifax, 1870," *Atlantis,* Vol. 5, No. 2 (Spring 1980), pp. 196-200.

APPENDIX E

A SERVANT'S DAILY DUTIES

The female servant the following refers to worked in a house with a cook, a chambermaid, and another female servant.[1]

As between maid she had to help both cook and housemaid, and her pre-breakfast duties were as follows:

Do kitchen range and light fire.

Fill kettles and put cook's tools ready on table.

Sweep floor. Do maids' sitting-room fire.

Sweep maids' room, dust and lay breakfast table.

Scrub front steps.

Clean taps and basins in cloakroom.

Scrub cloakroom floor, polish lavatory seat.

Scrub vestibule floor.

Make early morning tea and carry up to maids.

Take cans of hot water up to maids.

Do fires in dining-room, drawing-room, library, and morning-room.

Sweep first landing, front stairs and hall.

Wash, and put on clean apron for breakfast.

She had to rise by 5.30 each morning in order to complete her labours, and the rest of her day continued in much the same fashion:

After breakfast Mabel claimed me for help with bed making and other upstairs work. At twelve thirty she sent me down to Maud for half-an-hour's silver cleaning, or lessons in table and tray laying. Lunch over, up I went again to do the staff bathroom, back stairs, housemaid's cupboard, and the top landing; also to wash dusters and clean all the copper hot water cans. By 2.30 Daisy would be growling up the back stairs, 'Isn't that girl coming down yet? She's supposed to be between maid, not under-housemaid.' If Mabel felt like it, she would let me go, if not she made me finish the last little job. What a scene I went down to! Daisy would have died rather than wash one basin. In addition to breakfast and dinner dishes every pan, spoon, sieve, and dish used by her were piled on the table, in the sink, on the draining board and on the floor. She was an excellent cook, but a messy worker, and on my way to the sink I often slithered on gravy, milk and other greasy liquids. Daisy retired to wash and change and have a little rest, while I tackled the mess. After scrubbing the kitchen and larder floors, I washed our sitting-room floor, and prepared our tea. After tea, out to the kitchen again, to prepare vegetables, and wait on Daisy. Fetch and carry for her, stir or beat mixture, wipe up her spills and chop parsley.... When the gentry were at dinner I carried some of the dishes as far as the dining-room door, and if we had guests staying in the house Mabel collared me to help turn the beds down and put out night clothes. Not until our evening meal was over was I able to tackle another mountain of washing up, another sea of spills. This I did while my sisters-in-service sat by the fire with a tea tray. If we had no dinner party, I finished about 9.30 p.m., but guests meant that I chanted my Good Nights as late as 11.30.

The following extract from a 19th-century manual applies to a maid-of-all-work.[2]

The maid must be up by six o'clock, do her hair, ready herself and only go down to her kitchen when ready to go out to the market. Between six and nine o'clock, she has time to do many things. She will light the range and fires or stoke the stove. She will prepare the breakfasts, tidy the dining room, brush clothes and clean shoes. Here, the masters rise early; she shall do the rooms, put water in the washbasins, bring up wood or coal and take down rubbish. For all these duties she must wear sleeve protectors and a blue apron. She will do the market, if Madame does not go with her, and will not linger to talk; her time is precious. She will set the table, prepare luncheon, put on a white apron for serving and will be careful to wash her hands. Then, once the dining room has been tidied, the dishes washed and put away, the kitchen utensils cleaned, she may, before preparing dinner, carry out a special task for each day of the week. For instance, on Saturday thoroughly clean the kitchen and equipment; Monday the lounge and dining room; Tuesday, the brass in the bedrooms; Wednesday, washing; Thursday, ironing....

Timetable drawn up by Mme. Davaine:[3]

- Get up in order to be downstairs at six *precisely*.
- Light the fire with wood and coal set ready the evening before and quickly dust the kitchen.
- Put water on to heat and, meanwhile, fetch milk.
- Open shutters and windows, brush carpets in dining room and salon, sweep and wipe the floor cloth over everything.

- Properly swab the passageway, kitchen and scullery.
- Take up Madame's eggflip (at quarter past seven). While Madame is dressing, prepare children's bath and clothes.
- Heat milk and prepare coffee.
- While Madame is dressing the children, finish dusting the dining room, salon and passageway, not forgetting the hall stand.
- Wax Monsieur's shoes.
- Lay breakfast table.
- Tidy away bath articles.
- Breakfast around half past eight.
- Wash morning dishes.
- Peel vegetables fetched day before and start luncheon. Remember: on days when there is no soup, the small wash is boiled as soon as breakfast is over.
- Go upstairs and do Madame's room which should *never* normally take more than a half-hour, *even dusting properly.*
- Downstairs, pass feather duster over staircase windows, stairs and the lamp. In this way, the linen can be started at half past ten at the latest. I shall therefore be entitled to *demand* that the linen be finished in the morning.
- Finish luncheon.
- Set the table.
- Go upstairs and dress so as to be clean for waiting at the table.
- Luncheon.
- Wash up dishes.
- Fill the boiler.
- Fill oil lamps.
- Tidy kitchen.
- Iron or fold linen washed the day before or brush clothes or mend.
- Prepare tea. Teatime.
- After tea, see to next day's meals, errands to Mustin and the butcher, and attend to accounts.
- At six o'clock, fetch salad and other vegetables for next day. Clean salad.
- Fetch milk and heat supper.
- Prepare children's things, help them go to bed.
- Lay table.
- Supper.
- Wash up dishes.
- Prepare wood and coal for morning's fire.
- Prepare Madame's tray.
- Bed.

This timetable, which I have myself followed, can be carried out to the letter, provided that no time is lost in chatter nor in looking out the window.

---

1 Pamela Horn, *The Rise of the Victorian Servant* (New York: St. Martin's Press, 1975), pp. 175-76.
2 Pierre Guiral and Guy Thuillier, *La vie quotidienne des domestiques en France au XIXe siècle* (Paris: Hachette, 1978), pp. 79-80 (translation).
3 Anne Martin-Fugier, *La place des bonnes: la domesticité féminine à Paris en 1900* (Paris: Grasset, 1979), pp. 98-100 (translation).

APPENDIX F

LETTER FROM CHARLES BAILLAIRGÉ ON THE NEED FOR A SCHOOL TO TRAIN DOMESTIC SERVANTS*

Quebec City, 29 March 1897.

To The Reverend Sisters of the
Ursuline Order at Quebec City

I saw with pleasure in *L'Evénement* of yesterday's date that Ursulines have an institution at Roberval for preparing girls for work in the fields. This is an excellent thing.

Now, would it not be possible for them, or others, to also prepare girls for domestic service. It is a singular fact that everywhere one hears of the idleness of our population, many of whom beg through the streets or rely on public charity and yet one has the greatest hardship to obtain a maid-servant.

We have had them, on several occasions, from both Bon Pasteur and "La Maternité," but not knowing what to do and returning too often to their old habits.

I am convinced that all families in Quebec City would be most satisfied in seeing an Institution such as yours establishing a school for girls suitable for this purpose gathered from among the idle in Lac St. Jean or some other place. We would know then where to turn for a cook if need be; not top class, or $10 to $15 per month, but $7 or $10, knowing how to prepare a family meal — for instance: a soup made of beef, or with poultry or a leg of mutton but not so boiled that they lose all flavour but may be eaten after with or without a butter sauce — a roast of beef, veal, mutton (leg), a turkey, goose stuffed with bread or potatoes and with or without onions — jugged hare or rabbit — stew with meatballs, mutton or pigs' trotters with brown sauce (browned flour), beef or caribou steak not too well done — mutton or veal cutlet — a butt, cutlet of fresh pork with fat from the roast, to eat cold — fillets, kidneys, puddings, faggots, sweetbreads — calf's head split in two with a saw, brains removed, butter sauce with the brains (boiled separately in a muslin cloth) and hard boiled eggs, both chopped coarsely — stewed beef and carrots ("mode" as the French say) — Irish stew — partridge and cabbage — know how to put on the peas, cabbage early enough for them to cook — macaroni (with cheese) — know how to boil a salmon, etc., fry fish — make bread, rice or tapioca pudding, blancmange — caramel custard — know how to roast apples, potatoes — fried potatoes, apple fritters, pancakes, an omelette, etc. etc.

No need for sugar creams, charlotte russes, iced cream, flaky pastry, which one may do without or which the mistress of the house prepares herself, as she does her Christmas pudding with her own hands, and her small biscuits.

Aside from the kitchen, in a house where there is only one girl, she would have no business above stairs except to carry out waste water, wash dishes, polish the cutlery, silver, shoes, bring in the wood for the stove, placed nearby for the purpose, look after the hot water or steam boiler, found almost everywhere now, all winter; that is, light it once, stoke it with coal twice a day and take out the ashes daily or every second day and place them in the receptacle provided. As for the remaining refuse, nowadays most is [burned] — fats, small bones of all kinds being suitable and serving the flames, leaving little other than a few coffee grounds, tea leaves, vegetable and potato peelings, poultry innards and large bones that should be carried to the "garbage can."

Reverend Sisters, forgive such details — but they are to show you the need for teaching servants what they should know and what too often they do not — I will tell you that just yesterday, a new girl not only ruined my dinner by cutting the two ears off a calf's head and throwing them on the fire (they are the part I like the best) but was on the point of putting the whole head on to boil instead of sawing it in two to get the brain which otherwise would have been lost and the sauce spoiled.

The last girl we had spoiled the appearance of a beautiful turkey on Christmas Day by cutting off the parson's nose.

Last year I supped at a friend's house — a new girl had just arrived — the poultry did not arrive and finally Madame informed us that the poor girl had put the whole bird in to cook, that is without eviscerating it — she knew no better.

Worse, a friend assured me, a fresh arrival being told by her mistress to infuse the tea — put it on to boil; threw away the first water, which she found dirty, put it on the heat again with clean water, which since it was still somewhat dirty was, in turn, thrown down the drain — finally, it was only when washed three times that she found the water clean enough to consider the tea leaves presentable and, having arranged them with butter and seasoned them with pepper and salt, she served them in a dish as she would have done ordinary vegetables.

Servants must be told how to understand expressions such as: put the wine on ice, in order to avoid them uncorking the bottles and pouring the wine on the actual ice instead of putting the bottle in ice before uncorking, and other stupidities.

160

I do not need to say more, Reverend Sisters, for you to recognize the raison d'être of what I am taking the liberty of suggesting in the interests of thousands of families who suffer from servants' ignorance and their extravagant pretensions with respect to wages.

If you had a list or register of unemployed servants and people could apply to you if need be, it would remedy a situation which does not exist in other places where hundreds of servants advertise in the newspapers.

I have the honour to be,
Your obedient servant,
C. BAILLAIRGÉ

---

* Montreal. Bibliothèque municipale. Salle Gagnon, Collection Canadiana (translation).

APPENDIX G

THOUGHTS OF A CANADIAN LADY ON MASTER/SERVANT RELATIONSHIPS AT THE BEGINNING OF THE 20TH CENTURY*

Where are the servants of yesteryear? From one end of Canada to the other, in town and country, in homes with six servants as in households with just a maid-of-all-work, this same question is repeated with sadness; and, in other countries, our neighbours translate it into their own tongues.

The servants of yesteryear have disappeared and not been replaced. The famine is general and there is little reason to hope more for the future, since the seed necessary to a crop of good servants seems to be lost. And, once delivered of this observation, to heighten the bitterness each draws from his memory some family anecdote in praise of times past; the devoted features of an old serving woman who spent fifty years in Grandfather's or Great Uncle's service, and more than one of us, in childhood memories, sees again a good country face bending over the cradle, smiling under its white cap, one of those open, sweet faces full of innocence that we like to see today near the cradles of our own children.

Alas! The white caps have disappeared, the affectionate look, the tender innocent smiles have died away. During the last twenty-five years, the countryside has had time to become steeped in scepticism, covetousness, the follies whispered to it by the large cities. The countryside has lost and is losing more and more the faith, the simplicity, the love of work that once made it a haven of peace, and the final unbalancing of the already tormented minds of those who come to us is rapidly achieved by the abrupt change experienced in environment.

Weaker than before, because he has not received the good, solid education given to his predecessors in the family, no matter how modest, the servant today is also exposed to temptations that are much more redoubtable. Friends, workers, suppliers who are his normal companions make a point of "educating him," which, in their manner, means "corrupting him." His parents often only see him as a means of gain and push him to take advantage and help them take advantage of the facilities afforded by his situation. Evil comes to him from all sides and under all forms, through the conversation he hears, the newspaper he reads, the poster or caricature he sees, by the very letter he receives "from home" and, to counter these dangerous influences, he no longer has the two safeguards of before: the counsel of his parents, the protection of his master whose trust he has betrayed, solicitude rejected and goodness exhausted. Under such conditions, there is a very good chance that the servant will be bad and the master will have trouble in remaining good.

Poor servants creating poor masters, and vice versa: will this be the unavoidable situation in future? Many fear so, many point to towns in the United States where, servants having become unobtainable or unbearable, millionaires find themselves reduced to doing their own cooking unless they prefer to go and live in a hotel.

The situation does not appear so menacing to me and, while awaiting the moral development that will result in everything falling into place in the country, and in our homes at the same time, certain individual efforts, I believe, may be attempted. There should be some means of countering to some extent the inconveniences that tend to become afflictions and, if it is difficult to reason with domestics, perhaps reasoning with the masters might lead to appreciable results.

It is first important to establish wherein lies the great difference between our servants today and those of yesteryear whom we never cease to mourn.

The latter were not, however, nothing short of perfect. We have kept alive the memory of some who were distinguished by their devotion, but the others! The ordinary run of domestics!

Let the old authors remind us.

Marot could speak at length of his valet from Gascony, the lying, swearing thief, made to measure for the gallows tree!

But, nevertheless, the best son in the world. And Molière's Scapins, Sganarelles, Toinettes, Dorines, Martines embody the best collection of knaves, liars and impudent creatures conceivable, so much so that one wonders how our autocratic forefathers allowed them liberties that we would certainly not tolerate from their successors, a democratic system notwithstanding.

The reason is they had one advantage that will quickly be recognized and that is the secret of their master's patience and posterity's indulgence. One quality sufficed to counterbalance their faults, the first quality of a servant: attachment. The masters they tormented, railed at, willingly pillaged were not strangers to them; though they may have exploited them, they never thought to abandon them. Even while making life difficult for them at times, they suffered their troubles, helped in their plans, even defended them from outside enemies. They were part of the family — prodigals, perhaps — but part of it.

Domestics today are not part of it. It is not only social distance that separates them from their masters, but often hostility and nearly always indifference. I am not of those who see humanity too blackly painted and I consider that, among masters who do not inspire more attachment, most would deserve to inspire it, and that, among the servants, many would be capable of feeling it. This malaise between them does not so much come from themselves as from the new conditions of modern life, the prejudices that have been suggested on both sides and the consequent tension that is present from the beginning of their relationship, which is then very difficult to put on another footing. The result is a series of disappointments and problems for the master, misunderstandings, bitterness, continual and unjustified revolt on the part of the servant who, becoming cynical and proud, has not become — quite the contrary — wiser than his predecessors.

In order to remedy the present state of affairs that we deplore and return to the previous state of affairs so often regretted, or rather to return to what can suit with modern life, the bond of solidarity between master and servant that was so long their mutual support would have to be rekindled. True, this is not easy; but neither is it completely impossible; therefore one can, indeed one must, attempt it.

Let us not flatter ourselves. We will have to struggle against all types of obstacle, the most perfidious and the most disconcerting, against systematic poor faith or hypocritical good will, even against ourselves, our dislikes, our anger, our credulity and the weakness that can come either from goodness or lassitude.

The first error to avoid with regard to one's servants is to judge them according to one's own standards.

Requiring that what touches us should touch them, that they should be shocked by what shocks us, reproaching them for a lack of sensitivity, tact or openness as we would ourselves, would be naive towards ourselves and unjust towards them. Their nature, education, situation make certain of their weaknesses excusable, almost inevitable and make the fact that they even conserve an idea of their principle duties praiseworthy.

A servant who is honest, upright, sufficiently conscientious and never insolent is a good servant, even if he also sometimes be slow and clumsy, forgetful, stubborn, touchy, pernickety, a little lazy, even disagreeable. You would do well to keep him, for his successor will bring at least the equivalent of his faults and may not offer you the same guarantees. And such guarantees are to be required above all and masters who, for ease of service or reasons of economy, knowingly keep a corrupt, dissolute servant must expect all the unpleasantness to which they expose themselves.

Let us leave such masters and servants aside and return to the honest servant whom we hope to bind to us. We will not achieve our aim without much patience and a little skill. In order to reach the heart of a servant, you must destroy prejudice and distrust, and steal into his mind. One of the best ways to gain his attachment will be, first, to interest him.

One of the main causes for a servant's indifference is that he no longer feels at home in our home. Before, he knew he would have to live his entire life in the same house, he often put roots down there and his children remained after him. Today, our house is no more to him than a temporary lodging, where he behaves honestly, if he is honest, but where he likes nothing because nothing belongs to him. The only manner in which to react to this tendency is to give him the illusion of possessions and a shadow of authority. The cook who makes "her jams," the gardener who waters "his flowers" and the coachman who cares for "his horses" all accomplish their work better and with less trouble than servants who are equally conscientious but not stimulated by personal interest. In addition, this small measure of independence increases the servant's responsibility, strengthens his character and exercises his intelligence.

It is fitting, therefore, to be conciliatory on this point. If some arrangement in the kitchen or laundry room is not inconvenient and yet especially pleasing to the servant responsible, why not agree to it and, if necessary, remark on its usefulness and good taste? If some ways of doing things does not upset the order in the house and lightens the servant's work or satisfies his whim, why not leave him some latitude on the matter? Let me make myself clear: the liberty or authority allowed the servant must not, under any circumstances, go beyond the very narrow confines of his domain. A servant may enjoy what his master in fairness and kindness wishes him to have, but he must never presume upon such kindness, feel it bend or even falter under his pressure. A house conquered by a servant is a house that is lost, and I add that the servant who has conquered the house is also lost, so fatal to all are the consequences of the least breach in family order. Once freed from his master's authority, the servant will reduce him to submission, for no-one is as likely to become a tyrant as a usurper. It will be revolution in the home, the transfer of all influence, quarrels between those near to each other, extravagance, often the worst catastrophes.

Let me go further: even though the servant be well-intentioned, his reign will still be disastrous, since he does not have the ability necessary to lead. Much too advanced in some ways he is, in fact, and will always remain incomplete, a child, in others, and that is why the true practical, Christian way to act with him will always be to treat him as a child, to educate him and continue thus indefinitely, based on the same system we apply to our own children's education; by being as indulgent and patient in the little things as we are immovable on questions of principal, tolerating insofar as ourselves are concerned but suffering nothing, absolutely nothing, that could prejudice good order in the home or our dignity outside it.

Once these restrictions have been laid down, there is nothing to fear in granting the servant the satisfactions and kindnesses allowed.

166

We must not forget that our comfort, always close at hand, is a constant temptation to him and that, by letting him share in it to a small extent, we will weaken his covetousness.

The most celebrated founders of orders desired that their monks be content in their cells, and it is to be hoped that servants become attached to theirs; it is a way of attaching him to the house. It is not often possible to give him a large or commodious room, but a good bed, clean furniture, an odd end of carpet, gaily coloured wallpaper would all seem small luxuries to him.

His health and also his hygiene should not be neglected. He should never become too tired through our lack of foresight, nor really deprived through our parsimony or disorder. His dependence on us requires our solicitude and refusing him what is necessary would be to authorize him to take it. We would do well to add a little extra to what is necessary. A dish that he considers superior, cakes, candies that we think to let him taste, will cease to be forbidden fruits to him and celebrations, especially family celebrations, should not bring with them an excess of work. It is on the material level that we can make the most concessions since it is materially, physically, that his needs are identical to ours. On the other hand, let us avoid anything that could lead to the development of dangerous feelings. Do not give a chambermaid clothes above her station, do not encourage pretention or idleness in any way. Let us be attentive to the holidays granted, the use made of them, to books, newspapers, the visitors received in the kitchen.

A matter often discussed is the attitude to be taken towards servants. "I am an excellent master, I do not torment my servants, I barely speak to them," say some, most astonished that they garner even less approbation than demanding, difficult masters.

This is because a servant has no greater antipathy towards anything than that which seems to him distrust or coldness. He likes attention to be paid to him, a very human feeling; he wants to be closer to us, a natural tendency in inferiors. To attach him to us therefore, let us use some of the prestige that, despite everything, we have for him and that is our great strength. Do not let us compromise it by vulgar and dangerous familiarity, but do not let us fear it will be lessened if we remain accessible to the servants, sometimes speaking to them other than to give orders, showing interest in their families, their affairs, caring for them if they are ill, expressing fair ideas, high sentiments in front of them. They should not see us from too near, it is said. Why not, if we show ourselves to be as we should.

People, too often, believe they have fulfilled their responsibility to their servant when they have generously provided for his needs and paid his exact wages. This is an error. Material obligations have been fulfilled, but not the moral ones recognized by all Christian families. Our money pays for the servant's work. His care, the extra trouble

167

that he often willingly takes for us, the devotion that may perhaps grow in him deserve something more. So that he becomes attached to us, let us become attached to him or, at least, to the duty he represents. Whoever he may be, the servant always has a call on our interest. He needs our charity as much as the poor we assist, the ignorant we seek to instruct, and he has more right to it. Temporarily at least, he is one of those entrusted to us. He lives under our roof. He is, in the beautiful words of Saint François de Sales, "our nearest neighbour."

Aline Raymond

---

*   Aline Raymond, "Maîtres et serviteurs," *La Revue canadienne*, Vol. 41 (Feb. 1904), pp. 129-37 (translation).

ABBREVIATIONS USED

ANQ-M   Archives nationales du Québec, Montreal
ANQ-Q   Archives nationales du Québec, Quebec City
ANQ-TR   Archives nationales du Québec, Trois-Rivières
AO   Archives of Ontario
APJ-M   Archives du palais de justice, Montreal
APJ-Q   Archives du palais de justice, Quebec City
AVQ   Archives de la ville de Québec
IBCQ   Inventaire des biens culturels du Québec
NMC   National Map Collection
PAC   Public Archives Canada
PANS   Public Archives of Nova Scotia

ENDNOTES

Introduction

1 Two or three studies deal with servants but cover the French régime. See especially "La domesticité féminine de Québec au milieu du XVIIIe siècle" by Francine Barry (paper presented in Montreal at the 1974 meeting of the Institut d'histoire de l'Amérique française) and "La domesticité juvénile à Montréal pendant la première moitié du XVIIIe siècle (1713-1744)" by Daniel Lépine (MA thesis, Univ. de Sherbrooke, forthcoming). Little has been written about servants in the 19th century, but see Geneviève Leslie, "Domestic Service in Canada, 1880-1920," in Janice Acton et al., Women at Work: Ontario, 1850-1930 (Toronto: Canadian Women's Educational Press, 1974); Marilyn Barber, "The Women Ontario Welcomed: Immigrant Domestics for Ontario Homes, 1870-1930," Ontario History, Vol. 62, No. 3 (Sept. 1980), pp. 148-72; and Joy Parr, Labouring Children. British Immigrant Apprentices to Canada, 1864-1924 (London: Croom Helm, 1980).

2 This was certainly striking in the Campbell and Boulton (The Grange) houses in Toronto, and the Prescott, Uniacke, and Haliburton houses in the Halifax area. It is also surprising in the various houses in Upper Canada Village near Cornwall, Ont.

3 Bellevue House, Kingston, is an example of this. See Christina Bates, "Allocation and Functions of Domestic Offices at Bellevue N.H.P.," Manuscript Report Series, No. 429 (1981), Parks Canada, Ottawa.

4 See Bibliography, sect. 8, 9, 10.

5 See Bibliography, sect. 2, 3, 4, 6, 7.

6 Pierre Guiral and Guy Thuillier, "Les sources de l'histoire régionale des domestiques au XIXe siècle," Revue historique, No. 269 (April-June 1978), p. 444

Part One: 1816 to 1820

Introduction

1 J.-P. Bernard, P.-A. Linteau, and J.-C. Robert, "La structure professionnelle de Montréal en 1825," Revue d'histoire de l'Amérique française, Vol. 30, No. 3 (Dec. 1976), p. 386.

2 According to Curé Signay's 1818 census. There were several

omissions in the parish priest's listing: his total was 16 008 whereas it should have been 16 443. If members of religious orders and military personnel are included, the total becomes 18 626. See Joseph Signay, Recensement de la ville de Québec en 1818 (Quebec: Société historique de Québec, 1975) (hereafter cited as Signay, Recensement), p. 279.

3   For the Halifax census of 1816-17, see Thomas Beamish Akins, History of Halifax City (Belleville: Mika Publishing, 1973), p. 187.

4   This figure recurs frequently in a number of different works consulted; for example, see Gertrude A. Gunn, The Political History of Newfoundland, 1832-1864 (Toronto: Univ. of Toronto Press, 1966), p. 9.

5   Wills and statements of chattels for Halifax left much to be desired compared to the notarized documents in Quebec City.

6   For Quebec City, see Edward H. Dahl et al., La ville de Québec, 1800-1850: un inventaire de cartes et plans (Ottawa: Musées nationaux du Canada, 1975), p. 27. For Montreal, see Jean-Claude Robert, "Montréal (1821-1871). Aspects de l'urbanisation," PhD thesis, Univ. de Paris, No. I, 1977, p. 183. See also Fernand Ouellet, Éléments d'histoire sociale du Bas-Canada (Montreal: Hurtubise HMH, 1972), p. 181.

7   Fernand Ouellet, Le Bas-Canada, 1791-1840, Changements structuraux et crise (Ottawa: Ottawa Univ. Press, 1976) (hereafter cited as Le Bas-Canada), pp. 316-21.

8   Antonio Drolet, "La ville de Québec, histoire municipale; II: Régime anglais jusqu'à l'incorporation (1759-1833)," Cahiers d'histoire, No. 17 (1965), pp. 31-38. See also Jean-Claude Robert, op. cit., p. 43.

9   Claudette Lacelle, "La propriété militaire à Québec de 1760 à 1871," Histoire et archéologie, No. 57 (1982) (hereafter cited as "La propriété militaire"); Fernand Ouellet, Le Bas-Canada, p. 208.

10   Jean-Claude Robert, op. cit., p. 43.

11   See, among others, Helen I. Cowan, British Emigration to British North America, The First Hundred Years (Toronto: Univ. of Toronto Press, 1961), and Huguette Lapointe-Roy, "Paupérisme et assistance sociale à Montréal, 1832-1865," MA thesis, McGill Univ., Montreal, 1972.

12   Dictionnaire des oeuvres littéraires du Québec (Montreal: Fides, 1978-), Vol. 1: "Des origines à 1900," p. lvi.

13   See Hubert Charbonneau et al., La population du Québec: études rétrospectives (Montreal: Boréal Express, 1973), p. 13.

The People Involved – At the Beginning of the Century

1   Because of overlapping French definitions, my first job was to

172

check meanings in French dictionaries of the 17th, 18th, and 19th centuries.

The 1690 Furetière defines domestique as "one who is of a household" or as "officers, men paid by a Master"; fille covered "all types of female servant"; garçon was applied to "a man of all work, especially when the only servant and not wearing livery." A servante was "a girl or woman who serves in a household," and a serviteur "one paid by a Master." Antoine Furetière, Dictionnaire universel.... (Geneva: Slatkine Reprints, 1970).

The 1765 Dictionnaire de l'Académie française states that a domestique was one "who is of the household" and essentially "the male servants of a household"; fille was considered to be a chambermaid only, and garçon meant "a man who does not wear livery" and who sometimes "does the most menial work." A servante was a "woman or girl ... employed for the most menial work in a household for a wage," whereas a serviteur was "one who serves as a domestic."

L.N. Bescherelle's 1858 Dictionnaire national de la langue française defines a domestique as "a man or woman serving in a household, in a family, for a wage," but it specifies that this was the narrow sense of the word, which previously could have meant anyone attached to a prince or to a house. Fille was a "female servant" and garçon a "domestic, boy." A servante was a "woman or girl employed in household work, in the menial work of a household, and [who] receives a wage" whereas a serviteur was "someone in the service, payment of another," the word mainly being used "to describe domestics."

Finally, in Pierre Larousse's Grand Dictionnaire universel du XIXe siècle, 1865-75, Vol. 6, domestique chiefly referred to a manservant "living in his master's house," whereas serviteur often applied to those who "may have their own domicile and therefore find themselves slightly more independent."

Before 1850 engagé was only used as the past participle of the verb. Only when the Bescherelle appeared was the term treated as a noun ("hired hand") with the meaning "one who enters into a voluntary contract during a year."

2 Bas-Canada. Parlement, Statuts provinciaux du Bas-Canada (Quebec: P.E. Desbarats, 1811-20) (hereafter cited as Statuts provinciaux), Vol. 7: "1811-1814," 51 Geo. III, cap. 3, art. 3.

3 Signay, Recensement. The priest included 11 boys in the census, 10 of whom were in households with other servants.

4 I wish to thank Louise Dechêne for sharing with me the results of her research on George Pozer. In Signay's Recensement (p. 23), Pozer was shown as having only one female servant.

5 This corresponds to Hardy and Ruddel's point that "all domestics are hired, but not all those hired are domestics": Jean-Pierre

173

Hardy and David-Thiéry Ruddel, Les apprentis artisans à Québec, 1660-1815 (Montreal: Presses de l'univ. du Québec, 1977), p. 73, n. 50.

6   Signay, Recensement, s.v. "Isoir dit Provençal," p. 27.

7   As an example, see Mary Quayle Innis, ed., Mrs. Simcoe's Diary (Toronto: Macmillan, 1972), p. 147. The same situation existed in the U.S. around the same time; see Lucy Maynard Salmon, Domestic Service (New York: Macmillan, 1910), p. 57.

8   Bescherelle Dictionary, s.v. "valet."

9   Signay, Recensement.

10 PAC, MG17, A5, Vol. 5, Recensement de la ville de Montréal par Jacques Viger en 1825.

11 Jean-Paul Bernard et al., op. cit.

12 The youngest apprentice in a store often served as a domestic until a new apprentice arrived; see Pierre H. Audet, "Apprenticeship in Early Nineteenth Century Montreal, 1790-1812," MA thesis, Concordia Univ., 1975, p. 95. In fact, when first compiling data I included apprentices and clerks, only separating them at the final analysis.

13 Claudette Lacelle, "La garnison britannique dans la ville de Québec d'après les journaux de 1764 à 1840," Histoire et archéologie, No. 23 (1979); ibid., "La propriété militaire."

14 Quebec Mercury, 24 May 1817.

15 245 of the 1500 contracts recorded for 1816-20 concerned domestics; 196 of these were hired for the city, 33 for the surrounding country, and 16 for various places in Upper Canada. My analysis mainly deals with the 196 contracts covering servants who were to live in urban centres. The others were included only when they provided additional information or some significant detail. Also, various forays were made into previous years for comparative purposes, and 73 Quebec City and Montreal contracts were analyzed in the same way. Marthe Lacombe brought various Quebec City contracts from 1790 to 1800 to my attention, and Luce Vermette flagged a number of Montreal contracts from between 1780 and 1815. I gratefully acknowledge their assistance.

16 W. Kingsford's analysis of the 1784 Montreal census shows that 1 out of 9 servants was a child under 15 — slightly more than 11% — a ratio very closely corresponding to that reported here. See Louise Dechêne, Habitants et marchands de Montréal au XVIIe siècle (Paris and Montreal: Plon, 1974), p. 441, n. 93.

17 Jean-Paul Bernard et al., op. cit., p. 397.

18 My thanks to John Hare for informing me of this point.

19 See Theresa M. McBride, The Domestic Revolution: The Modernization of Household Service in England and France, 1820-1920

(New York: Holmes and Meier, 1976) (hereafter cited as <u>Domestic Revolution</u>), p. 9.

20 Ibid., p. 35.   She stated that in 1820, 61% of servants in Versailles were born elsewhere, and she compared these data with data Adeline Daumard cited for Paris in 1831, when 60% of servants who died there were from outside the city. See Adeline Daumard, <u>La bourgeoisie parisienne de 1815 à 1848</u> (Paris: SEVPEN, 1963) (hereafter cited as <u>La bourgeoisie</u>). See also Theresa M. McBride, "The Modernization of Woman's Work," <u>The Journal of Modern History</u>, Vol. 49, No. 2 (June 1977) (hereafter cited as "Modernization"), p. 233.

21 ANQ-M, Registres de décès pour la paroisse Notre-Dame. I also consulted registers for the parish of Notre-Dame de Québec in the ANQ-Q for 1813-17 (those for 1818-20 were not available), but no servants' deaths were recorded.

22 Jean-Paul Bernard et al., op. cit., pp. 408-415.

23 Using Signay's figures, we obtain:
4611 souls in St-Roch,
1035 in the <u>banlieue</u>,
3959 for the Upper Town <u>faubourgs</u>,
3243 for the Lower Town,
3595 for the Upper Town.
These figures do not take into account members of religious orders nor the garrison, so 450 people at the Hôpital général should be added to the <u>banlieue</u>, and 133 priests and nuns, the 18 inhabitants of the château, and the 1582 members of the garrison should be added to the Upper Town. The proportions would then become 24.8% in St-Roch, 8% in the <u>banlieue</u>, 21.3 in the <u>faubourgs</u>, 17.4 in the Lower Town, and 28.6 in the Upper Town. However, I do not think the garrison should be included and have therefore omitted it from my recalculations. The percentages are therefore: St-Roch, 27.1%; <u>banlieue</u>, 8.7%; <u>faubourgs</u>, 23.3%; Lower Town, 19%; and Upper Town, 22%.

24 Theresa M. McBride, <u>Domestic Revolution</u>, pp. 117-18. See also ibid., "Modernization," p. 232.

25 PAC, MG23, GII, 10, Vols. 12 and 13: trial records of 272 cases Judge Sewell heard at Quebec City between 1808 and 1820.

26 Theresa M. McBride, <u>Domestic Revolution</u>; see also Pierre Guiral and Guy Thuillier, <u>La vie quotidienne des domestiques en France au XIXe siècle</u> (Paris: Hachette, 1978) (hereafter cited as <u>Vie quotidienne</u>).

27 Cissie Fairchilds noted that in Toulouse, men servants came from more favourable circumstances than women servants did: see "Masters and Servants in Eighteenth Century Toulouse," <u>Journal of Social History</u>, Vol. 12, No. 3 (Spring 1979), p. 371.

See also Maurice Garden, Lyon et les Lyonnais au XVIIIe siècle (Paris: Belles Lettres, 1975), p. 250.

28 My thanks to Luce Vermette for having shared her observations on this subject. Parishes surrounding Quebec City and Montreal are concerned here.

29 Theresa M. McBride, "Modernization," p. 232. Towards the middle of the century the proportion would have been 1 to 4 for Hamilton; see Michael Katz, The People of Hamilton, Canada West; Family and Class in a Mid-Nineteenth Century City (Cambridge, Mass.: Harvard Univ. Press, 1975), p. 25.

30 According to Signay's figures, domestic help in Quebec City constituted 7.2% of the total population. However, he omitted Protestants and did not include the château, which most certainly had more than one domestic. Nor did he include the servants of all the religious orders even though they had been included in previous censuses. Finally, he mentioned no servants from the various hotels or inns except for the Union Hotel and the Neptune Inn.

Also, certain domestics did not live in their employers' houses; I found five of them in the course of research, which perhaps explains the priest's silence concerning inns and hotels. In addition, some others may possibly have been included in the census as labourers. An example drawn from previous censuses is Louis Lefebvre, 2 rue Laval, who in 1792 was classified as a domestic, was down as a labourer in 1795, and in 1805 was once again counted as a domestic. On this point see Joseph-Octave Plessis, "Dénombrements de Québec faits en 1792, 1795, 1798 and 1805 par le curé Joseph-Octave Plessis," in Rapport de l'archiviste de la province de Québec pour 1948-1949 (Quebec: Rédempti Paradis, 1949), pp. 1-250. Taking "Possibilities" into account, the figure would come to 8.2%.

Domestic Service

1 Denise Helly's observation in "Anthropologie et différentiation sexuelle," paper presented at the October 1979 meeting of the Institut d'histoire de l'Amérique française, University of Ottawa.

2 See Philippe Ariès, L'enfant et la vie familiale sous l'ancien régime (Paris: Plon, 1960), specifically the chapter "De la famille médiévale à la famille moderne."

3 Ibid. p. 412.

4 The phenomenon of employing relations was also observed in France at the same period in instances where account books could be consulted. Ronald-Henri Hubscher noted that 1/3 of the servants with the Flahaut family were related; see "Une contribution à la connaissance des milieux populaires ruraux au XIXe siècle. Le livre de compte de la famille Flahaut (1811-1877),"

Revue d'histoire économique et sociale, Vol. 47, No. 3 (1969) (hereafter cited as "Contribution"), p. 396.

5   Robert de Roquebrune, Testament de mon enfance (Montreal: Fides, 1979), p. 20, in which he recounts Sambo's arrival. These memoirs date from the end of the century, but the actual method of hiring was certainly common.

6   Four newspapers were examined for the period 1816-20: La Gazette de Québec, La Gazette de Montréal, Quebec Mercury, and Montreal Herald.

7   Marjory Whitelaw, ed., The Dalhousie Journals (Ottawa: Oberon Press, 1978), p. 148.

8   Montreal Herald, 4 Mar. 1820.

9   ANQ-M, greffe de Jean-Marie Cadieux, acte no. 239, 15 May 1816; greffe de Henry Griffin, acte no. 3253, 13 July 1820; greffe de Jean-Guillaume Delisle, acte no. 1376, 8 Sept. 1817; greffe de Louis-Huguet Latour, acte, 15 July 1818. The last involves a young girl who was both servant and apprentice.

10 ANQ-M, greffe de Jean-Marie Cadieux, acte no. 386, 30 Aug. 1816; greffe de Henry Griffin, acte no. 1797, 9 Apr. 1817.

11 John Lambert, Travels through Lower Canada and the United States of North America, in the Years 1806, 1807 and 1808 (London: Richard Phillips, 1816), p. 475; Albert Babeau, Les artisans et les domestiques d'autrefois (Paris: Firmin-Didot, 1886), p. 286; Abel Chatelain, "Migrations et domesticité féminine urbaine en France, XVIIIe-XXe siècles," Revue d'histoire économique et sociale, Vol. 47, No. 4 (Dec. 1969), p. 508.

12 See Article 5 of "Rules and Regulations of Police for the City and Suburbs of Montreal," Montreal Herald, 21 June 1817.

13 PAC, MG23, GII, 10, Vol. 13, pp. 6213-4.

14 Clarissa Packard (nom-de-plume for Caroline Howard Gilman), Recollections of a Housekeeper (New York: Harper and Brothers, 1836).

15 Jean-Pierre Hardy and David-Thiéry Ruddel, op. cit., p. 172.

16 ANQ-M, greffe de Jean-Marie Cadieux, acte no. 27, 24 Jan. 1816; greffe de Nicolas-Benjamin Doucet, acte no. 5058, 1 Apr. 1818; greffe de Charles Huot, acte no. 808, 30 Aug. 1816.

17 Pierre H. Audet, op. cit., p. 151, Table 20.

18 Jean-Pierre Hardy and David-Thiéry Ruddel, op. cit., pp. 173-75.

19 ANQ-Q, greffe de Jean Bélanger, acte no. 6872, 27 June 1817.

20 ANQ-M, greffe de Henry Griffin, acte no. 2451, 12 Jan. 1819; greffe de Louis-Huguet Latour, acte, 15 July 1816; greffe de Henry Griffin, acte no. 1803, 14 Apr. 1817.

21 ANQ-M, greffe de John Gerband Beek, acte no. 2265, 19 May 1817; acte no. 2348, 21 Aug. 1819; greffe de Charles Prévost, acte, 26 Oct. 1818.

22 This was covered by law in Great Britain. See Thomas Coznett,

The Footman's Directory and Butler's Remembrance; or, the Advice of Onesimus to his Young Friends (London: printed for the author, 1823), p. 260.

23 ANQ-Q, greffe de Jean Bélanger, acte no. 7184, 24 Jan. 1818.

24 Theresa M. McBride, Domestic Revolution, p. 63.

25 ANQ-TR, greffe de Joseph Badeaux, acte no. 2126, 24 Dec. 1817, and acte no. 2140, 27 Dec. 1818.

26 ANQ-M, greffe de Henry Griffin, acte no. 2965, 22 Feb. 1820.

27 Judith Fingard dealt with this problem in "The Winter's Tale: The Seasonal Contours of Pre-industrial Poverty in British North America, 1815-1860," Historical Papers/Communications historiques (1974), pp. 65-94.

28 ANQ-M, greffe de Thomas Barron, acte no. 2979, 30 Oct. 1816. This contract gives the impression that the youngster had been in his master's employ for some time.

29 See Theresa M. McBride, Domestic Revolution, as well as Pierre Guiral and Guy Thuillier, Vie quotidienne.

30 Theresa M. McBride, Domestic Revolution, chap. 5, and also "Social Mobility for the Lower Class: Domestic Servants in France," Journal of Social History, Vol. 8, No. 1 (Fall 1974) (hereafter cited as "Social Mobility"), pp. 63-78.

Everyday Life

1 See, for example, Jean-Pierre Hardy and David-Thiéry Ruddel, op. cit., p. 130; Pierre Guiral and Guy Thuillier, Vie quotidienne, p. 78; and Theresa M. McBride, Domestic Revolution, p. 55. With respect to apprentices, see Jean-Pierre Hardy and David-Thiéry Ruddel, op. cit., pp. 52-54. For journeymens' hours, see greffe de Roger Lelièvre, acte no. 8871, 25 Mar. 1816.

2 See, for example, Theresa M. McBride, (Domestic Revolution, p. 55) quoting from Samuel and Sarah Adams's handbook The Complete Servant (London: Knight and Lacey, 1825), p. 286: "Those who thrive, must rise by five." See also PAC, MG23, GII, 10, Vol. 12, p. 5845: in December 1811 Mr. Organ in evidence stated that the family prepared for bed between 9 and 10 o'clock, as did the servant; in Vol. 13, p. 6195, Françoise Godbout stated that she went to bed at 9 in the evening (June 1816); in 1817 Marguerite Langevin, a servant, said she went to bed at 10 o'clock (p. 6715); and Amable Courteau, who was also in service, said "She returned at 10 o'clock I was abed" (p. 6766).

3 Pierre Guiral and Guy Thuillier, Vie quotidienne, p. 79; Pamela Horn, The Rise and Fall of the Victorian Servant (New York: St. Martin's Press, 1975), p. 50.

4 PAC, MG23, GII, 10, Vol. 12, p. 6091.

5 Pierre H. Audet, op. cit., p. 92.

6 In the 24 turn-of-the-century houses known, 27 servants' rooms

were found, 24 of which were near the kitchen (next to, opposite, behind, or above); the 3 others each opened onto attic storage rooms.

7   ANQ-M, Plans de l'architecture domestique, no. CAR 40/6/9; this plan is also cited as A-74-8 in A. Giroux, N. Cloutier, and R. Bédard, "Plans de l'architecture domestique inventoriés aux Archives nationales du Québec à Montréal," Histoire et archéologie/History and Archeology, No. 4 (1975); PAC, MG23, GII, 10, Vol. 13, p. 6986-8.

8   ANQ-M, Plans de l'architecture domestique, no. 1625. This plan is also cited as A-2-1 in A. Giroux, N. Cloutier, and R. Bédard, op. cit. See also Marthe Lacombe, "La maison George-Etienne Cartier, rue Notre-Dame à Montréal," Travail inédit, No. 240 (1977), Parks Canada, Ottawa, for a plan of the Perry house in 1835.

9   ANQ-M, greffe de Nicolas-Benjamin Doucet, acte no. 6600, 15 Sept. 1819.

10 Clarissa Packard, op. cit., pp. 80-84.

11 ANQ-Q, QBC 28, Vol. 45, Juges de paix et sessions de la paix, Jan.-June 1829.

12 ANQ-Q, greffe de Laughlan T. McPherson, acte, 19 March 1817.

13 PAC, MG23, GII, 10, Vol. 13, pp. 6715-6716.

14 Ibid., Vol. 12, p. 6092.

15 Theresa M. McBride estimated that feeding a servant could cost 2 to 3 times her salary; see Domestic Revolution, p. 51. And Lady Aylmer mentioned that it cost ₤25 per year to board with the Ursulines (PAC, MG24, A43, p. 76), which was 2-1/2 times a female servant's wage.

16 Albert Babeau, "La domesticité d'autrefois," Le Correspondant, Vol. 139 (1885), p. 247; Louis Bergeron, "Approvisionnement et consommation à Paris sous le premier empire," Fédération des Sociétés historiques et archéologiques de Paris et de l'Ile de France, Vol. 14 (1963), p. 232; Pierre Guiral and Guy Thuillier, Vie quotidienne, pp. 50-59; Theresa M. McBride, Domestic Revolution, p. 54.

17 See Luce Vermette, "Les donations 1800-1820: activités domestiques et genres de vie," Rapport sur microfiches, No. 16 (1982), Parks Canada, Ottawa.

18 ANQ-M, greffe de Jean-Guillaume Delisle, acte no. 7462, 26 Feb. 1816.

19 Pierre Guiral and Guy Thuillier, Vie quotidienne, p. 45.

20 ANQ-Q, greffe de Joseph-Bernard Planté, acte no. 7770, 20 July 1819.

21 Mary Quayle Innis, op. cit., p. 147.

22 Pamphile Lemay, Rouge et Bleu, Comédies (Quebec: C. Darveau, 1891); one is entitled En livrée.

23 La Gazette du Québec, 1 June 1820.

24 Dorothy Marshall, The English Domestic Servant in History (London: The Historical Association, 1949), p. 20. Phyllis Cunnington, Costumes of Old Servants from the Middle Ages to 1900 (London: Adam and Charles Black, 1974).

25 More than one writer noted a certain propensity for luxury in Canadian women; see Albert Faucher, "La notion de luxe chez les Canadiens français au dix-neuvième siècle," Mémoire de la Société royale du Canada, 4th ser., Vol. 11 (1973), pp. 177-82.

26 PAC, MG23, GII, 10, Vol. 12, pp. 6018-21; Vol. 13, pp. 6227-31.

27 James Lomax, "Behind the Green Baize Door," Country Life, No. 4186 (Sept. 1977), pp. 762-64.

28 See mainly Pierre Guiral and Guy Thuillier, Vie quotidienne, chap. 5; also Jean-Louis Flandrin, Famille, parenté, maison, sexualité dans l'ancienne société (Paris: Hachette, 1976) (hereafter cited as Famille); Pamela Horn, op. cit.; Dorothy Marshall, op. cit.; and Edward Shorter, Naissance de la famille moderne, XVIIIe - XIXe siècle (Paris: Seuil, 1977) (hereafter cited as Naissance).

29 Reported by Pierre Guiral and Guy Thuillier (Vie quotidienne, p. 132) quoting Raymond Ryckère, La servante criminelle (Paris: Maloine, 1908).

30 This is one of the oldest complaints about servants. Philippe Ariès (op. cit., p. 428) wrote of a treatise on the subject dating from 1642. See also Daniel Calhoun, The Intelligence of a People (Princeton: Princeton Univ. Press, 1973), which discusses children's upbringing in the 18th and 19th centuries and which notes that several authors decried children's close contact with domestics. See also Jean-Louis Flandrin, "L'attitude à l'égard du petit enfant et les conduites sexuelles dans la civilisation occidentale: structures anciennes et évolution," Annales de démographie historique, 1973, pp. 143-210 (hereafter cited as "L'attitude"), and Blaine E. McKinley, " 'The Stranger in the Gates': Employer Reactions Toward Domestic Servants in America, 1825-1875," PhD thesis, Michigan State Univ., 1969; and Barbara Stein Frankle, "The Genteel Family: High Victorian Conceptions of Domesticity and Good Behaviour," PhD thesis, Wisconsin Univ., 1969, especially the chapter "Intruders in the Home: Servants in the Genteel Family." Clifford E. Clark, Jr., "Domestic Architecture as an Index to Social History: The Romantic Revival and the Cult of Domesticity in America, 1840-1870," Journal of Interdisciplinary History, Vol. 8, No. 1 (Summer 1976), p. 50, deals with the importance of service stairs in a house.

31 See Quebec. Ministère des Affaires culturelles, C. Baillairgé, Dessins architecturaux (Quebec: Ministère des Affaires culturelles, 1979), p. 23; it is the catalogue for the autumn 1979

180

exhibition of Charles Baillairgé's architectural plans in the Quebec City archives.

32 Evenings round the fire, visits, and card parties have already been mentioned. In evidence Agathe Lapointe spoke of going to a dance at Joanet's on 28 December and only leaving there at 4 o'clock in the morning (PAC, MG23, GII, 10, Vol. 13, p. 6253).

33 These can be found with various amendments in Bas-Canada. Parlement, Statuts provinciaux, Vol. 7: "1811-1814," 57 Geo. III, cap. 16, art. 10.

34 See, for example, Michelle Perrot, "Délinquance et système pénitentiaire en France au XIXe siècle," Annales E.S.C., Vol. 30, No. 1 (Jan.-Feb. 1975), pp. 67-92; Robert M. Mennel, Thorns and Thistles: Juvenile Delinquents in the United States, 1825-1940 (Hanover, N.H.: New England Univ. Press, 1973); John R. Gillis, "Youth in History: Progress and Prospects," Journal of Social History, Vol. 7, No. 2 (Winter 1974), pp. 201-207; Harvey Graff, "Crime and Punishment in the Nineteenth Century: A New Look at the Criminal," Journal of Interdisciplinary History, Vol. 7, No. 3 (Winter 1977) (hereafter cited as "Crime and Punishment"), pp. 477-91; Leonard Berlanstein, "Vagrants, Beggars and Thieves: Delinquent Boys in Mid-Nineteenth Century Paris," Journal of Social History, Vol. 12, No. 4 (Summer 1979), pp. 532-52; John W. Fierheller, "Approaches to the Study of Urban Crime: A Review Article," Revue d'histoire urbaine, Vol. 8, No. 2 (Oct. 1979), pp. 104-112.

35 The contracts show that the children had a great deal to do and were closely supervised.

36 Bulletin des recherches historiques, "Une servante d'autrefois," Vol. 46, No. 11 (Nov. 1940) (hereafter cited as BRH-"Servante"), p. 324.

37 ANQ-Q, Register of the Quebec Gaol, Vol. 6, Entry No. 1006, 12 Aug. 1818.

38 No verdict was given in the case of Louis Isabel; see PAC, MG23, GII, 10, Vol. 12, pp. 6211-6212.

39 ANQ-Q, Register of the Quebec Gaol, Vol. 6, Entry No. 569, 3 July 1817; ibid., greffe de Antoine-Archange Parent, acte no. 1327, 2 Feb. 1820.

Social Relationships

1 Georges d'Avenel, Découvertes d'histoire sociale, 1200-1910 (Paris: Flammarion, 1910), p. 142; see also Dorothy Marshall, op. cit.

2 PAC, MG23, GII, 10, Vol. 12, pp. 6117-1628; BRH-"Servante," p. 324; La Gazette de Montréal, 10 Feb. 1819; PAC, MG23, GII, 10, Vol. 13, pp. 6334-6335, and Vol. 12, pp. 6091-6095.

3 La Gazette de Québec, 14 Mar. 1771. Although this document

predates our period slightly, it is nevertheless one of the most revealing I found.

4   PAC, MG23, GII, 10, Vol. 12, pp. 6018-6021; Vol. 13, pp. 6227-6231; Vol. 12, p. 5845; Vol. 13, pp. 6213-6214, 6227-6231; Vol. 12, pp. 6087-6088; Vol. 13, pp. 6986-6990.

5   ANQ-M, greffe de Nicolas-Benjamin Doucet, acte no. 5080, 9 Apr. 1818.

6   ANQ-Q, greffe de Joseph-Bernard Planté, acte no. 8091, 15 June 1821.

7   Signay, Recensement, pp. 237-38.

8   For example see ANQ-M, greffe de Jean-Marie Cadieux, acte no. 67, 19 Feb. 1817; greffe de Joseph Desautels, acte no. 3511, 14 Feb. 1818; greffe de Jean-Guillaume Delisle, acte no. 7552, 23 Mar. 1819.

9   Yves Durand, Les fermiers généraux au XVIIIe siècle (Paris: Presses universitaires de France, 1971), p. 607; Cissie Fairchilds, op. cit., p. 373.

10 ANQ-Q, greffe de Antoine-Archange Parent, acte no. 1327, 2 Feb. 1820.

11 PAC, MG24, A57, Journals of Lady Katherine Sherbrooke, Pt. 2, Vol. 10, 2 May 1818.

12 Ronald-Henri Hubscher, "Contribution," p. 364.

13 Pierre Guiral and Guy Thuillier, Vie quotidienne, p. 23. In ANQ-M, greffe de Nicolas-Benjamin Doucet (acte no. 5058, 1 Apr. 1818) the servant Angélique Poirier is called Marguerite on four occasions.

14 ANQ-Q, greffe de Pierre Laforce, acte no. 1545, 2 Oct. 1817; Isabel Foulché-Delbosc, "Women in Three-Rivers: 1651-53" in Susan Mann Trofimenkoff and Alison Prentice, eds., The Neglected Majority: Essays in Canadian Women's History (Toronto: McClelland and Stewart, 1977), pp. 14-26.

15 ANQ-Q, Register of the Quebec Gaol, Vol. 6: 1813-1823, Entry Nos. 185-1867 (1816-20) were analyzed; PAC, MG23, GII, 10, Vols. 12 and 13.

16 This is the only case where no example was found in archival documents but every single book mentioned it. See especially Alain Lottin, "Naissances illégitimes et filles-mères à Lille au XVIIIe siècle," Revue d'histoire moderne et contemporaine, Vol. 17 (Apr.-June 1970), p. 318; Jean-Louis Flandrin, Famille and Les amours paysannes; amour et sexualité dans les campagnes de l'ancienne France (XVIe- XIXe siècles) (Paris: Gallimard Juillard, 1975), pp. 205-218.

17 ANQ-Q, Register of the Quebec Gaol, Vol. 6, Entry No. 569. This involved Sally Brass, servant of Roger Lelièvre, notary.

18 Lewis A. Coser, "Servants: The Obsolescence of an Occupational Role," (Social Forces, Vol. 52 [Sept. 1973], pp. 31-40), is one

example among many; Cissie Fairchilds, op. cit., p. 368; Pierre Guiral and Guy Thuillier, Vie quotidienne, pp. 35-36; Theresa M. McBride, Domestic Revolution, pp. 118-119.

19 ANQ-Q, greffe de Antoine-Archange Parent, acte no. 239, 26 Nov. 1816. The mother added that she would take her daughter back if the girl were ill-treated.

20 Philippe Aubert de Gaspé, Mémoires (Montreal: Fides, 1971) (hereafter cited as Mémoires).

21 BRH-"Servante," p. 324.

22 All French and British authors stressed the importance of references, and newspaper advertisements show that they were also important here.

23 Several American authors have studied the power of gossip; see also Melissa Clark, "Les formes alternatives de prise de conscience politique chez les femmes," paper presented at the meeting of the Institut d'histoire de l'Amérique française, Univ. of Ottawa, Oct. 1979.

24 PAC, MG23, GII, 10, Vol. 12, pp. 6091-6092; Molly Harrison, The Kitchen in History (Reading, Eng.: Osprey Publishing, 1972), p. 86; PAC, MG23, GII, 10, Vol. 13, pp. 6195-97; Vol. 12, p. 6887, Vol. 13, pp. 6986-88; Ronald-Henri Hubscher, "Contribution," p. 396.

25 J. Jean Hecht, The Domestic Servant Class in Eighteenth Century England (London: Routledge and Kegan Paul, 1956), p. 129.

26 Pierre Petitclair, Griphon, ou la vengeance d'un valet (Quebec: William Cowan, 1837), p. 6: "I do not know why a valet is always pleased when his masters depart.... We feel freer ... we can enjoy ourselves...." See other extracts from plays in Etienne Duval, Anthologie thématique du théâtre québécois au XIXe siècle (Montreal: Théâtre Leméac, 1978).

27 PAC, MG23, GII, 10, Vol. 12, p. 5669, Vol. 13, pp. 6197-6200, 6211-6212, 6294-6295; ANQ-Q, Register of the Quebec Gaol, Vol. 6, Entry No. 769.

28 Peter N. Moogk, "The Craftsmen of New France," PhD thesis, Univ. of Toronto, 1973, p. 280.

29 ANQ-Q, greffe de Charles Huot, acte no. 808, 30 Aug. 1816; greffe de Antoine-Archange Parent, acte no. 239, 26 Nov. 1816; ANQ-M, greffe de Jean-Marie Cadieux, acte no. 271, 24 May 1820; PAC, MG23, GII, 10, Vol. 13, pp. 6986-6989.

30 PAC, MG23, GII, 10, Vol. 13, pp. 6227-6231, 6715-6722.

Part Two: 1871 to 1875

Introduction

1 Major analyses, as well as monographs for the cities, agree on

this point. For examples of both, see W.T. Easterbrook and Hugh G.J. Aitken, Canadian Economic History (Toronto: Macmillan, 1956), p. 350; and Jean-Claude Robert, op. cit., pp. 246-47.

2   Jean Hamelin and Yves Roby, Histoire économique et sociale du Québec, 1851-1896 (Montreal: Fides, 1971), pp. 62-63, 76; Thomas H. Raddall, Halifax, Warden of the North (Toronto: McClelland and Stewart, 1948), p. 224; P.-A. Linteau, R. Durocher, and J.-C. Robert, Histoire du Québec contemporain (Montreal: Boréal Express, 1979), p. 42.

3   Canada. Parliament, Census of Canada/Recensement du Canada, 1870-71 (Ottawa: I.B. Taylor, 1873) (hereafter cited as Census of Canada), Vol. 1.

The People Involved — In 1871

1   This is the census of individuals for Toronto, Quebec City, Halifax, and the St-Antoine district of Montreal that I consulted in the Public Archives of Canada (hereafter cited as PAC, Census ... 1871).

2   This was the case in Division 2 of the St-Jean district in Quebec City where the enumerator identified all servants as being "domestics."

3   The St-Antoine district of Montreal can serve as an example here: although divided into 13 sections, details on servants' functions were only given for 3. Indeed, out of the 190 households with at least 4 servants in all 4 cities, servants' duties have been determined in barely 35 cases.

4   PAC, Census ... 1871, Halifax Ward 1, G-1, household 444; Ward 1, A-2, household 213; ibid., Toronto, St. James, B-2, household 258.

5   Census of Canada, Vol. 2, pp. 262-71, 286-97, 310-21, 334-45.

6   See, among others, W.A. Armstrong, "The Use of Information about Occupation," in E.A. Wrigley, ed., Nineteenth Century Society. Essays in the Use of Quantitative Methods for the Study of Social Data (Cambridge: Cambridge Univ. Press, 1972), pp. 284-93; Adeline Daumard, "Une référence pour l'étude des sociétés urbaines en France aux XVIIIe and XIXe siècles: projet de code socio-professionnel," Revue d'histoire moderne et contemporaine, Vol. 10, No. 2 (July-Sept. 1963), pp. 185-210; Michael Flinn, ed., Scottish Population History from the 17th Century to the 1930s (Cambridge: Cambridge Univ. Press, 1977). Finally, Ronald-Henri Hubscher's excellent article "Société globale et population agricole: un essai de classification des catégories socio-professionnelles non agricoles" (Revue d'histoire moderne et contemporaine, Vol. 27 [Apr.-June 1980], pp. 312-19) contains a fairly good list of reference works on the subject.

7   In the case of the 1842 Quebec City census which I also used.

My analysis was based on Jean-Pierre Hardy's notes. My warmest thanks to him for having put his data at my disposal.

8 The exact figures, according to Census of Canada, Vol. 2, are 4.1 for Montreal, 4.3 for Quebec City, 5.1 for Toronto, and 5.9 for Halifax; overall, servants represented 5% of the cities' populations. This percentage is far higher than the proportion of servants to the total population of the country (1.45%) and confirms servants' tendency to come to the city to search for work. Thus, whereas in 1871 the 10 Canadian cities with more than 10 000 inhabitants accounted for 10.6% of the population, they drained off 31.8% of total servants. In 1921, people whose occupation was given as "personal service" still accounted for around 5% of the population for the 4 cities under study, whereas in 1971 they were just under 1%. These figures have been taken from the compilation tables of the 1921 and 1971 censuses.

9 I considered the wealthiest to be those with the highest number of households with live-in servants: Palais/St-Louis in Quebec City (1 out of 2), St-Antoine in Montreal, Ward 1 of Halifax (1 out of 4), and St. James in Toronto (1 out of 5).

10 I have grouped areas together that previously only formed one district, such as St-Roch, which comprised St-Sauveur, Jacques-Cartier, and St-Roch Nord in 1871. I have likewise grouped together the Montcalm districts and the banlieues as well as the two districts that made up the Upper Town intra muros — St-Louis and du Palais.

11 The figures were virtually the same for the U.S. in 1870 (see Blaine E. McKinley, op. cit., p. 7) and England in 1871 and 1872, where 92% of servants were women. However, in France the ratio appeared to be 71% women, 29% men for the same period; see Theresa M. McBride, Domestic Revolution, p. 45.

12 These data strongly resemble the results of Allan Greer's study of literacy in 19th-century Quebec: "The Pattern of Literacy in Quebec, 1754-1899," Histoire sociale/Social History, Vol. 11, No. 22 (Nov. 1978), pp. 295-335. See, in particular, Table 11 (p. 327), showing that 81.8% of city dwellers over 20 knew how to read in 1861.

13 In England in 1871 the average age seems to have been 26.8 according to Theresa M. McBride ("'As the Twig is Bent': The Victorian Nanny," in A.S. Wohl, ed., The Victorian Family [London: Croom Helm, 1978], p. 49), and the situation was similar in the U.S. according to Daniel E. Sutherland ("Americans and Their Servants, 1800-1920: Being an Inquiry into the Origins and Progress of the American Servant Problems," PhD thesis, Wayne State Univ., Detroit, 1976, p. 106). The average age of domestics working in institutions was slightly higher (by 1 or 2 years) than the average age of live-in domestics working in

households; this brings the figure for servants in Canada closer to that for elsewhere because McBride's 26.8 seems to be based on servants as a whole whereas the average age for our live-in servants as a whole (70% of the servant population) is 26 years.

14 These statistics have been compiled from domestic help identi- fied through Signay's 1818 Quebec census; see Part I, "The People Involved — At the Beginning of the Century."

15 Montreal is a good example: 51 of the 59 contracts drawn up in French between 1816 and 1820 concerned masters and servants who were both Francophones; 49 of the 50 in English concerned masters and servants who were both Anglophones; the remaining 9 were in the servants' language (ANQ-M, greffes des notaires).

16 In the U.S., where the situation was the same, the servant problem was identified as the Irish problem; see Blaine E. McKinley, op. cit., chap. 4. However, in Halifax, where there were few immigrant servants, Irish domestics were in proportion to the city's Irish population — which is in line with A. Gordon Darroch and Michael D. Ornstein's thoughts in "Ethnicity and Occupational Structure in Canada in 1871: The Vertical Mosaic in Historical Perspective," Canadian Historical Review, Vol. 61, No. 3 (Sept. 1980), pp. 305-333.

17 Jean-Claude Robert, op. cit.

18 In ANQ-M I consulted the death registers for the parish of Notre-Dame for the years 1816-20 and 1871-75. I also re- searched those for St. Patrick's parish for the latter period, as well as those for the Anglican cathedral and the Methodist church. However, only the Notre-Dame registers were of use because, for one thing, deaths in St. Patrick's were registered at Notre-Dame, and for another, the deceased's occupation was rarely noted in non-Catholic parishes. As far as Quebec City was concerned, efforts were fruitless: in the ANQ-Q the death records for 1818-20 for the parish of Notre-Dame de Québec were not available. I therefore searched through those for 1813 to 1817 without finding any mention of servants. A similar problem arose for 1871-75: the deceased's occupation was rarely listed for servants and it is hardly likely that only 7 servants died in the city during this 5-year period. For the second period I consulted registers for the Catholic parishes of Notre-Dame de Québec, Notre-Dame de Foy, St-Jean-Baptiste, St-Roch, St- Sauveur, and St. Patrick, and the Protestant churches of St. Andrew and St. Matthew. I was no more fortunate in Halifax and Toronto since information concerning occupation was rarely given there too.

19 I have no figures for Europe and the U.S. for these specific periods, but Theresa M. McBride set the number of those from rural areas at 60% around 1830 in France; see "Modernization,"

p. 233. She based her figures on the work of Adeline Daumard (La bourgeoisie), who had consulted death registers for this information.

20   This was not the only stereotype current at the time. Contemporary literature also depicted a servant as a little country girl, gauche, lost, and confused in her master's city home. This, at least, was the image prevalent in Europe; see Theresa M. McBride, Domestic Revolution, p. 37, and in particular, Edmond and Jules Goncourt, Germinie Lacerteux (Paris: Flammarion et Fasquelle, 1864), p. 44: "The child, fresh from her village and suddenly finding herself [in Paris], was bewildered, totally frightened in such a place, such a service."

21   Blaine E. McKinley, op. cit., and Theresa M. McBride, Domestic Revolution.

22   According to analysis of Signay's Quebec City census; however, at that time Quebec was the largest city in the country, the seat of government, and the army headquarters. Consequently, many influential people lived there as well as British army officers.

23   This is what Theresa M. McBride stated for France from 1830 to 1880 (see Domestic Revolution, p. 14). The same method was used in the U.S. Blaine E. McKinley (op. cit., p. 5) considered that there was one servant per 5.8 families in New York State around the same period (1825-75).

24   Theresa M. McBride, "Rural Tradition and the Process of Modernization: Domestic Servants in Nineteenth Century France," PhD thesis, Rutgers Univ., New Brunswick, N.J., 1973, (hereafter cited as "Rural Tradition"), p. 10.

25   Blaine E. McKinley, op. cit., p. 17.

26   Theresa M. McBride, "Rural Tradition," p. 31.

27   This means 4.8 people per household in Quebec City in 1818, and 5.2 in Toronto, 4.9 in Quebec City (Signay, Recensement), and 4.8 in Halifax in 1871 (PAC, Census ... 1871).

28   Many have noted this: see Georges d'Avenel, op. cit., p. 153; Dorothy Marshall, op. cit., p. 15; Theresa M. McBride, Domestic Revolution, p. 31.

29   Andrew Allentuck, "Vanishing Pleasures," En Route (Nov. 1980), p. 34.

30   For example, a recent study estimated that only 13% of the Montreal population would have been in the bourgeois class in 1871; see Marcel Bellavance, "Les structures de l'espace montréalais à l'époque de la confédération," Cahiers de géographie du Québec, Vol. 24, No. 63 (Dec. 1980), pp. 363-84. The same applied to England and Wales in 1867 according to the picture Harold Perkin painted in The Origins of Modern English Society 1780-1880 (Toronto: Univ. of Toronto Press, 1969), p. 420. Perkin stated that the upper class, those whose income was over

£1000, comprised 0.48% of families; the middle class (between £300 and £1000 income), 1.46% of families; and the lower middle class (with around £100 to £300), 8.29% of families. He also added to this lower middle class a group that apparently had income of less than £100 and accounted for 15.35% of families. Together these groups (upper, middle, and lower middle classes) represented 25.6% of families, and manual labourers, 74.4% of families. However, not everybody in the so-called "middle" class (25.1%) could afford even a maid-of-all-work; it was estimated at the time that this would require an income of at least £150; see Isabella Beeton, The Book of Household Management.... (London: S.O. Beeton, 1861), p. 8. This therefore means that around 10 to 11% of people could afford a maid, very close to my own estimates.

Domestic Service

1 ANQ-M, ANQ-Q, APJ-M, and APJ-Q, records of notaries practising in Montreal and Quebec City between 1871 and 1875. Six of the 684 contracts listed covered domestics. The change in the custom of hiring by contract seems peculiar to the second half of the century. Although I have only systematically analyzed the years 1816-20 and 1871-75, I have benefited from the efforts of Montreal students who, under Robert Sweeney's direction, researched hiring contracts deposited in notaries' records in Montreal between 1820 and 1840. At the time I consulted the contracts at McGill University, only a few Anglophone notaries had been researched, but 60 or so servants' contracts had already been found. Apart from the fact that women's wages had increased slightly, the clauses were the same as 20 years earlier, and it also seemed that there were as many contracts. However, 30 years later, they were practically non-existent. I am grateful to Mr. Sweeney and his students for making this material available to me.

2 See respective lists in "Bibliography," sect. 3, 4.

3 At the beginning of the 1850s Abbé Mailloux published Le manuel des parents chrétiens (4th ed., Quebec: L'Action sociale, 1910). In 1855 The Canadian Settler's Guide by Catherine Parr Traill was published (Toronto: McClelland and Stewart, 1969), but as its title indicates, it was mainly intended for families arriving in the country. Books appearing between 1860 and 1890 were nearly all on cookery or recipes: a dozen or so titles are featured in Hilary Russell's "Bibliography of Domestic Manuals," manuscript on file, National Historic Parks and Sites Branch, Environment Canada — Parks, Ottawa (1980). Religious orders published treatises on household management and recipe books for their pupils, and cookbooks published in England at the beginning of the century

were also published here. One manual on household management that was published here in 1896 is Benjamin-A. Testard de Montigny's Manuel d'économie domestique (Montreal: Cadieux et Derome, 1896).

4   Several French novelists of the time were serialized in the newspapers. For instance, La Patrie in Montreal published Lamartine in the 1850s (Séraphin Marion, Les lettres canadiennes d'autrefois [Ottawa: Editions de l'université d'Ottawa, 1948-54], Vol. 4, p. 30), and l'Evénement in Quebec City published 27 serials between 1871 and 1875, including 3 novels by Paul Féval, 2 by Emile Gaboriau and Gustave Aymard, and 1 each by Henri de Suskau, Mme. Léonie d'Aunel, Paul Duplessis, Ponson du Terrail, Emile Chevalier, Alfred des Essarts, Jules Sandeau, Edmond Aborit, Eugène Dick, F. de Boisgobey, and 10 other unknown authors. The Acadian Reporter in Halifax published the translation of an Alexandre Dumas novel in 1871. According to Yves Dostaler (Les infortunes du roman dans le Québec du XIXᵉ siècle [Montreal: Hurtubise HMH, 1977], pp. 17-30), widely read French authors were: Victor Hugo, Emile Zola, J.-J. Rousseau, Eugène Sue, Mme. de Genlis, Lesage, Voltaire, Montesquieu, Bernardin de Saint-Pierre, Mme. de Staël, Chateaubriand, Lamartine, Mérimée, Alphonse Daudet, Louis Veuillot, Alexandre Dumas, Paul Féval, Mme. Craven, and Jules Verne.

As far as English authors are concerned, Walter Scott seems to have been the most popular in Quebec according to Yves Dostaler (op. cit., p. 33), as he was in England (David Roberts (Paternalism in Early Victorian England [New Brunswick, N.J.: Rutgers Univ. Press, 1979], p. 59). Aside from Scott, Charles Dickens was read a great deal (see numerous references in Henriette Dessaulles, Fadette, Journal d'Henriette Dessaules, 1874-1880 [Montreal: Hurtubise HMH, 1971], pp. 45-80), as well as James Fenimore Cooper, Harriet Beecher Stowe, Jane Austen, and the Brontë sisters.

The books most frequently needing repair in military garrison libraries and therefore the most read were the works of Walter Scott, Charles Dickens, Jane Austen, Maria Edgeworth, James Fenimore Cooper, and Henry Fielding; see Carol M. Whitfield, "Tommy Atkins: le soldat britannique en garnison au Canada, de 1759 à 1870," Histoire et archéologie, No. 56 (1981), p. 102. When researching the Quebec garrison in 1975 I was struck by the same fact: between 1845 and 1860 the books requiring repair were by these same authors; see PAC, RG8, I, British Military and Naval Records, Vols. 519-528, form no. 1, listing the books to be repaired during that period.

I read quite a few 19th-century novels in order to see how servants were portrayed. As far as French works in which the central figure is a servant are concerned, I owe much to Johanne Cloutier, who informed me of several, including La Rabouilleuse by Balzac (Paris: Livre de poche, 1972), which otherwise I might well not have read. Her help is much appreciated.

5   These were useful in that they gave impressions of the great size of the houses in which servants worked, the number of floors they constantly had to cover, and therefore the number of stairs they had to climb countless times a day; see Figs. 17-20.

6   Those of Lady Dufferin (My Canadian Journal, 1872-1878 [Don Mills: Longmans, 1969]) and Henriette Dessaulles (op. cit.) were the most useful.

7   See La Gazette de Québec, 3 Sept. 1818, and Montreal Herald, 4 Mar. 1820.

8   In the U.S., for example, employers generally paid twice as much as the servants: David Katzman, Seven Days a Week: Women and Domestic Service in Industrializing America (New York: Oxford Univ. Press, 1978), p. 101.

9   This was what happened in France, at least (Theresa M. McBride, Domestic Revolution, p. 78), and also in the U.S., where the fee could be as much as a quarter of a week's wages (David Katzman, op. cit., p. 101).

10   According to Theresa M. McBride (Domestic Revolution, p. 78) this was so in France but not in England, where information was shared, at least towards the end of the century.

11   On the whole, these agencies were thought to be involved in procuring prostitutes for brothels, the arrival of young girls in search of help suiting their purposes very well. See Pamela Horn (op. cit., p. 40) for England, Theresa M. McBride ("Rural Tradition," p. 177) for France, and David Katzman (op. cit., p. 103) and Daniel E. Sutherland (op. cit., p. 48) for the U.S.

12   David Katzman, op. cit., p. 104.

13   For charitable associations, see Blaine E. McKinley's analysis (op. cit., chap. 3) for the U.S., Theresa M. McBride ("Rural Tradition," chap. 4) for France, Pamela Horn (op. cit., pp. 40-42) and Brian Harrison ("For Church, Queen and Family: The Girls' Friendly Society, 1874-1920," Past and Present, Vol. 61 [Nov. 1973], pp. 107-138), among others, for England.

14   Blaine E. McKinley, op. cit., p. 101. He specified that this was an annual contribution and that employers referred to agencies several times a year. In Halifax, however, the payment made by a servant who wanted to stay in a "shelter" was equivalent to her weekly wage.

15   Many of the organizations dealt with children; see, among others, Micheline Dumont-Johnson, "Des garderies au XIXe siècle: les salles d'asile des Soeurs Grises à Montréal," Revue d'histoire de l'Amérique française, Vol. 34, No. 1 (June 1980), pp.

27-56. People often contacted these organizations in order to employ orphans as servants; see G.E. Fenwick, "The Medical Statistics of the City of Montreal" (British American Journal, Vol. 3 [Jan. 1862], p. 32), which states that orphans were sent into service; see also Joy Parr, op. cit.

16 See Rainer Baehre, "Paupers and Poor Relief in Upper Canada," Historical Papers/Communications historiques (1981), pp. 57-80; see also Huguette Lapointe-Roy, op. cit., chap. 2, and Suzanne Cross, "The Neglected Majority: The Changing Role of Women in 19th Century Montreal," in Susan Mann Trofimenkoff and Alison Prentice, eds., op. cit., pp. 66-68. I have no specific information on this suject for Quebec City, but charitable works were just as flourishing there; see, among others, René Hardy, "L'Activité sociale du curé de Notre-Dame de Québec; aperçu de l'influence du clergé au milieu du XIXe siècle," Histoire sociale/Social History, Vol. 3, No. 6 (Nov. 1970), pp. 5-32.

17 Figures quoted by Marian Brown in "Report on Newspaper Articles, Women's Columns and Domestic Labour Advertisements," manuscript presented July 1981, COSEP project, which deals mainly with food; British Columbia newspapers were researched for the late 19th and early 20th centuries. I thank Marilyn Barber for bringing this work to my attention.

18 Comment by Daniel E. Sutherland (op. cit., pp. 43-44). He also stated that few employers took advantage of classified advertisements.

19 Stated by Theresa M. McBride for France ("Rural Tradition," p. 182) for example. It is also the method recommended in household management books because it was considered far more effective than others; for example, see Isabella Beeton, op. cit., pp. 6-7.

20 The servant who ran errands often met her friends in the market and quickly learned "so-and-so was leaving such-and-such."

21 Ernest Doin, Le dîner interrompu, ou nouvelle farce de Jocrisse (Montreal: Beauchemin, 1885) (hereafter cited as Le dîner interrompu); Jocrisse asked his master to hire his cousin.

22 This is what the compilations show, and it is not unique. In France, in the Flahaut family, 1/3 of the servants working for the family between 1811 and 1877 were related. See Ronald-Henri Hubscher, "Contribution," p. 396.

23 Young girls entering service very often did not know what certain objects were called: see, among others, Pamela Horn, op. cit., p. 34. Also, see the letter from Charles Baillairgé to the Ursulines of Quebec City at the end of the century (Appendix E). I thank Christina Cameron for having advised me of this.

24 This no doubt happened with orphan girls who were taught how to do the heavy work but rarely how to perform more delicate tasks

such as handling porcelain. And the servants who had spent some time in charitable institutions no doubt had little time to improve their skills.

25 At least, this is what Lady Dufferin did in Quebec City in 1872; see her diary, op. cit., p. 17.

26 In France, for example, servants were usually required to carry a book containing their employment history (Theresa M. McBride, "Rural Tradition," p. 175). In England a character reference was so important that it was often used as blackmail (Dorothy Marshall, op. cit., p. 11). It was also important in the U.S. because private employment agencies only offered their services to servants with such references (Blaine E. McKinley, op. cit., p. 101). See also M.E.W. Sherwood, "The Lack of Good Servants," North American Review, Vol. 153, No. 420 (Nov. 1891), p. 552.

27 See Isabella Beeton, op. cit., p. 7, for example.

28 All offers and requests for employment appearing in Quebec City and Montreal newspapers at the beginning of the century required a "character."

29 Lady Dufferin, op. cit., p. 17.

30 Acadian Recorder, 29 Oct. 1875.

31 This seems to be indicated by the fact that servants working in households with large staffs were, on average, much older than other servants. It is also borne out by Margaret Powell (Below Stairs [London: Peter Davies, 1968]) and Paul Chabot (Jean et Yvonne, domestiques in 1900 [Paris: Téma-éditions, 1977]).

32 The analysis of well-staffed houses is our guide here; however, few enumerators gave details on the position each held.

33 House plans consulted in PANS, ANQ-Q, AVQ, ANQ-M, AO, and the Baldwin Room of the Toronto Metropolitan Public Library. In all, 4.3% had 1 storey, 43.5% had 2, 39.2% had 3, 8.7% had 4, and 4.3% had 5. All, of course, had basements or cellars, and several had attics that could be lived in.

34 Leonore Davidoff and Ruth Hawthorn (A Day in the Life of a Victorian Domestic Servant [London: George Allen and Unwin, 1976], p. 78) state that a bucket of coal weighed 20 to 30 lbs. and a medium-sized water pitcher for filling baths, around 30 lbs.; see Margaret Powell, op. cit., p. 37.

35 All authors agree on this point. See, for England, Mark Ebury and Brian Preston, Domestic Service in Late Victorian and Edwardian England, 1871-1914 (London: George Over, 1976) p. 28. A 100-hour week was not unusual for a servant. For France, see Theresa M. McBride, Domestic Revolution, p. 55; for the U.S., see David Katzman, op. cit., p. 20. In fact, maids have to work 15 or 16 hours at a stretch even today according to Rachel Epstein ("'I Thought There Was No More Slavery in Canada.' West Indian Domestic Workers on Employment Visas," Canadian

Women's Studies/Les cahiers de la femme, Vol. 2, No. 1 [1980], p. 26); and Mirjana Vukman-Tenebaum ("Domestic Workers and Organizing Strategies," Resources for Feminist Research/Documentation sur la recherche féministe, Vol. 10, No. 2 [July 1981], p. 32).

36 Geneviève Fraisse (Femmes toutes mains. Essai sur le service domestique [Paris: Seuil, 1979], p. 39) reported what Elisabeth Renaud, an old governess, said before the Congrès sur la condition et des droits des femmes, September 1900.

37 The custom of eating around 8 p.m. instead of 6 p.m. seems to have been fairly widespread: "between 1850 and 1900 ... people dined around 8 o'clock in Paris, which delayed servants' bedtimes: 'a servant's working day ends much later now than before' " (Pierre Guiral and Guy Thuillier, Vie quotidienne, p. 80). The same applied in England according to Leonore Davidoff and Ruth Hawthorn (op. cit., p. 75): "By the 1850s middle-class families, often in the imitation of the upper-class ... began to expect more complicated meals ... people dined at 7 or 8 p.m." People apparently followed the same tide in the U.S.: "people dine later than they did formerly" (E.F. Ellet, ed., The New Cyclopaedia of Domestic Economy and Practical Housekeeper [Norwich, Conn.: Henry Bill Publishing, 1873]). Fanny Joseph's diary (1871-79) clearly shows that the same applied to Quebec City since, on 14 October 1877, she deplored the fact that the doctor had recommended that her father eat earlier: "We will have to give up our old habits." On 5 November she stated that "We are taking ... tea at 1/2 past six, the latter hitherto an unknown meal but necessary now on account of father's health" (PAC, MG24, 161, reel M-200).

38 At the beginning of the century, servants were in the kitchen around 9 p.m. talking or playing cards, but this became impossible from the moment that a meal had to be prepared for 8 o'clock and the kitchen tidied after the meal was finished. Information on servants' free time is from Judge Sewell's notes on the 272 Quebec City trials he heard between 1808 and 1820 (PAC, MG23, GII, 10; on spare time see, among others, Vol. 13, pp. 6227-6231, 6715-6722).

39 David E. Sutherland noted this (op. cit., pp. 225-26); according to him, servants' great mobility was partly due to the fact that it was one of the few ways they could show their independence.

40 Abel Chatelain, op. cit., p. 508.

41 Blaine E. McKinley, op. cit., p. 101. Reference is made here to the "Registry Offices" in New York and Philadelphia. See also, for the U.S., Clarissa Packard's satirical work (op. cit.).

42 See Catherine E. Beecher and Harriet Beecher Stowe, Principles of Domestic Science as Applied to the Duties and Pleasures of

<u>Home</u> (New York: J.B.K. Ford, 1870), p. 279. Judge Sewell's trial accounts were also very informative for the beginning of the century: PAC, MG23, GII, 10, Vol. 13, pp. 6213-6214, and Vol. 12, pp. 6117-6128; <u>see</u> Appendix B. <u>See also</u> Emma Newman's diary for 1864-65; she wrote of a cook who arrived on 5 January 1865 and left on 12 March (Great Britain. National Army Museum, Newman papers).

43   Quebec, Archives du séminaire, Fonds manuscrits, MS No. 301, Servants Wages, booklet kept by Jules Quesnel, Quebec City, 1830-40, 47 pages. We do not know who Jules Quesnel was, but he may have been a merchant because he employed many more men than women. His booklet reveals many interesting points. Firstly, women were paid the same as men: $5 a month on average. However, when taken individually, some of the men only received $3 per month, whereas all the women earned $5. Could they all have been cooks, since this position was better paid? Another finding: once servants stayed for a full year, they usually remained for slightly more than 3. They therefore fall into 2 categories: those (55%) who stayed an average of 5 months and those (45%) who stayed 3 years and 2 months. However, the number of mobile domestics was greater than these figures seem to indicate because the booklet mainly deals with men, who represented 83% of the servants. Quesnel commented on the poor conduct of 12% of the servants he employed; the remainder seem to have been satisfactory workers. My thanks to the historians of the Quebec Regional Office of Environment Canada — Parks for sending me a copy of this document.

44   Marilyn Barber, op. cit., p. 162.

45   That men were only hired when a master was able to employ 3 servants is good proof of this.

46   Frank E. Huggett, <u>Life Below Stairs. Domestic Servants in England from Victorian Times</u> (London: John Murray, 1977), p. 36.

47   This is what Theresa M. McBride (<u>Domestic Revolution</u>, p. 51) gives for Europe and Blaine E. McKinley (op. cit., p. 23) for the U.S. For Canada we only have J.G. Snell's figures, which readily confirm this theory since he estimated that in Ontario towns in 1870 a woman would spend an average of $3.25 for her weekly board ($13 per month), whereas a servant's average monthly salary was $5.50; <u>see</u> J.G. Snell, "The Cost of Living in Canada in 1870," <u>Histoire sociale/Social History</u>, Vol. 12, No. 23 (May 1979), pp. 189, 191.

48   This is what appears from J.G. Snell's table, op. cit., p. 189; however, some female servants received a little less, such as those working for James Malcom in Halifax in 1876 and 1877 (PANS, RG48, reel 485, file No. 1608, inventory of James

Malcom's estate). The executor's account book specifies that the two female servants each received $4 a month.

49 See, for example, the hiring contract for Théophile Dupont, a servant employed by Joseph Barsalou, which states that Dupont's monthly salary would be 16 piasters per month, more than double that of a female servant (ANQ-M, greffe de L.-Arthur Desrosiers, acte no. 3875, 2 Aug. 1873). It appears that women's salaries had increased by 1/3 in 50 years, but men's, if we can rely on the few details available, appear to have doubled.

50 England: Theresa M. McBride, Domestic Revolution, p. 62; U.S.: Blaine E. McKinley (op. cit., p. 20) states that the weekly salary was $2.45, whereas David Katzman (op. cit., p. 312) suggests a figure of $4.76 per week.

51 Reported by Theresa M. McBride (Domestic Revolution, p. 62) for Europe and Daniel Sutherland (op. cit., p. 173) for the U.S.

52 Mark Ebury and Brian Preston, op. cit., p. 90; Anne Martin-Fugier, La place des bonnes. La domesticité féminine à Paris en 1900 (Paris: Grasset, 1979), pp. 226-27; Theresa M. McBride, Domestic Revolution, p. 59; Pierre Guiral and Guy Thuillier, Vie quotidienne, p. 61.

53 Information from Leonore Davidoff and Ruth Hawthorn (op. cit., p. 80) for England; David Katzman (op. cit., p. 113) for the U.S.; and Theresa M. McBride ("Rural Tradition," pp. 129-30) for France.

54 John Leefe, "Sidney Morton's Diary," Acadiensis: Journal of the History of the Atlantic Region/Revue de l'histoire de la région atlantique, Vol. 4, No. 1 (Fall 1974), p. 126; Leonore Davidoff and Ruth Hawthorn, op. cit., p. 80; David Katzman, op. cit., p. 114.

55 Leonore Davidoff and Ruth Hawthorn, op. cit., p. 80. No Canadian source really gives detailed information on servants' time off.

56 Several authors made this observation. Indeed, one can only be surprised at the number of young Montreal servants who died in hospital between 1871 and 1875: 46% of the female servants who died in Montreal during that period expired at the Hôtel-Dieu; their average age was 25.5 although 1/3 of them were not yet 20. A third of the menservants, averaging 26.5 years of age, died in the hospital. Considering how wretched dying in hospital was thought to be in those days (Louis Fréchette, Mémoires intimes [Montreal: Fides, 1977], pp. 100-101), the servants who did so must have been without other shelter. See ANQ-M, Registres de décès, Notre-Dame de Montréal, 1871-75.

57 See, as examples, those given by Mark Ebury and Brian Preston (op. cit., p. 93) for 1868-72: a maid-of-all-work could earn ₤12 while a cook received ₤24.

58 Isabella Beeton, op. cit., pp. 988-98.

59 From the census (PAC, Census ... 1871) I was able to establish that 75-80% of Montreal and Quebec City households employed servants who spoke the same language.

60 See, as examples, Leonore Davidoff and Ruth Hawthorn, op. cit., p. 78; Pierre Guiral and Guy Thuillier, Vie quotidienne, pp. 81 and 86.

61 All authors emphasize servants' inferior status and several analyze the consequences and implications. See Albert Memmi, L'Homme dominé (Paris: Payot, 1968).

62 An aspect the Beecher sisters mentioned in their book (op. cit., p. 281).

63 All authors agree on this point. See, for the different countries, David Katzman, op. cit., p. 242; Leonore Davidoff and Ruth Hawthorn, op. cit., p. 82; Geneviève Fraisse, op. cit., pp. 115-26.

64 Theresa M. McBride, who studied the question of savings in France at length, found that servants there represented the largest group of savers and accounted for 20-25% of savings-bank depositors ("Rural Tradition," pp. 219-34). On the other hand, David Katzman (op. cit., p. 308) said that according to a survey of Kansas cities, only 30% of female servants seemed to have saved anything during the year. Nevertheless, this percentage is no doubt much higher than for other working women of the time, maybe because as Michelet mentioned, workers who preferred to live in pleasant, clean environments saved less than servants who did not have to purchase furniture. See Jules Michelet, Le peuple (Paris: Flammarion, 1974), p. 59, n. 1.

65 Huguette Lapointe-Roy, op. cit., pp. 138-39.

66 In 1876 when Lady Dufferin (op. cit., pp. 189-90) was travelling in the West with her servants, they stopped at the Palmer House, a magnificent hotel. They "settled into these magnificences," but Lady Dufferin agreed with her maidservant who, after a long train journey, did not feel ready to be "bothered with so much splendour." A servant would have had to be accustomed to luxury in order to make such a remark.

67 See statements reported by Pierre Guiral and Guy Thuillier (Vie quotidienne, pp. 36, 115, 116) for France, as well as the servants in literature such as Germinie (the Goncourts), Geneviève (Lamartine), Célestine (Mirbeau), and Jean and Yvonne (Paul Chabot). For England see, among others, Pamela Horn, op. cit., and Clementina Black, "The Dislike to [sic] Domestic Service," Nineteenth Century, Vol. 33 (Jan.-June 1893), pp. 454-56; for the U.S. see David Katzman, op. cit.

68 See, for example, what Pierre Guiral and Guy Thuillier say (Vie quotidienne, pp. 38-39) about the 1906 "Exposition de la

Tuberculose," or for the U.S., Lucy Maynard Salmon's comments on inquest results (op. cit.).

69 See, for France, Yvonne Cretté-Breton, Mémoires d'une bonne (Paris: Scorpion 1966), or for England, Margaret Powell, op. cit.

Everyday Life

1 Catherine E. Beecher and Harriet Beecher Stowe, op. cit., p. 285.

2 Blaine E. McKinley, op. cit., p. 253, quoting Henry Hudson.

3 See Leonore Davidoff and Ruth Hawthorn, op. cit., p. 82; Frank Dawes, Not in Front of the Servants (New York: Taplinger, 1973), p. 67; Pierre Guiral and Guy Thuillier, Vie quotidienne, pp. 37-39; Pamela Horn, op. cit., p. 116; David Katzman, op. cit., p. 20; Theresa McBride, Domestic Revolution, pp. 51-52; Blaine E. McKinley, op. cit., pp. 250-55; Margaret Powell, op. cit., p. 61; Daniel E. Sutherland, op. cit., pp. 182-83.

4 Helen Campbell, Household Economics (New York: G.P. Putnam's Sons, 1898), p. 223; and Aymar Embury, The Livable House. Its Plan and Design (New York: Moffat Yard, 1917), p. 123.

5 On the subject of kitchens, see Catherine E. Beecher and Harriet Beecher Stowe, op. cit., p. 280; Geneviève Fraisse, op. cit., pp. 151, 189; Pierre Guiral and Guy Thuillier, Vie quotidienne, p. 83; Molly Harrison, op. cit; Theresa M. McBride, Domestic Revolution, pp. 52-53; Blaine E. McKinley, op. cit., pp. 242-45; Daniel E. Sutherland, op. cit., pp. 182, 188. Émile Zola (Pot-Bouille [Paris: Garnier-Flammarion, 1969], p. 53) has Mme. Josserand say that the kitchen "is an eyesore."

6 Blaine E. McKinley stated that this was the case in the U.S. (op. cit., p. 242) as did Arthur C. Downs ("Downing's Newburgh Villa," Association for Preservation Technology Bulletin/Bulletin de l'Association pour la préservation et ses techniques, Vol. 4, Nos. 3-4 [1972], pp. 1-113). Some house plans show this well; all the post-1870 collections I consulted recommended that the kitchen be on the ground floor. See Bibliography, sect. 9: "Collections of House Plans," including Robert Kerr, E.C. Hussey, Robert W. Edis, S.B. Reed, Louis H. Gibson, George W. Kinzer, and Aymar Embury.

7 Blaine E. McKinley specified that in the cities, kitchens were still in the basement during the 1860s and 1870s (op. cit., p. 242), while Daniel E. Sutherland stated that this was still the case in cities like New York in 1890 (op. cit., p. 68).

8 A common room only existed when the number of servants warranted it, i.e., when they were 3, 4, or more in a house. This is clear from house-plan collections; see, as an example, Robert

W. Edis, Decoration and Furniture of Town Houses (Wakefield, Yorkshire: E.P. Publishing, 1972), p. 231.

9 Margaret Powell, op. cit., pp. 41, 49.

10 AO, Horwood Collection, Toronto house plans, 1850-80; Toronto, Metropolitan Toronto Library, Baldwin Room, Howard Collection, architectural plans from 1840 on; PAC, NMC, post-1840 house plans; ANQ-M, post-1840 house plans listed by A. Giroux, N. Cloutier, and R. Bédard, op. cit.; ANQ-Q, post-1840 house plans, especially fonds Stavely; AVQ, post-1840 house plans, especially Fonds Baillairgé. I also consulted plans reproduced in agenda papers for post-1840 houses (Canada. Department of the Environment. Parks. National Historic Parks and Sites Branch, Agenda papers, 1962-78). I have not taken Halifax plans into consideration: several microfilms were consulted, but almost all postdate 1890 and few have anything to do with the town itself.

  I also consulted some 100 pre-1840 drawings during the course of research on the first part of the century. In a May 1982 article I stated that kitchens were in basements in 2/3 of cases, but at that time I had not yet consulted the 125 or so plans in the Toronto collections. Therefore, when the 100 or so plans from the beginning of the century were replaced by the 100 or so from Toronto, the number changed from 2/3 to 1/2 for the second half of the century.

  Various books on architectural drawings were also consulted, such as those of L. Noppen, C. Paulette, and M. Tremblay, Québec. Trois siècles d'architecture ([Montreal], Libre Expression, 1979); France Gagnon-Pratte, L'architecture et la nature à Québec au dix-neuvième siècle: les villas (Quebec: Ministère des Affaires culturelles, 1980); Raymonde Gauthier, Les manoirs du Québec (Montreal: Fides & Éditeur officiel du Québec, 1976); Michel Lessard and Huguette Marquis, Encyclopédie de la maison québecoise, 3 siècles d'habitation (Montreal: Editions de l'Homme, 1971); and Michel Lessard and Gilles Villandré, La maison traditionnelle au Québec: construction, inventaire, restauration (Montreal: Éditions de l'Homme, 1972). Curiously, these books rarely mention servants' quarters, which speaks volumes on the scant importance they have always been given.

11 AO, RG22, 05/109/6-10 and 05/121/25, York County, Estate Files, 1871-75, boxes 89-124; 7 of the 431 inventories in these records give details on servants' rooms. In ANQ-M and APJ-M are records of the 48 notaries practising in Montreal between 1871 and 1875 and of 20 others practising in the surrounding areas. The Tableau de l'ordre des notaires (Quebec [Province]. Chambre des notaires, Le tableau de l'ordre des notaires de la province du Québec [n.p.: 1967]) lists 156 notaries who appear to have practised in the area at that period; 48 were not in the two

sets of records mentioned above and I discarded 40 more who only practised for part of the period concerned. ANQ-Q and APJ-Q records of 48 notaries practising in Quebec between 1871 and 1875 were consulted, but I did not analyze records of notaries in the surrounding areas except for F.A. Mercier's, which are extensive, because they would neither add nor change anything judging from the Montreal records examined. According to the Tableau de l'ordre des notaires, 95 notaries appear to have practised in the Quebec City region between 1871 and 1875; of those, 49 were actually in the city itself, but I consulted only 48 sets of records because the remaining set is unavailable. In Montreal 19 of the 377 inventories traced cover houses with servants' quarters; in Quebec City 5 out of 127 inventories listed have information on servants' quarters. In Halifax 6 of the 323 inventories mention servants (PANS, RG48, reels 478-469). I also referred to the Macaulay inventory during the 50s, reproduced in Jeanne Minhinnick and Elizabeth Wylie's "Extracts from the Macaulay Papers Relating to Furnishings, Architecture and Gardens," Association for Preservation Technology Bulletin/Bulletin de l'Association pour la préservation et ses techniques, Vol. 5, No. 3 (1973), pp. 34-76.

12   Which is very different from the situation in England at the time, the men sleeping in the basement and the women in the attic. I would like to know how this division was established and if it was not simply a deduction based on what was known of the great houses.

13   There seems to be increasing evidence that this document is typical. See Yves Morin, "La représentativité de l'inventaire après décès — l'étude d'un cas: Québec au début du XIXe siècle," Revue d'histoire de l'Amérique française, Vol. 34, No. 4 (Mar. 1981), pp. 515-34.

14   See, for example, AO, RG22, 05/109/6-10, box 95, file 1336; ANQ-M, greffe de James S. Hunter, acte no. 20580; ANQ-Q, greffe de John Clapham, acte no. 4849; PANS, RG48, reel 478, file 1458. All these documents date from the early 1870s except for the last, which is from 1867.

15   See, for example, ANQ-M, greffe de James S. Hunter, acte no. 20814, 14 Apr. 1875, and J.-Hilarion Jobin, acte no. 12914, 4 Sept. 1872; ANQ-Q, greffe de W.D. Campbell, acte no. 3074, 1 Mar. 1875.

16   Servants' room in the home of R. Sewell, former mayor of Quebec City; see ANQ-Q, greffe de William D. Campbell, acte no. 3084, 1 Mar. 1875.

17   B.G. Jefferis and J.L. Nichols, The Household Guide; or, Domestic Cyclopaedia (Toronto: J.L. Nichols, 1894), p. 396.

18   Henriette Dessaulles, op. cit., p. 210.

19 ANQ-M, greffe de James S. Hunter, acte no. 21252, 8 Sept. 1875.

20 Leonore Davidoff and Ruth Hawthorn, op. cit., p. 81; Anne Martin-Fugier, op. cit., p. 278; Daniel E. Sutherland, op. cit., pp. 172, 179.

21 Theresa M. McBride, Domestic Revolution, p. 54; Blaine E. McKinley, op. cit., p. 216; Pierre Guiral and Guy Thuillier, Vie quotidienne, p. 50 (referring to Mme. Pariset's 1852 edition of the Manuel de la maîtresse de maison, ou lettres sur l'économie domestique [Paris: Audot], p. 66); Blaine E. McKinley, op. cit., p. 215; Anne Martin-Fugier, op. cit., p. 279.

22 Bernard O'Reilly, The Mirror of True Womanhood: A Book of Instruction for Women in the World (New York: Peter F. Collin, 1879), p. 315.

23 See Pierre Guiral and Guy Thuillier, Vie quotidienne, p. 52.

24 Leonore Davidoff and Ruth Hawthorn, op. cit., p. 80. See also Phyllis Cunnington (op. cit., pp. 17-18), who clearly stated that gentlemen avoided wearing blue and similar colours that were very often used for livery.

25 Leonore Davidoff and Ruth Hawthorn, op. cit., p. 80.

26 David Katzman, op. cit., pp. 237-38; Lucy Maynard Salmon, op. cit., p. 57; Catherine E. Beecher and Harriet Beecher Stowe, op. cit., p. 289; Douglas T. Miller, "Immigration and Social Stratification in Pre—Civil War New York," New York History, Vol. 49, No. 2 (Apr. 1968), p. 164.

27 M. Jeanne Peterson, "The Victorian Governess: Status Incongruence in Family and Society," Victorian Studies, Vol. 14, No. 1 (Sept. 1970), p. 8.

28 Pierre Guiral and Guy Thuillier, Vie quotidienne, p. 46; Catherine E. Beecher and Harriet Beecher Stowe, op. cit., p. 281. See also Pamela Horn, op. cit., p. 114, who mentioned that certain conditions were also imposed by masters; for example, when crinolines were fashionable, some masters did not permit their servants to wear such clothing.

29 See, for example, Jean-Pierre Gutton's Domestiques et serviteurs dans la France de l'Ancien Régime (Paris: Aubier-Montaigne, 1981), p. 179.

30 Pamphile Lemay, op. cit.: play entitled En livrée.

31 Henriette Dessaulles, op. cit., 11th page of illustrations between pp. 288 and 289, "Kate McGinley, employed as children's nurse for 14 years by Casimir Dessaulles, holding Henriette on her lap as a child."

32 Lady Dufferin, op. cit., p. 17.

33 Ernest Doin, Le dîner interrompu, p. 6; Luce Vermette, "Les donations, 1850-1870: activités domestiques et genres de vie," Rapport sur microfiches, No. 17 (1982), Parks Canada, Ottawa;

Suzanne Cross, op. cit., in Susan Mann Trofimenkoff and Alison Prentice, eds., op. cit., p. 72.

34 Poverty was rife throughout the cities of the time. See, among others, James H. Treble, Urban Poverty in Britain, 1830-1914 (London: Batsford, 1979), and James A. Hammerton, Emigrant Gentlewomen: Genteel Poverty and Female Emigration, 1830-1914 (London: Croom Helm, 1979), for England; Leonard Berlanstein, op. cit., and Léon Murard and Patrick Zylberman, Le petit travailleur infatigable, ou le prolétaire (Fontenay-sous-Bois: Recherches, 1976), for France; Sean Wilentz, "Crime, Poverty and the Streets of New York City: The Diary of William H. Bell, 1850-51," History Workshop. A Journal of Socialist Historians, Vol. 7 (Spring 1979), pp. 126-55, for the U.S. And, especially, the popular novels of the day that described and exploited this poverty: Paul Féval, Les mystères de Londres (Paris: Nouvelles éditions Oswald, 1978), first serialized during 1843 and 1844, and Eugène Sue, Les mystères de Paris (Paris: C. Gosselin, 1844).

The poor were obviously in Canadian cities as well: see Harvey J. Graff, "Pauperism, Misery and Vice: Illiteracy and Criminality in the Nineteenth Century," Journal of Social History, Vol. 11, No. 2 (Winter 1977), pp. 245-68; Judith Fingard, op. cit.; Huguette Lapointe-Roy, op. cit.; Bettina Bradbury, "The Family Economy and Work in an Industrializing City: Montreal in the 1870s," Historical Papers/Communications historiques (1979), pp. 71-96; and Jean-Claude Robert, op. cit., pp. 225-28.

35 Observation by Jean-Pierre Gutton (op. cit., pp. 170, 171) when speaking of servants under the Ancien Régime. I believe it was still current in the latter half of the 19th century.

36 See Pierre Guiral and Guy Thuillier, Vie quotidienne, pp. 86, 127.

37 Theresa M. McBride, "Rural Tradition," p. 124; Elaine Showalter, "Victorian Women and Insanity," Victorian Studies, Vol. 23, No. 2 (Winter 1980), p. 157.

38 Alphonse de Lamartine, Geneviève, histoire d'une servante (Paris: Michel Lévy, 1863), p. 63.

39 Daniel E. Sutherland, op. cit., p. 186. This may be surprising, but according to Sutherland, bathtubs were not commonplace in middle-class families before the 1870s nor were inside toilets commonplace before the 1890s.

40 See, among others, Catherine E. Beecher and Harriet Beecher Stowe, op. cit., pp. 280-81; Anne Martin-Fugier, op. cit., pp. 264-83; and Daniel E. Sutherland, op. cit., pp. 191-92.

41 As Anne Martin-Fugier reminds us (op. cit., pp. 266-68). In addition, Mirbeau's character, Célestine, reads Paul Bourget;

Madame Celnart recommended that servants read something "sensible and amusing," such as Poor Richard's Almanack, the first popular book by Franklin; and Lamartine had Geneviève read the gospels, the lives of the saints, Robinson Crusoe, Imitation de Jésus-Christ, Télémaque, and Paul et Virginie.

42 PAC, Census ... 1871, Toronto, St. David district, listing of deceased persons.

43 ANQ-M, Registres de décès de Notre-Dame de Montréal, 1871-75; see previous chapter, n. 56. Louis Fréchette (op. cit., p. 101) clearly indicated that at that time to die in hospital was to die poor.

44 PAC, Census ... 1871, Toronto, St. Andrew district, B-4, last number.

45 This was, at any rate, what happened at the beginning of the century according to Sewell's trial reports; see PAC, MG23, GII, 10, Vol. 13, pp. 6227-6231, 6715-6722.

46 Ernest Doin, Le dîner, p. 19. We do not know if Doin deliberately chose Le Juif errant (a very popular 19th-century novel by Eugène Sue) in order to insinuate that servants would have greatly liked the novel, a long diatribe against the Jesuits.

47 Ibid., p. 9. See also Henriette Dessaulles, op. cit., pp. 82, 87, 88; BRH-"Servante," p. 324.

48 P.G.M. Bouniceau-Gesmon, Domestiques et maîtres, ou Sécurité de la famille à propos de crimes récents (Paris: E. Dentu, 1886).

49 Pierre Guiral and Guy Thuillier, Vie quotidienne, p. 142. L'Evénement (Quebec) is a good example, and articles concerning crime in the servant classes were featured frequently.

50 Theresa M. McBride, Domestic Revolution, p. 107. I have found the same thing in Sewell's trial notes for Quebec City between 1808 and 1820.

51 P.G.M. Bouniceau-Gesmon, op. cit., p. 111; Geneviève Fraisse (op. cit., p. 180) quotes Raymond Ryckère (op. cit.).

52 See, among others, Anne Martin-Fugier, op. cit., pp. 226-34.

53 Geneviève Fraisse, op. cit., p. 189; Pamela Horn, op. cit., p. 146.

54 Edward Shorter, "Illegitimacy, Sexual Revolution and Social Change in Modern Europe," Journal of Interdisciplinary History, Vol. 22, No. 2 (Fall 1971), p. 250.

55 See, among others, P.G.M. Bouniceau-Gesmon, op. cit., pp. 172-73; Pierre Guiral and Guy Thuillier, Vie quotidienne, p. 133; Edward Shorter, Naissance, p. 172; John R. Gillis, "Servants, Sexual Relations and the Risks of Illegitimacy in London, 1801-1900," Feminist Studies, Vol. 5, No. 1 (Spring 1979), p. 160.

56 Anne Martin-Fugier, op. cit., p. 77.

57 Daniel E. Sutherland, op. cit., pp. 122-23.

58 Ample proof is found in Nathaniel Hawthorne's The Scarlet

Letter (Franklin Center, Pa.: Franklin Library, 1978), written in 1850; I consulted a reprint of the second (1852) edition.

59 John R. Gillis, op. cit., pp. 114-15.

60 Anne Martin-Fugier, op. cit., p. 294.

61 Ibid.

62 See, among others, R.M. Mennel, op. cit.; Michelle Perrot, op. cit.; Paul Boyer, *Urban Masses and Moral Order in America, 1820-1920* (Cambridge, Mass.: Harvard Univ. Press, 1978); also John W. Fierheller (op. cit.), who analyzed several.

63 This column appeared frequently, although irregularly, in *L'Evénement*. In July 1871, for example, articles on servants' infractions appeared on the 4th, 6th, 13th, 14th, 20th, 24th, and 27th.

64 *Acadian Recorder*, 29 Oct. 1875.

65 See, for example, *L'Evénement*, 1 June 1871, and *Acadian Recorder*, 10 Nov. and 20 Dec. 1875.

66 ANQ-Q, Ministère de la Justice. Prison de Québec, Mandats, Jan. 1871–Dec. 1875. I had hoped to obtain this information from other legal sources, but the fact that the recorders did not give the parties' occupations prevented me from doing so.

In PANS I consulted Vols. 4 to 6 in RG34-312, Halifax Country, ser. J. Vols. 4 and 5 have nothing of interest, and while Vol. 6 (Visiting Committee, Jail, 1868-79) holds interesting information on prison conditions, it is far outside our subject. Records of cases in the Supreme Court (RG39, J112 to 114) contain no occupation information. I then tried the actual documents (RG39, ser. C, Halifax Supreme Court), consulting the first three boxes (255-257) for 1871. Only one servant was mentioned (Case 11168) and he was acquitted. It would have taken several weeks to cover the whole 1871-75 period (boxes 255-303), and I doubted that the results would justify the effort.

Toronto research was just as fruitless. In the AO I consulted the following documents without finding anything of the least use: RG22, 05/112/29, York County, Quarter Session Minutes, 1870-79, and 05/99/17A, York County, King's Bench Civil Assize Minutes, 1867-75.

67 Harvey J. Graff, "Crime and Punishment," p. 487.

68 Jean-Claude Robert, op. cit., p. 315.

69 The total number of servants recorded is considered here because some convicted servants were listed as housewives; 1530 were live-in servants. Only women have been considered because no manservant was convicted in 1871. However, men were guilty of 70% of the total offences committed between 1871 and 1875.

Social Relationships

1   See, among others, M.E.W. Sherwood, op. cit., p. 553; Elizabeth A.M. Lewis, "A Reformation of Domestic Service," Nineteenth Century, Vol. 33 (Jan.-June 1893), pp. 127-38; George S. Layard, "The Doom of the Domestic Cook," Nineteenth Century, Vol. 33 (Jan.-June 1893), pp. 309-319; Ellen W. Darwin, "Domestic Service," Nineteenth Century, Vol. 28 (Aug. 1890), pp. 286-96; and P.G.M. Bouniceau-Gesmon, op. cit., pp. 64-65.

2   Several authors have found this. See, for example, Dorothy Marshall, op. cit., p. 15; Theresa M. McBride, Domestic Revolution, p. 31; Blaine E. McKinley, op. cit.; Daniel E. Sutherland, op. cit., p. 17; Geneviève Fraisse, op. cit., p. 18. In recalling her childhood at the turn of the century, Agatha Christie said the same thing; see An Autobiography (London: Butler & Tanner, 1977), p. 30.

3   P.G.M. Bouniceau-Gesmon, op. cit., p. 68.

4   M.E.W. Sherwood, op. cit., p. 554. The Beecher sisters believed that the English were the best (Catherine E. Beecher and Harriet Beecher Stowe, op. cit., p. 279).

5   See Blaine E. McKinley, op. cit., chap. 4; Pierre Guiral and Guy Thuillier, Vie quotidienne, p. 167; and the Irish caricatures reproduced here (Figs. 14, 21, 32).

6   According to Paul Allard, the bourgeoisie renews by half each generation: "La composition de la bourgeoisie d'Arles sous le Second Empire," paper presented at the annual meeting of the Historical Society of Canada, Halifax, June 1981, pp. 6-7.

7   Theresa M. McBride, "Rural Tradition," p. 34. The same was true of previous centuries too (Jean-Pierre Gutton, op. cit., p. 133).

8   J.B. Brown, "The Pig or the Stye: Drink and Poverty in Late Victorian England," International Review of Social History, Vol. 18, Part 2 (1973), p. 381.

9   Among the individual sources analyzed for France are plays (Ludovic Leclerc, Les valets au théâtre [Geneva: Slatkine Reprints, 1970]); for the U.S., household management manuals and women's magazines (see Blaine E. McKinley, op. cit.).

10 For 19th-century authors see M.A. Baines, op. cit., p. 9; Rose Mary Crawshay, Domestic Service for Gentlewomen: A Record of Experience and Success (London: Mrs. Crawshay's Office for Lady-helps, 1876), p. 15; Catherine E. Beecher and Harriet Beecher Stowe, op. cit., p. 245; M.E.W. Sherwood, op. cit., p. 549; P.G.M. Bouniceau-Gesmon, op. cit., p. 78; Elizabeth F. Bayle-Mouillard (pseud. Madame Celnart), Manuel complet d'économie domestique (Paris: Roret, 1826), p. 11. See also Pierre Larousse's perception analyzed by Pierre Simoni, "Science anthropologique et racisme à l'époque de l'expansion coloniale: le

cas du Grand dictionnaire universel du XIXe siècle de Pierre Larousse," Historical Papers/Communications historiques (1980), pp. 167-84.

For contemporary authors, see Lewis A. Coser, op. cit., pp. 32, 36; Arthur Downs, op. cit., p. 58; Jean-Louis Flandrin, "L'Attitude," pp. 143-210; Geneviève Fraisse, op. cit., p. 20; Barbara Stein Frankle, op. cit; John Gillis, op. cit., p. 163; Pierre Guiral and Guy Thuillier, Vie quotidienne, pp. 188-91; Gaston Jolivet, "Les domestiques parisiens," Le Correspondant (10 Aug. 1908), p. 462; Theresa M. McBride, "Rural Tradition," p. 39.

11 See, for example, Daniel Calhoun, op. cit., p. 171. He reported remarks by Mrs. J. Blackwell, Mother's Practical Guide in the Early Training of Her Children (New York: 1843).

12 For 19th-century authors, see Rose Mary Crawshay, op. cit., p. 15; Edmond and Jules Goncourt, op. cit.; Alphonse de Lamartine, op. cit., p. 65 (portrait of Geneviève); Eugène Sue, op. cit. (Pt. 4, chap. 8); Émile Zola, op. cit., p. 54.

For contemporary authors, see Barbara Stein Frankle, op. cit. p. 238; Anne Martin-Fugier, op. cit., p. 156 (she pointed out that this was a true image of Bécassine); M. Jeanne Peterson, op. cit., p. 13.

13 These portraits are mainly taken from period novels; for example, Louisa May Alcott (Little Women; or, Meg, Jo, Beth and Amy [New York: Collier Books, 1962 (1st ed. 1869)], p. 24) and especially the books of Jules Verne. See related analyses by Brian Harrison (op. cit., pp. 107-138), Anne Martin-Fugier (op. cit., pp. 140-156), and Ghislain de Diesbach (Le tour de Jules Verne en quatre-vingts livres [Paris: Julliard, 1969]).

14 The Beecher sisters on the subject: "The higher up in the social scale one goes, the more courteous seems to become the intercourse of master and servant" (Catherine E. Beecher and Harriet Beecher Stowe, op. cit., p. 279).

15 See Geneviève Fraisse (op. cit., pp. 104-106), who noted several such portraits in the French production.

16 L. Perry Curtis, Jr., (Apes and Angels: The Irishman in Victorian Caricature [Washington, D.C.: Smithsonian Institution Press, 1871]) studied this image the most. It is evident from the caricatures of the time.

17 L. Perry Curtis, Jr., op. cit., p. 95.

18 All authors who have studied domestic service agree; see, among others, Barbara Stein Frankle, op. cit., chap. 6.

19 This idea is always evident in collections of house plans. See also Clifford E. Clark Jr., op. cit., p. 50; Jill Franklin, "Troops of Servants: Labour and Planning in the Country House, 1840-1914," Victorian Studies, Vol. 19, No. 2 (Dec. 1975), p. 211; Mark Girouard, The Victorian Country House (New Haven: Yale Univ.

Press, 1979); and T.R. Slater, "Family, Society and the Ornamental Villa on the Fringes of English Country Towns," <u>Journal of Historical Geography</u>, Vol. 4, No. 2 (Apr. 1978), pp. 129-44.

20   David Katzman, op. cit., p. 10; Daniel E. Sutherland, op. cit., p. 233; Brian Harrison, op. cit., p. 136; Geneviève Fraisse, op. cit., p. 29.

21   Margaret Powell, op. cit., p. 37; Geneviève Fraisse, op. cit., p. 169.

22   <u>Canadian Illustrated News</u>, 13 July 1878, p. 22.

23   Alexis Mailloux, op. cit., p. 237; Benjamin A. Testard de Montigny, op. cit., p. 37.

24   Philippe Aubert de Gaspé, <u>Mémoires</u>, p. 66; AO, MU303, 308-309, Andrew Buell Papers, 1848-81, Addie Thorp to her sister Mrs. A.N. Buell, 13 Sept. 1875.

25   Joy Parr, op. cit., p. 115.

26   Philippe Aubert de Gaspé, <u>Mémoires</u>, p. 66; Lady Dufferin, op. cit., p. 64; Robert de Roquebrune, op. cit., pp. 36, 168-69; Henriette Dessaulles, op. cit., p. 263.

27   Henriette Dessaulles, op. cit., p. 88.

28   Ibid., p. 28.

29   See article by Marilyn Barber, op. cit.

30   Daniel E. Sutherland, op. cit., p. 267; P.G.M. Bouniceau-Gesmon, op. cit., p. 82; Ellen W. Darwin, op. cit., p. 287.

31   Anne Martin-Fugier, op. cit., p. 299. Also <u>see</u> Deborah Gorham, "The 'Maiden Tribute of Modern Babylon' Re-examined: Child Prostitution and the Idea of Childhood in Late-Victorian England," <u>Victorian Studies</u>, Vol. 21, No. 3 (Spring 1978), p. 371; and Yvonne Knibiehler, "Les médecins et la "nature féminine" au temps du code civil," <u>Annales, E.S.C.</u>, Vol. 31, No. 4 (July-Aug. 1976), pp. 829-33. Gorham mentioned the 19th-century belief that venereal disease would be cured if the sufferer had sexual relations with a virgin. Knibiehler pointed out that only at the beginning of the century did people realize that pregnancy could result from rape; they had believed that conception could only occur during intercourse with consenting partners.

32   Pierre Guiral and Guy Thuillier, <u>Vie quotidienne</u>, p. 122.

33   See, for example, Frank Dawes, op. cit., p. 67; David Katzman, op. cit., pp. 16-17; Theresa M. McBride, "Rural Tradition," p. 43; Leonore Davidoff and Ruth Hawthorn, op. cit., p. 82; Pierre Guiral and Guy Thuillier, <u>Vie quotidienne</u>, pp. 123-27.

34   Pierre Guiral and Guy Thuillier, <u>Vie quotidienne</u>, pp. 50-59.

35   Much ink has flowed on this subject. As a general rule, attempts were made to convince servants that, in following their master's wishes, they were following God's will (Anne Martin-Fugier, op. cit., p. 143; Pamela Horn, op. cit., p. 111; <u>see also</u> Blaine E. McKinley, op. cit., preface).

36 Barbara Stein Frankle (op. cit., p. 236) quotes here from Mrs. Mary Motherly, The Servants' Behaviour Book (London: Bell and Daldy, 1859), pp. 20-21.

37 Geneviève Fraisse, op. cit., quotes the child Simplicie's remark, demonstrating the importance of children's books in transmitting stereotypes. The Comtesse de Ségur's books are still widely read by children between 9 and 12.

38 The same remarks as above apply to Jules Verne's novels (from which this image was drawn); they are still popular. See Ghislain de Diesbach, op. cit., p. 152.

39 P.G.M. Bouniceau-Gesmon, op. cit., p. 78.

40 L'Evénement, 13 and 16 Jan. 1871, for example.

41 Ibid., 24 Feb. 1871.

42 For instance, those of Philippe Aubert de Gaspé, Lady Dufferin, Robert de Roquebrune, Louis Fréchette, and Henriette Dessaulles that have already been mentioned. See also Casgrain's memoirs quoted in BRH-"Servante," p. 324.

43 Toronto wills for 1871-75 are deposited in the AO, RG22, 05/109/6-10 and 05/121/25, York County Estate Files, 1871-75, boxes 89-124. Montreal and Quebec City wills are deposited in notaries' records in the ANQ-M and APJ-M as well as ANQ-Q and APJ-Q (see Bibliography, "Manuscript Sources"). Halifax wills are deposited in PANS, RG48, Court of Probate, Halifax County Will Books, Vol. 8 (1870-77), reel 360. I found 253 in Toronto, 2336 in Montreal, 1077 in Quebec City, and 208 in Halifax. Of these, 6 covered servants in Toronto, 13 in Montreal, 23 in Quebec City, and 8 in Halifax. The variance between the Anglophone and Francophone cities arises from the fact that the Courts of Probate in English Canada only covered people who had drawn up wills, had sufficient property to have files, and had died during that period. The notaries' records in French Canada contained all the wills drawn up during 1871-75, regardless of when the people died.

44 This average is inflated by two pensions of $300 and $100 respectively; see ANQ-Q, greffe de John Clapham, acte no. 4954, 27 Sept. 1872, and APJ-Q, greffe de Jean-Alfred Charlebois, acte no. 625, 14 Jan. 1873.

45 For examples, see AO, RG22, 05/121/25, box 122, file 2069, 27 May 1874, and ANQ-M, greffe de James S. Hunter, acte no. 19036, 6 Nov. 1873.

46 See ANQ-M, greffe de J.-Hilarion Jobin, acte no. 13285, 31 Dec. 1873; ANQ-M greffe de James S. Hunter, acte no. 19036, 6 Nov. 1873; and APJ-M, greffe de L.-Ovide Hétu, acte no. 7219, 28 Aug. 1875, respectively.

47 This is the overall view for I found 50 wills concerning servants out of the 3874 in the various archives. The figure is, nonethe-

less, ambiguous because people making wills did not necessarily have servants.

48 This is perhaps one of the reasons why so many servants were found in asylums.

49 See ANQ-Q, greffe de Alexandre Lemoine, acte no. 4053, 4 Feb. 1874.

50 See, among others, Leonore Davidoff, "Mastered for Life: Servant and Wife in Victorian and Edwardian England" (Journal of Social History, Vol. 7, No. 4 [Summer 1974], pp. 406-428), which is based on Max Weber's writings and in particular on his Economy and Society. In this connection, see G. Roth and C. Wittich, eds., Max Weber, Economy and Society: An Outline of Interpretive Sociology (New York: Bedminster Press, 1968), Vol. 3, p. 1066. See also Theresa M. McBride, Blaine E. McKinley, and Pierre Guiral and Guy Thuillier.

51 David Roberts, op. cit., p. 45.

52 See "The People Involved — In 1871" on the question of whether servants came from the city or country. For family support, see Joan W. Scott and Louise A. Tilly, "Women's Work and the Family in Nineteenth Century Europe," Comparative Studies in Society and History. An International Quarterly, Vol. 17, No. 1 (1975), pp. 36-64; and Mary Lynn McDougall, "Women's Work in Industrializing Britain and France," Atlantis, Vol. 4, No. 3 (Spring 1979), pp. 143-51.

53 Henriette Dessaulles (op. cit., p. 82) recounted that their seamstress wrote to her nephew who was a priest. Was she an exception?

54 In Canada members of the same family worked together in about 10% of cases, as mentioned in the first chapter. I have also found cases of sisters working in neighbouring houses.

55 See Geneviève Fraisse, op. cit., p. 111, and Deborah Gorham and Maurianne Adams, "Victorian Reform as A Family Business: The Hill Family" and "Family Disintegration and Creative Reintegration: The Case of Charlotte Brontë and Jane Eyre" respectively, in Anthony S. Wohl, ed., The Victorian Family, Structure and Stresses (London: Croom Helm, 1978), pp. 119-47, 148-79.

56 Daniel T. Rodgers, "Socializing Middle-Class Children: Institutions, Fables and Work Values in Nineteenth Century America," Journal of Social History, Vol. 13, No. 3 (Spring 1980), p. 361.

57 See, for example, Pierre Guiral and Guy Thuillier, Vie quotidienne, chap. 7; P.G.M. Bouniceau-Gesmon, op. cit., p. 80; Frank Huggett, op. cit.

58 Frank E. Huggett, op. cit., p. 116.

59 Frank Dawes, op. cit., p. 80.

60 Ernest Sackville Turner, What the Butler Saw; Two Hundred and

Fifty Years of the Servant Problem (London: Michael Joseph, 1962), p. 223.

61 Catherine E. Beecher and Harriet Beecher Stowe, op. cit., p. 289.

62 Helen Campbell, op. cit., p. 221.

Conclusion

1 As far as women's work in the 19th century is concerned, the following works (detailed in Bibliography, sect. 11) have proved most helpful: Thomas Dublin, Margaret Gibson Wilson, Tamara K. Hareven and Maris A. Vinovskis, Lee Holcombe, Isaac Joseph and Philippe Fritsch, Evelyne Sullerot, Janice Acton, and John Baltye.

2 Among the thought-provoking books were those of Patricia Branca, Carl N. Degler, Mary Kelley, Katherine Kish Sklar, Barbara Welter, Renata Bridenthal and Claudia Koonz, Sally Mitchell, Rosalind Rosenberg, Donald D. Slone, Françoise Basch, Laura S. Strumingher, Edward R. Tannenbaum, Margaret R. Conrad, Ramsay Cook and Wendy Mitchinson, Micheline Dumont-Johnson, Linda Kealy, Marie Lavigne and Yolande Pinard, and Kathleen McCrone.

3 Lady Darling, A Handy Book for Domestic Service (London: Griffon Bohn, 1863), p. 3; Pamela Horn, op. cit., p. 111: text taken from Advice to Young Women on Going into Service (Society for Promoting Christian Knowledge, 1835); Anne Martin-Fugier, op. cit., p. 140; Bible (King James Version), I Peter 2, 18-19.

4 In addition to Lewis A. Coser (op. cit.), David Katzman (op. cit.) considered that service was practically anachronistic in the second half of the 19th century.

5 Louis Chevalier, La formation de la population parisienne au XIXᵉ siècle (Paris: INED/PUF, 1950), p. 79.

6 Theresa M. McBride, "Rural Tradition," pp. 265-66; several people have qualified domestic service as a "bridging occupation."

7 Thus, as Raymond Grew observed, if we fix a goal to modernism, we commit the classic error of believing that history ends with us ("More on Modernization," Journal of Social History, Vol. 11, No. 2 Winter 1980 , pp. 179-87). See also the interesting articles by Peter N. Stearns, "The Effort of Continuity in Working Class Culture," The Journal of Modern History, Vol. 52, No. 4 (Dec. 1980), pp. 626-55, and "Modernization and Social History: Some Suggestions, and a Muted Cheer," Journal of Social History, Vol. 14, No. 2 (Winter 1980), pp. 189-209; and Tony Judt, "A Clown in Regal Purple: Social History and the

Historians," History Workshop. A Journal of Socialist Historians, Vol. 7 (Spring 1979), pp. 66-94.

8   At least this is what Theresa M. McBride ("Social Mobility") and Lewis A. Coser (op. cit.) maintain.

9   I was able to establish this number for the 1870s; it was no doubt similar around 1820. Signay's Recensement of 1818 did not allow a figure to be set since not all institutions were taken into account and only 5 servants were enumerated as heads of families; that is, living with their families and not with their masters.

10   It is to be hoped that other studies similar to Michael B. Katz's work will clarify the make-up of the "middle class" and its behaviour. See Katz, "Social Class in North American Urban History" (Journal of Interdisciplinary History, Vol. 11, No. 4 [Spring 1981], pp. 579-605), in which he stated that, given equal incomes, a merchant would hire a servant whereas a tradesman would buy a house.

11   Anne Martin-Fugier, op. cit., p. 104.

12   Daniel E. Sutherland, op. cit., chap. 8.

Illustration Sources

1   PAC, NMC, C-55480.

2   Ibid., 129382/2.

3   ANQ-Q, H772-22.

4   La Gazette de Québec/Quebec Gazette, 1 May 1817, 30 Oct. 1817, 24 Feb. 1820; La Gazette de Montréal/Montreal Gazette, 12 Sept. 1816; Quebec Mercury, 24 June 1817, 26 Jan. 1819; Montreal Herald, 23 Mar. 1816, 29 Nov. 1817.

5   ANQ-M, Plan No. 1625.

6   ANQ-Q, greffe de Joseph Planté, acte no. 7108, 8-17 Oct. 1816; ibid., acte no. 7368, 18-27 Oct. 1817; ANQ-M, greffe de Nicolas-Benjamin Doucet, acte no. 6600, 15 Sept. 1819.

7   IBCQ, 18,2890-11.

8   IBCQ, 17,213A-11.

9   ANQ-Q, N274-38.

10   The New Standard Atlas of the Dominion of Canada.... (Montreal and Toronto: Walker and Miles, 1875), pp. 80-81 (PAC, NMC, C-118009).

11   Ibid., pp. 66-67 (PAC, NMC, C-118008).

12   Ibid., p. 59 (PAC, NMC, C-37130).

13   Ibid., p. 35 (PAC, NMC, C-118010).

14   Canadian Illustrated News, 22 Apr. 1871 (PAC, C-54365).

15   Ibid., 17 Mar. 1877 (PAC, C-65717).

16   AVQ, Plans d'architecture domestique, fonds Baillairgé, folder No. 1: Les maisons privées, No. 46.

17   Ibid., No. 47.

18 Ibid., No. 48.
19 Ibid., No. 49.
20 Canadian Illustrated News, 12 May 1877 (PAC, C-65833).
21 Ibid., 4 Jan. 1873 (PAC, C-58960).
22 Ibid., 28 Dec. 1872 (PAC, C-58947).
23 AO, Horwood Collection, domestic architecture plans, 136/2.
24 AVQ, Plans d'architecture domestique, fonds Charles Baillairgé, folder No. 1: Les maisons privées, No. 98.
25 Ibid., No. 97.
26 AO, Horwood Collection, domestic architecture plans, 638/32.
27 ANQ-Q, Plans d'architecture domestique, fonds Staveley, N78-8-45.
28 APJ-M, greffe de L.-O. Hétu, acte no. 5646, 10 Sept. 1873; ANQ-Q, greffe de W.D. Campbell, acte no. 3084, 1 Mar. 1875.
29 Leonore Davidoff and Ruth Hawthorn, A Day in the Life of a Victorian Domestic Servant (London: George Allen and Unwin, 1976), p. 13.
30 Canadian Illustrated News, 21 Apr. 1883 (PAC, C-78158).
31 Ibid., 6 May 1882 (PAC, C-77137).
32 Ibid., 15 July 1871 (PAC, C-56375).

BIBLIOGRAPHY

I Manuscript Sources

Canada. Public Archives. Manuscript Division.
MG17, A5, Archevêché de Montréal, 1725-1891, Vol. 5, correspondance des familles Viger et Lartigue, 1788-1858.
MG23, GII, 10, Sewell, Jonathan (1766-1839), Vols. 12 and 13, Records of cases heard, 1808-20.
MG23, GII, 19, Monk Family, Vol. 8, Anne Amelia Gugy Monk Diary.
MG23, GIII, 18, Labadie, Louis-Généreux (1765-1824).
MG23, HI, 3, Jarvis Family, Vol. 2, Hannah Peters Jarvis and Family, 1762-1822.
MG24, A2, Ellice Papers, Vol. 50, Diary of Mrs. Edward Ellice Junior.
MG24, A12, Dalhousie, George Ramsay, ninth Earl of (1746-1839), Journals, 1816-28.
MG24, A43, Whitworth-Aylmer, Louisa Anne, Baroness, Journals.
MG24, A57, Sherbrooke, Sir John Coape (1764-1830), Vols. 6-13, Journals of Lady Katherine Sherbrooke, 1811-18.
MG24, B2, Papiers Papineau, Vol. 1, correspondance, 1815-66.
MG24, B9, Robinson, Sir John Beverley (1791-1863), Vols. 1 & 2, correspondence, 1803-22.
MG24, B66, Mercy Ann Coles, Reminiscences of Canada, 1864-78.
MG24, I28, Sandys, Charles, 1813-14, letters received from Alicia Cockburn.
MG24, I61, Abraham Joseph Papers, Diary of Fanny Joseph, 1871-79.
MG29, E74, J.C.A. Campbell, Memoirs of Charlotte Oillie, 1835-60.
MG30, C85, J.E.G. Curran Papers, Vol. 5, Manual for Female Servants (1867).
Census for Toronto, Montreal, Quebec City, and Halifax in 1871:
       Toronto: C-9969 to 9973;
       Montreal (quartier Saint-Antoine): C-10046 to 10048;
       Quebec City: C-10095 to C-10097, 10344 to 10346;
       Halifax: C-10550 to 10552.
RG8, I, British Military and Naval Records.
National Map Collection, Architectural Records Section.
Domestic architecture plans.
Picture Division.
Picture collection.

Great Britain. National Army Museum (London).
Newman Papers, Diary of Emma Newman (manuscript in Italian, translated by the Department of the Secretary of State, Ottawa; copy on file, Halifax Defense Complex, Atlantic Regional Office, Environment Canada – Parks, Halifax).

McGill University
Collection Canadiana: illustrations, maps, and plans.

Montreal. Archives du palais de justice.
Greffes (contrats d'engagement, inventaires après décès, testaments), 1871-75:

Archambault, Amable	Jobin, André-D.
Arnould, François-E.	Kittson, G.-R. William
Beauchesne, Pierre-C.	Lepailleur, A.-Narcisse
Bélanger, Léandre	Lighthall, William F.
Bélanger, Théophile	Longtin, Moïse
Blain, Jean	Mainville, Philéas
Brault, H.-Alexandre	Payette, Antoine-E.
Cushing, Charles	Pelland, Basile-E.
Doucet, Théodore	Pépin, Henri-P.
Forest, Léon	Phaneuf, Antoine
Garand, Moïse	Prud'homme, Eustache
Germain, Clément-P.	Quintal, Isaïe-A.
Hart, L.-Alexandre	Renaud, François-P.
Hétu, L.-Ovide	Rieutord, Félix
Huot, Tancrède-A.	Terreau, Pierre
Isaacson, John H.	Wright, Henry B.

Montreal. Bibliothèque municipale. Salle Gagnon.
Collection Canadiana.

Montreal. Université.
Collection Baby.
Collection Melzac.

Nova Scotia. Public Archives.
Picture Collection.
Plans of domestic architecture.
RG32, Vital Statistics, 4, Deaths – Halifax County, Vols. 39-42, 1871-1875.
RG34-312, Halifax County, J Series, Halifax City Gaol, Vols. 4-6, 1868-79;
RG34-312, Halifax County, P Series, Grand Jury Book, Vol. 21, 1867-1875.
RG38, County Courts, Halifax County, Vol. 1, 1872-75.

RG39, Supreme Court, Halifax County, J 112-114, Original Entries, Cause Book—Supreme Court.

RG39, C Series, Halifax Supreme Court, Causes, Vols. 255-303, 1871-1875.

RG48, Court of Probate (inventories of possessions), 1867-71, reels 478-496.

Halifax County Will Books, Vol. 8, 1870-77, reel 360.

Ontario. Archives.
Horwood Collection: Domestic architecture plans
MS 522, Rogers Papers.
MU105, Thomas Fraser Papers, 1825-63.
MU135, Birchard Family Papers, 1808-1938.
MU282, Margaret Bowlby Collection, 1852-78.
MU303, 308-309, Andrew Buell Papers, 1848-81.
MU759, Cronkite Papers.
MU866, Frances T. Milnes, Diary, 1867-75.
MU1054, Ford Papers.
MU1147, Gowan (James and Ogle) Papers, 1833-43.
MU1962, F.D. McLennan Collection.
MU3062, Van Buren Collection, Diary of H. Meade.
Picture Collection.
RG22, 05/112/29, York County, Quarter Session Minutes, 1870-79.
RG22, 05/99/11B, York County, Civil Assize Minutes, 1867-72.
RG22, 05/99/17A, York County, King's Bench, Civil Assize Minutes (Home Circuit), 1872-75.
RG22, 05/124/08, York County, Clerk of the Peace, Coroner's Inquest Book, 1865-95.
RG22, 05/109/6-10, York County, Estate Files, 1871-73.
RG22, 05/121/25, York County, Estate Files, 1873-75.

Quebec (City). Archives.
Plans d'architecture domestique, especially Fonds Charles Baillairgé.

Quebec (City). Archives du palais de justice.
Greffes (contrats d'engagement, inventaires après décès, testaments):
1871 to 1875:

Austin, Henry C.	Mercier, François-A.
Chaperon, J.-Alphonse	Nolet, Isaïe
Charlebois, Jean-Alfred	Pageau, Charles
Delage, Jean-Baptiste	Parkins, John B.
Giroux, Elzéar	Pelletier, Elzéar
Labrèque, Cyprien	Shaw, Peter A.
Lapointe, J.-Alfred	Strang, John
Laurin, Jos.-Octave	Tourangeau, Guillet-A.

Tremblay, Georges-T.   Walsh, James
Vocelle, Augustin

Quebec (Province). Archives nationales du Québec à Montréal.
Collection iconographique.
Greffes (contrats d'engagement, inventaires après décès, testaments):
  1816 to 1820

Barron, Thomas	Guy, Louis
Bédouin, Thomas	Huot, Charles
Beek, John Gerband	Jobin, André
Cadieux, Jean-Marie	Lanctôt, Pierre
Constantin, Jean-Baptiste	Latour, Louis-Huguet
Dandurand, R.-François	Lukin, Peter, fils
Daveluy, P.-Édouard	Mailloux, Joseph
Deguire, Jean-Baptiste	Mondelet, Jean-Marie, fils
Demers, Joseph	Nolin, Charles
Desautels, Joseph	Papineau, Joseph
Delisle, Jean-Guillaume	Payment, Joseph
Doucet, Nicolas-Benjamin	Pinet, Alexis
Dubois, Antoine-Alexis	Pinsonneault, Théophile
Gauthier, J.-Pierre	Prévost, Charles
Gauthier, Pierre-Antoine	Thibodeau, Louis
Griffin, Henry	Vallée, Pierre

  1871 to 1875:

Auger, J.-Cyrille	Hurteau, P.-O.
Beaubien, P.-Desrivières	Jeannotte, Hormidas
Beaufield, Ramon	Jobin, J.-Hilarion
Bourbonnière, E.-Narcisse	Lamontagne, C.-Hormidas
Bureau, J.-Olivier	Lamothe, Pierre
Caron, Michel	Leclair, Ovide
Champoux, Elzéar	McIntosh, Edward
Coutu, J.-F. Gilbert	Normandeau, Pierre-E.
Dagan, Gaspard	Normandin, Louis
Desrosiers, L.-Arthur	Papineau, J.-Godefroy
Dubreuil, Joseph	Paré, Alexis-P.
Dumesnil, Hyacinthe	Reignier, Octave
Durand, François-J.	Robert, Charles
Fréchette, E.-Pantaléon	Robert, J.-T. Amédée
Grenier, Louis-A.	Ross, William
Griffin, John C.	Sanborn, Myron H.
Horan, John	Smith, James
Hunter, James S.	Terroux, Charles

Plans d'architecture domestique.
Plumitifs de la cour du banc du roi, 1816-20.

216

Registres de décès des paroisses:
    1816 to 1820:
        Notre-Dame
    1871 to 1875:
        Cathédrale anglicane
        Église méthodiste
        Notre-Dame
        Notre-Dame de Grâce
        St. Patrick

Quebec (Province). Archives nationales du Québec à Québec.
Collection iconographique.
Greffes (contrats d'engagement, inventaires après décès, testaments):
    1816 to 1820:

Bélanger, Jean
Bernier, François
Bernier, Louis
Berthelot, Michel
Besserer, Louis-Théodore
Bigué, Paul
Boucher, Jacques
Boudreault, Étienne
Campbell, Archibald
Chavigny de la Chevrotière,
    Ambroise
Côté, Alexis
Côté, Joseph
Demers, Julien
Duclos, Pierre-Louis
Dugal, Charles
Faribault, Barthélemy, fils
Gagnon, Pierre
Glackmeyer, Édouard
Guay, Louis

Laforce, Pierre
Larue, Damase
Larue, François-Xavier
Lee, Thomas
Lefebvre, François-Xavier
Lefrançois, Dominique
Lelièvre, Roger
Martineau, Jean-Marie
McPherson, Laughlan T.
Panet, Louis
Parent, Antoine-Archange
Planté, Joseph-Bernard
Ranvoyze, Louis
Sauvageau, Michel
Scott, William Fisher
Tessier, Michel
Têtu, Félix
Vaillancourt, François-X.
Voyer, Charles
Voyer, Jacques

    1871 to 1875:

Bernier, L.-Octave
Bolduc, Henri
Campbell, William D.
Campeau, Olivier
Cannon, Edward G.
Cinq-Mars, Charles
Clapham, John
Côté, Jean
Couillard de Beaumont, R.

Doyle, John
Falardeau, Louis
Fraser, Alexandre
Fraser, John
Gauvreau, François-L.
Glackmeyer, Édouard
Guay, Germain
Hébert, Célestin
Huot, Philéas

Huot, Philippe
Launière, Wilfrid
Laurin, Joseph
Leclair, Louis
Lemoine, Alexandre
Lemoine, Édouard

Matte, J.-Baptiste
McPherson, Daniel
Panet, Louis
Pruneau, J.-Baptiste
Rousseau, Louis-B.
Sirois Duplessis, Alexandre-B.

Quebec. Bas-Canada.
    28: Cours de Justice, 1760-1880:
      Cour supérieure, 1767-1867.
      Cour du banc du roi, 1764-1863.
      Cour de circuit, 1811-65.
       Cour d'oyer et terminer, 1777-1865.
       Juges de paix et sessions de la paix, 1765-1856.
Ministère de la Justice, Prison de Québec, Mandats, Jan. 1871—Dec. 1875.
Plans d'architecture domestique, especially fonds Staveley.
Register of the Quebec Gaol, Vol. 6, 1813-23.
Registres de décès des paroisses:
    1813 to 1817:
      Notre-Dame.
    1871 to 1875:
      Église protestante St. Andrew
      Église protestante St. Matthew
      Notre-Dame de Foy
      Notre-Dame de Québec
      Saint-Jean-Baptiste
      St. Patrick
      Saint-Roch
      Saint-Sauveur

Quebec (Province). Archives nationales du Québec à Trois-Rivières.
Greffe de Joseph Badeaux, 1817-18.

Quebec (Province). Bibliothèque nationale. Pavillon Fauteux.
Collection Canadiana.

Quebec (Province). Ministère des Affaires culturelles.
Inventaire des biens culturels, collection iconographique.

Quebec (Province). Musée du Québec. Bibliothèque.
Collection iconographique.

Quebec (Seminary). Archives.
Fonds manuscrits, MS No. 301, Servants Wages, livret tenu par Jules Quesnel de Québec, 1831-40.

Toronto. Metropolitan Public Library. Baldwin Room.
Arthur Jarvis papers.
L.W. Smith papers.
Howard Collection: Architectural plans.

II   Printed Sources

1.   Anthologies, Dictionaries, Collections

Bas–Canada. Parlement.
Statuts provinciaux du Bas-Canada. P.E. Desbarats, Quebec, 1811-20.
Vols. 7-9.

Bescherelle, L.N.
Dictionnaire national de la langue française. Garnier, Paris, 1858. 3
vols.

Canada. Parliament.
Census of Canada/Recensement du Canada, 1870-71. I.B. Taylor,
Ottawa, 1873. 5 vols.
Statuts du Canada, 1871-1875. Brown Chamberlin, Ottawa, 1871-75.

Dahl, Edward H., et al.
La ville de Québec, 1800-1850: un inventaire de cartes et plans.
Musées nationaux du Canada, Ottawa, 1975. Division de l'histoire,
Dossier No. 13.

Dictionnaire de l'Académie française
Rev. ed. Libraires Associés, Paris, 1765. 2 vols.

Dictionnaire des oeuvres littéraires du Québec
Ed. Maurice Lemire. Fides, Montreal, 1978-. Vol. 1: Des origines à
1900.

Duval, Étienne
Anthologie thématique du théâtre québécois au XIXe siècle. Théâtre
Leméac, Montreal, 1978.

Furetière, Antoine
Dictionnaire universel contenant généralement tous les mots français
tant vieux que modernes et les termes de toutes les sciences et des
arts. Reprint of 1690 ed. Slatkine Reprints, Geneva, 1970. 3 vols.

Hayne, David M., and Marcel Tyrol
Bibliographie du roman canadien-français, 1837-1900.   Presses de l'université Laval, Quebec, 1969.

Larousse, Pierre
Grand Dictionnaire universel du XIXe siècle. Administration du Grand Dictionnaire universel, Paris, 1865-75. 17 vols.

The New Standard Atlas of the Dominion of Canada
Walker and Miles, Montreal, 1875.

Oxford English Dictionary
Reprint of 1933 ed. Clarendon Press, Oxford, 1970. 12 vols.

Plessis, Joseph-Octave
"Dénombrements de Québec faits en 1792, 1795, 1798 et 1805 par le curé Joseph-Octave Plessis." In Rapport de l'archiviste de la province de Québec pour 1948-1949, Rédempti Paradis, Quebec, 1949, pp. 1-250.

Quebec (Province). Chambre des notaires.
Tableau de l'ordre des notaires de la province de Québec. N.p., 1967.

Revue de l'université d'Ottawa
"Histoire littéraire du Québec, I." Vol. 42, Nos. 1-2 (Jan.-April 1979). Ottawa.

Russell, Hilary
"Bibliography of Domestic Manuals." Manuscript on file, National Historic Parks and Sites Branch, Environment Canada — Parks, Ottawa, 1980.

Signay, Joseph
Recensement de la ville de Québec en 1818. Preface by H. Provost. Société historique de Québec, Quebec, 1976.

2.   Period Studies of Domestic Service

Babeau, Albert
"La domesticité d'autrefois." Le Correspondant, Vol. 139 (1885), pp. 231-56.
Les artisans et les domestiques d'autrefois. Firmin-Didot, Paris, 1886.

Black, Clementina
"The Dislike [sic] to Domestic Service." Nineteenth Century, Vol. 33 (Jan.-June 1893), pp. 454-56. London.

Crawshay, Rose Mary
Domestic Service for Gentlewomen: A Record of Experience and Success. Mrs. Crawshay's Office for Lady-helps, London, 1876.

Darwin, Ellen W.
"Domestic Service." Nineteenth Century, Vol. 28 (Aug. 1890), pp. 286-96. London.

Jollivet, Gaston
"Les domestiques parisiens." Le Correspondant, 10 Aug. 1908, pp. 458-475.

Layard, George S.
"The Doom of the Domestic Cook." Nineteenth Century, Vol. 33 (Feb. 1893), pp. 309-319. London.

Lewis, Elizabeth
"A Reformation of Domestic Service." Nineteenth Century, Vol. 33 (Jan.-June 1893), pp. 127-38. London.

Packard, Clarissa, pseud. (Caroline Howard Gilman)
Recollections of a Housekeeper. Harper and Brothers, New York, 1836.

Raymond, Aline
"Maîtres et serviteurs." La revue canadienne, Vol. 41 (Feb. 1904), pp. 129-37. Montreal.

Ryckère, Raymond
La servante criminelle. Maloine, Paris, 1908.

Salmon, Lucy Maynard
Domestic Service. Macmillan, New York, 1901.

Sherwood, M.W.E.
"The Lack of Good Servants." North American Review, Vol. 153, No. 420 (Nov. 1891), pp. 546-58. New York.

Sykes, Ella C.
A Home-help in Canada. Smith Elder, London, 1913.

3. Manuals for Domestics

Adams, Samuel, and Sarah Adams
The Complete Servant. Knight and Lacey, London, 1825.

Baines, M.E.
Domestic Servants As They Are and As They Ought To Be. W. Tweedie, London, 1859.

Beecher, Catherine E.
Letters to Persons who are Engaged in Domestic Service. Leavitt and Trow, New York, 1842.

Coznett, Thomas
The Footman's Directory and Butler's Remembrance; or, The Advice of Onesimus to his Young Friends. Printed for the author, London, 1823.

Darling, Lady E.
A Handy Book for Domestic Service. Griffin Bohn, London, 1863.

Guide du domestique, à l'usage du simple domestique, du valet de chambre ... et de la cuisinière
2nd ed. Martinton, Paris, 1852.

Instructions in Household Matters; or, The Young Girl's Guide to Domestic Service
John W. Parker, London, 1844.

Motherly, Mary
The Servants' Behaviour Book. Bell and Daldy, London, 1859.

National and Industrial Schools of Holy Trinity
Household Work; or, The Duties of Female Servants Practically and Economically Illustrated through the Respective Grades of Maid-of-all-Work, House and Parlour Maid, and Laundry-Maid, with many Valuable Recipes for Facilitating Labour in Every Department, Prepared for the Use of the National and Industrial Schools of Holy Trinity, at Finchley. 15th ed. Joseph Master, London, 1867.

The Young Housekeepers' Essential Aid to the Thorough Understanding of the Duties of the Maidservants
Thomas Dean and Son, London, 1852.

4. Household Management Treatises

Arthur, T.S.
Advice to Young Ladies on their Duties and Conduct in Life. J.A. Bradley, Philadelphia, 1861.

Bassanville, Anaïs Lebrun, comtesse de
L'art de bien tenir une maison. A. Broussois, Paris, 1878.

Bayle-Mouillard, Elizabeth-F. (pseud. Madame Celnart)
Manuel complet d'économie domestique. Roret, Paris, 1826.

Beecher, Catherine E.
A Treatise on Domestic Economy. Reprint of 1841 ed. Schochen, New York, 1977.

Beecher, Catherine E., and Harriet Beecher Stowe
Principles of Domestic Science as Applied to the Duties and Pleasures of Home. J.B.K. Ford, New York, 1870.

Beeton, Isabella
The Book of Household Management; Comprising Information for the Mistress, Housekeeper, Cook, Kitchen-maid, Butler, Footman, Coachman, Valet, Upper and Under House-maids, Lady's Maid, Maid-of-all-work, Laundry-maid, Nurse and Nurse-maid, Monthly, Wet and Sick Nurses, etc., etc., also, Sanitary, Medical and Legal Memoranda; with a History of the Origin, Properties, and Uses of All Things Connected with Home Life and Comfort. S.O. Beeton, London, 1861.

Bouniceau-Gesmon, P.G.M.
Domestiques et maîtres, ou sécurité de la famille à propos de crimes récents. E. Dentu, Paris, 1886.

Campbell, Helen
Household Economics. G.P. Putnam's Sons, New York, 1898.

Ellet, Elizabeth F.
The New Cyclopaedia of Domestic Economy, and Practical Housekeeper. Henry Bill Publishing, Norwich, Conn., 1873.

Jefferis, B.G., and J.L. Nichols
The Household Guide, or Domestic Cyclopaedia. J.L. Nichols, Toronto, 1894.

Leslie, Miss
Miss Leslie's Behaviour Book. Reprint of 1859 ed. Arno Press, Philadelphia, 1972.

Mailloux, Alexis
Le manuel des parents chrétiens. 4th ed. (1st ed. published by Côté in 1851). L'Action sociale, Quebec, 1910.

O'Reilly, Bernard
The Mirror of True Womanhood: A Book of Instruction for Women in the World. 12th ed. Peter F. Collin, New York, 1879.

Pariset, Madame
Manuel de la maîtresse de maison, ou lettres sur l'économie domestique. Audot, Paris, 1823.

Putman, Elizabeth
Mrs. Putman's Receipt Book and Young Housekeeper's Assistant. Sheldon, New York, 1867.

Testard de Montigny, Benjamin-A.
Manuel d'économie domestique. Cadieux and Derome, Montreal, 1896.

Traill, Catherine Parr
The Canadian Settler's Guide. Reprint of 1855 ed. McClelland and Stewart, Toronto, 1969. New Canadian Library, No. 64.

Webster, Thomas, and Frances Parkes
An Encyclopaedia of Domestic Economy; Comprising such Subjects as Are Most Immediately Connected with Housekeeping. Harper and Brothers, New York, 1845.

5.   Contemporary Studies of Domestic Servants

Barber, Marilyn
"The Women Ontario Welcomed: Immigrant Domestics for Ontario Homes, 1870-1930." Ontario History, Vol. 62, No. 3 (Sept. 1980), pp. 148-72. Toronto.

Barry, Francine
"La domesticité féminine de Québec au milieu du XVIIIᵉ siècle." Paper presented at the conference of the Institut d'histoire de l'Amérique française, Montreal, 1974.

Bates, Christina
"Allocation and Functions of Domestic Offices at Bellevue, N.H.P."
Manuscript Report Series, No. 429, Parks Canada, Ottawa, 1981.

Bled, Yves
"La condition des domestiques antillaises à Montréal." MA thesis,
Faculté d'anthropologie, université de Montréal, 1965.

Brown, Marian
"Report on Newspaper Articles, Women's Columns and Domestic
Labour Advertisements." Manuscript presented July 1981, COSEP
project.

Bulletin des recherches historiques
"Une servante d'autrefois." Vol. 46, No. 11 (Nov. 1940), pp. 324.
Lévis.

Chabot, Paul
Jean et Yvonne, domestiques en 1900. Téma-éditions, Paris, 1977.

Chatelain, Abel
"Migrations et domesticité féminine urbaine en France, XVIIIe-XXe
siècles." Revue d'histoire économique et sociale, Vol. 47, No. 4 (Dec.
1969), pp. 506-28. Paris.

Coser, Lewis A.
"Servants: The Obsolescence of an Occupational Role." Social Forces,
Vol. 52 (Sept. 1973), pp. 31-40. Chapel Hill, N.C.

Cretté-Breton, Yvonne
Mémoires d'une bonne. Scorpion, Paris, 1966.

Davidoff, Leonore
"Mastered for Life: Servant and Wife in Victorian and Edwardian
England." Journal of Social History, Vol. 7, No. 4 (Summer 1974), pp.
406-28. Pittsburg.

Davidoff, Leonore, and Ruth Hawthorn
A Day in the Life of a Victorian Domestic Servant. George Allen and
Unwin, London, 1976.

Dawes, Frank
Not in Front of the Servants. Taplinger Publishing, New York, 1973.

Ebury, Mark, and Brian Preston
Domestic Service in Late Victorian and Edwardian England, 1871-1914.
George Over, London, 1976.

Epstein, Rachel
" 'I Thought There Was no More Slavery in Canada.' West Indian Domestic Workers on Employment Visas." Canadian Women's Studies/Les cahiers de la femme, Vol. 2, No. 1 (1980), pp. 22-29. Ottawa.

Fairchilds, Cissie
"Masters and Servants in Eighteenth Century Toulouse." Journal of Social History, Vol. 12, No. 3 (Spring 1979), pp. 368-95. Pittsburg.

Fraisse, Geneviève
Femmes toutes mains. Essai sur le service domestique. Seuil, Paris, 1979.

Frankle, Barbara Stein
"The Genteel Family: High Victorian Conceptions of Domesticity and Good Behaviour." PhD diss., Wisconsin University, 1969.

Franklin, Jill
"Troops of Servants: Labour and Planning in the Country House, 1840-1914." Victorian Studies, Vol. 19, No. 2 (Dec. 1975), pp. 211-40. Leicester and Bloomington.

Genet, Jean
Les bonnes. Marc Barbizat-L'Arbalète, Paris, 1947.

Gillis, John R.
"Servants, Sexual Relations and the Risks of Illegitimacy in London, 1801-1900." Feminist Studies, Vol. 5, No. 1 (Spring 1979), pp. 142-73. College Park, Md.

Guiral, Pierre, and Guy Thuillier
La vie quotidienne des domestiques en France au XIXe siècle. Hachette, Paris, 1978.
"Les sources de l'histoire régionale des domestiques au XIXe siècle." Revue historique, Vol. 259 (April-June 1978), pp. 441-51. Paris.

Gutton, Jean-Pierre
Domestiques et serviteurs dans la France de l'Ancien Régime. Aubier-Montaigne, Paris, 1981.

226

Hecht, J. Jean
The Domestic Servant Class in Eighteenth-Century England. Routledge and Kegan Paul, London, 1956.

Horn, Pamela
The Rise and Fall of the Victorian Servant. St. Martin's Press, New York, 1975.

Huggett, Frank E.
Life Below Stairs. Domestic Servants in England from Victorian Times. John Murray, London, 1977.

Katzman, David
Seven Days a Week: Women and Domestic Service in Industrializing America. Oxford University Press, New York, 1978.

Lacelle, Claudette
"Les domestiques dans les villes canadiennes au XIXe siècle: effectifs et conditions de vie." Histoire sociale/Social History, Vol. 15, No. 29 (May 1982), pp. 181-207. Ottawa.
"Les domestiques en milieu urbain au XIXe siècle: première étape de recherche." Bulletin de recherches, No. 101 (1979). Parks Canada, Ottawa. (Published in English as "Domestic Servants in Urban Areas in the 19th Century: Preliminary Research," Research Bulletin, No. 101 [1979], Parks Canada, Ottawa.)
"Les domestiques en milieu urbain au XIXe siècle: deuxième étape de recherche." Bulletin de recherches, No. 109 (1979). Parks Canada, Ottawa. (Published in English as "Urban Domestic Servants in the Nineteenth Century: Second Stage of the Research," Research Bulletin, No. 109 [1979], Parks Canada, Ottawa.)
"Maîtres et domestiques en milieu urbain: le recensement de 1871." Bulletin de recherches, No. 166 (1981). Parks Canada, Ottawa. (Published in English as "Employers and Domestic Servants in Urban Centres: The 1871 Census," Research Bulletin, No. 166 [1981], Parks Canada, Ottawa.)

Lépine, Daniel
"La domesticité juvénile à Montréal pendant la première moitié du XVIIIe siècle (1713-1744)." MA thesis, Université de Sherbrooke, forthcoming.

Lomax, James
"Behind the Green Baize Door." Country Life, No. 4186 (Sept. 1977), pp. 762-64. London.

Marshall, Dorothy
The English Domestic Servant in History. The Historical Association, London, 1949.

Martin-Fugier, Anne
La place des bonnes: la domesticité féminine à Paris en 1900. Grasset, Paris, 1979.

McBride, Theresa M.
"Rural Tradition and the Process of Modernization: Domestic Servants in Nineteenth Century France." PhD thesis, Rutgers University, New Brunswick, N.J., 1973.
"Social Mobility for the Lower Class: Domestic Servants in France." Journal of Social History, Vol. 8, No. 1 (Autumn 1974), pp. 63-78. Pittsburg.
The Domestic Revolution: The Modernization of Household Service in England and France, 1820-1920. Holmes and Meier, New York, 1976.
"The Modernization of Woman's Work." The Journal of Modern History, Vol. 49, No. 2 (June 1977), pp. 231-45. Chicago.

McKinley, Blaine E.
" 'The Stranger in the Gates': Employer Reactions Towards Domestic Servants in America, 1825-1875." PhD diss., Michigan State University, 1969.

Memmi, Albert
L'Homme dominé. Payot, Paris, 1968.

Parr, Joy
Labouring Children. British Immigrant Apprentices to Canada, 1864-1924. Croom Helm, London, 1980.

Peterson, M. Jeanne
"The Victorian Governess: Status Incongruence in Family and Society." Victorian Studies, Vol. 14, No. 1 (Sept. 1970), pp. 7-26. Leicester and Bloomington.

Powell, Margaret
Below Stairs. Peter Davies, London, 1968.

Sutherland, Daniel
"Americans and their Servants, 1800-1920; Being an Inquiry into the Origins and Progress of the American Servant Problems." PhD diss., Wayne State University, Detroit, 1976. 2 vols.

Turner, Ernest Sackville
What the Butler Saw; Two Hundred and Fifty Years of The Servant Problem. Michael Joseph, London, 1962.

Vukman-Tenebaum, Mirjana
"Domestic Workers and Organizing Strategies." Resources for Feminist Research/Documentation sur la recherche féministe, Vol. 10, No. 2 (July 1981), pp. 32-39. Toronto.

6. Local Newspapers

Acadian Recorder (Halifax)
1871-75.

L'Événement (Québec)
1871-75.

La Gazette de Montréal
1816-20.

La Gazette de Québec
17 Mar. 1771; 1816-20.

Montreal Herald
1816-20.

Quebec Mercury
1816-20.

7. Period Literature: Novels, Short Stories, Plays

Alcott, Louisa May
Little Women; or, Meg, Jo, Beth and Amy. First publication 1869. Collier Books, New York, 1962. Pts. 1 and 2.

Aubert de Gaspé, [Philippe], fils
Le chercheur de trésor ou l'influence d'un livre. Reprint of 1837 ed. Nouvelle édition de poche, Montreal, 1968.

Aubert de Gaspé, Philippe
Les anciens Canadiens. Reprint of 1864 ed. Fides, Montreal, 1971.

Balzac, Honoré de
La Rabouilleuse. Reprint of Vol. 6 of La Comédie humaine (1843). Paris, Livre de poche, 1972.

Boucher de Boucherville, Georges
Une de perdue, deux de retrouvées. Reprint of 1st (1849) ed. Preface by Réginald Hamel. Hurtubise HMH, Montreal, 1973.

Brontë, Charlotte
Jane Eyre. Reprint of 3rd (1848) ed. The Franklin Library, Franklin Center, Pa., 1981.

Brooke, Frances
The History of Emily Montague by the author of Lady Julia Mandeville. J. Dodsley, London, 1769.

Chauveau, P.J.O.
Charles Guérin. Reprint of article published in La Revue canadienne in 1900 (1st published 1853). Marc-A. Guérin, Québec, 1973.

Doin, Ernest
Le désespoir de Jocrisse, ou les folies d'une journée. Beauchemin, Montreal, 1880.
Le dîner interrompu, ou nouvelle farce de Jocrisse. Beauchemin, Montreal, 1885.

Faucher de Saint-Maurice, Édouard
Contes et récits. Originally published between 1868 and 1877. Preface by Serge Provencher. VLB Éditeur, Montreal, 1977.

Féval, Paul
Les mystères de Londres. Nouvelles éditions Oswald, Paris, 1978. 2 vols.

Goncourt, Edmond, and Jules Goncourt
Germinie Lacerteux. Flammarion et Fasquelle, Paris, 1864.

Hare, John, ed.
Contes et nouvelles du Canada français 1778-1859. Éditions de l'université d'Ottawa, Ottawa, 1971. Vol. 1.

Hawthorne, Nathaniel
The Scarlet Letter. Reprint of 2nd (1852) ed. The Franklin Library, Franklin Center, Pa., 1978.

Lamartine, Alphonse de
Geneviève, histoire d'une servante. Michel Lévy, Paris, 1863.

Leclerc, Ludovic
Les valets au théâtre. Reprint of 1875 ed. Slatkine Reprints, Geneva, 1970.

Lemay, Pamphile
Picounoc le Maudit. Reprint of 1878 ed. Hurtubise HMH, Montreal, 1972.
Rouge et bleu, comédies. C. Darveau, Quebec, 1891.

Marion, Séraphin
Les lettres canadiennes d'autrefois. Éditions de l'université d'Ottawa, Ottawa, 1948-54. 8 vols.

Mirbeau, Octave
Le journal d'une femme de chambre. Reprint of 1937 ed. (1st published 1900). Livre de poche, Paris, 1976.

Petitclair, Pierre
Griphon, ou la vengeance d'un valet. William Cowan, Quebec, 1837.

La Revue canadienne
1864-1907. Montreal.

Sue, Eugène
Les mystères de Paris. C. Gosselin, Paris, 1844.

Zola, Émile
Pot-Bouille. Reprint of 1882 ed. Garnier-Flammarion, Paris, 1969.

8.   Travel Accounts, Memoirs, Private Diaries

Arusmont, Fanny Wright D'
Views of Society and Manners in America: in a Series of Letters from that Country to a Friend in England during the Years 1818, 1819 and 1820 by an Englishwoman. Longman, Hurst, Rees, Orme and Brown, London, 1821.

Aubert de Gaspé, Philippe
Mémoires. Reprint of 1866 ed. Fides, Montreal, 1971.

Bernhard, Karl
Travels through North America during the Years 1825 and 1826. Carey, Lea and Carey, Philadelphia, 1828. 2 vols.

Bouchette, Robert S.M.
Mémoires de Robert S.M. Bouchette, 1805-1840. Comp. Errol Bouchette, notes by A.D. Decelles. La Revue Canadienne, Montreal, 1903.

Campbell, Patrick
Travels in North America. Greenwood Press, New York, 1968.

Chassé, Béatrice, ed.
"Les journaux d'Émilie Berthelot-Girouard." Rapport des Archives du Québec, Vol. 53, (1975). Quebec.

Chevalier, Michel
Lettres sur l'Amérique du Nord. Charles Gosselin, Paris, 1837.

Christie, Agatha
Autobiographie. Trans. Marie-Louise Navarro. Libre Expression, [Montreal], 1981.

Dessaulles, Henriette
Fadette, Journal d'Henriette Dessaulles, 1874-1880. Hurtubise HMH, Montreal, 1971.

Dorwin, J.H.
Montreal in 1816, Reminiscences. Montreal Daily Star, Montreal, 1881.

Dufferin, Lady Hariot
My Canadian Journal, 1872-1878. Preface and notes by Gladys Chantler Walker. Longmans, Don Mills, 1969.

Duncan, John M.
Travels through Part of the United States and Canada in 1818, 1819. W.B. Gilley, New York, 1823.

Fowler, Thomas
The Journal of a Tour Through British America. Lewis Smith, Aberdeen, 1832.

Fréchette, Louis
Mémoires intimes. Ed. and annotated by George A. Klinck. Fides, Montréal, 1977.

Graig, Gerald M.
Early Travellers in the Canadas, 1791-1867. Macmillan, Toronto, 1955.

Hall, Francis
Travels in Canada and the United States in 1816 and 1817. Longman, Hurst, Rees, Orme and Brown, London, 1818.

Innis, Mary Quayle, ed.
Mrs. Simcoe's Diary. Macmillan, Toronto, 1971.

Lambert, John
Travel through Lower Canada and the United States of North America, in the Years 1806, 1807 and 1808. 3rd ed. Richard Phillips, London, 1816. 2 vols.

Leefe, John, ed.
"Sydney Morton's Diary." Acadiensis: Journal of the History of the Atlantic Region/Revue de l'histoire de la région atlantique, Vol. 4, No. 1 (Autumn 1974), pp. 121-29. Fredericton.

Maleuvrier, comte Colbert de
Voyage dans l'intérieur des États-Unis et au Canada. John Hopkins Press, Baltimore, 1935.

Roquebrune, Robert de
Testament de mon enfance. Reprint of 1951 ed. Fides, Montreal, 1979.

Silleman, Benjamin
A Tour to Quebec in the Autumn of 1819. Richard Phillips, London, 1822.

Talbot, Edward A.
Five Years Residence in the Canadas. Longman, Hurst, Rees, Orme and Brown, London, 1824. 2 vols.

Whitelaw, Marjory, ed.
The Dalhousie Journals. Oberon Press, Ottawa, 1978.

9. Collections of House Plans

Benjamin, Asher
The Architect; or, Practical House Carpenter. B.B. Mussey, Boston, 1845.

Bicknell, A.J.
Victorian Village Builder. Reprint of 1878 ed. A.J. Bicknell, New York, 1976.

Canada. Department of the Environment. Parks. National Historic Parks and Sites Branch.
Agenda papers. Ottawa, 1962-81.

Downing, Andrew Jackson
The Architecture of Country Houses Including Designs for Cottages, and Farmhouses, and Villas, with Remarks on Interiors, Furniture and the Best Modes of Warming and Ventilating. Reprint of 1850 ed. Dover Publications, New York, 1969.

Edis, Robert W.
Decoration and Furniture of Town Houses: A Series of Cantor Lectures Delivered Before the Society of Arts, 1880, Amplified and Enlarged. Reprint of 2nd ed. (1881). E.P. Publishing, Wakefield, Yorkshire, 1972.

Embury, Aymar
The Livable House. Its Plan and Design. Moffat Yard, New York, 1917.

Gibson, Louis-H.
Convenient Houses with Fifty Plans for the Housekeeper. Thomas Y. Crowell, New York, 1889.

Giroux, A., N. Cloutier, and R. Bédard
"Plans de l'architecture domestique inventoriés aux Archives nationales du Québec à Montréal." Histoire et archéologie, No. 4 (1975), 3 vols. Ottawa.

Hussey, E.C.
Victorian Home Building. A Transcontinental View. E.C. Hussey, New York, 1876.

Jourdain, M.
English Interiors in Smaller Houses: From the Restoration to the Regency, 1660-1830. B.T. Batsford, London, 1923.

Kerr, Robert
The Gentleman's House; or, How to Plan English Residences from the Parsonage to the Palace. Reprint of 1871 ed. Johnson Reprint, New York, 1972.

Kinzer, George W.
The Radford American Homes, 100 House Plans.   The Radford Architectural Company, Riverside, Ill., 1903.

Loudon, J.C., ed.
An Encyclopedia of Cottage, Farm, and Villa Architecture and Furniture; Containing Numerous Designs for Dwellings from the Villa to the Cottage and the Farm Including Farm Houses, Farmeries, and Other Agricultural Buildings; Country Inns, Public Houses, and Parochial Schools: with the Requisite Fittings-up, Fixtures, and Furniture; and Appropriate Offices, Gardens, and Garden Scenery; Each Design Accompanied by Analytical and Critical Remarks. Rev. ed. Longman, Brown, Green and Longmans, London, 1846.

Reed, S.B.
House-Plans for Everybody. For Village and Country Residences, Costing from $250 to $8,000; Including Full Descriptions and Estimates in Detail of Materials, Labor and Costs, with Many Practical Suggestions and 175 Illustrations. 5th ed. Orange Judd, New York, 1882.

Vaux, Calvert
Villas and Cottages. A Series of Designs Prepared for Execution in the United States. Reprint of 1864 ed. Dover Publications, New York, 1970.

Watson, Rosamund M.
The Art of the House. George Bell and Sons, London, 1897.

10.   Collections of Pictorial Material

Allodi, Mary
Canadian Watercolours and Drawings in the Royal Ontario Museum. Royal Ontario Museum, Toronto, 1974. 2 vols.

Bartlett, William H.
Bartlett's Canada; A Pre-Confederation Journey.   Intro. Henry C. Campbell. McClelland and Stewart, Toronto, 1968.

Bell, Michael
Painters in a New Land. McClelland and Stewart, Toronto, 1973.

Cameron, Christina, and Jean Trudel
The Drawings of James Cockburn: A Visit through Quebec's Past.
Gage Publishing, Toronto, 1976.

Campbell, Henry C.
Early Days on the Great Lakes: The Art of William Armstrong.
McClelland and Stewart, Toronto, 1971.

Cunnington, Phyllis
Costumes of Old Servants from the Middle Ages to 1900. Adam and
Charles Black, London, 1974.

Curtis, L. Perry, Jr.
Apes and Angels: The Irishman in Victorian Caricature. Smithsonian
Institution Press, Washington, D.C., 1971.

Fischel, Oskar, and Max Von Boehn
Modes and Manners of the Nineteenth Century as Represented in the
Pictures and Engravings of the Time. Trans. M. Edwardes, intro.
Grace Rhys. Benjamin Blom, New York, 1970. 2 vols.

Gagnon-Pratte, France
L'architecture et la nature à Québec au dix-neuvième siècle: les villas.
Ministère des Affaires culturelles, Quebec, 1980.

Harper, Russell
La peinture au Canada des origines à nos jours. Presses de l'université
Laval, Quebec, 1966.

Hawkins, Alfred
Hawkin's Picture of Quebec with Historical Recollections. Neilson and
Cowan, Quebec, 1834.

Hayes, J.
Rowlandson, Watercolours and Drawings. Phaidon Press, London,
1972.

Jouvancourt, Hughes de
Cornelius Krieghoff. Musson Book Company, Toronto, 1973.

Maurice, Arthur B., and Frederick T. Cooper
The History of the Nineteenth Century in Caricature. Cooper Square
Publishing, New York, 1970.

236

Noppen, L., C. Paulette, and M. Tremblay
Québec. Trois siècles d'architecture. Libre Expression, [Montreal], 1979.

Quebec (Province). Ministère des Affaires culturelles.
C. Baillairgé, dessins architecturaux. Quebec, 1979.

Ross, A.M.
William Henry Bartlett, Artist, Author and Traveller. University of Toronto Press, Toronto, 1973.

Searle, R., C. Roy, and B. Bornemann
La caricature. Art et manifeste du XVIe siècle à nos jours. Albert Skira, Geneva, 1974.

Smith, C.
Sketches in the Canadas. N.p., London, n.d.

Spendlove, F. St. George
The Face of Early Canada; Pictures of Canada which Have Helped to Make History. Illustrated by Examples from the Sigmund Samuel Canadiana Collection, Royal Ontario Museum. Ryerson Press, Toronto, 1958.

UNESCO
Catalogue de reproductions en couleurs de peintures antérieures à 1860. 7th ed. UNESCO, Paris, 1964.

Willis, N.P.
Canadian Scenery. N.p., London, 1842. 2 vols.

11. General Works and Journals

Acadiensis: Journal of the History of the Atlantic Region/Revue de l'histoire de la région atlantique
1971-81. Fredericton.

Acton, Janice, et al.
Women at Work: Ontario, 1850-1930. Canadian Women's Educational Press, Toronto, 1974.

Akins, Thomas Beamish
History of Halifax City. Reprint of 1895 ed. Mika Publishing, Belleville, 1973.

Allard, Paul
"La composition de la bourgeoisie d'Arles sous le second empire."
Paper presented at the Historical Society of Canada meetings, Halifax, June 1981.

Allentuck, Andrew
"Vanishing Pleasures." En Route (Nov. 1980), pp. 35-46. Weston, Ont.

American Historical Review
1970-81. Bloomington, Ind.

American Quarterly
1966-81. Philadelphia.

Annales canadiennes d'histoire/Canadian Journal of History
1966-81. Saskatoon.

Annales de démographie historique
1964-81. Paris.

Annales, Économies, Sociétés, Civilisations
1970-81. Paris.

Archivaria
1975-81. Ottawa.

Archives
1975-81. Quebec.

Ariès, Philippe
L'enfant et la vie familiale sous l'ancien régime. Plon, Paris, 1960.

Association for Preservation Technology Bulletin/Bulletin de l'Association pour la préservation et ses techniques
1969-81. Ottawa.

Atlantis: A Women's Studies Journal/Revue d'études sur la femme
1975-81. Wolfville, N.S.
"Report on the Home for Young Women Seeking Employment, Halifax, 1870." Vol. 5, No. 2 (Spring 1980), pp. 196-200.

Audet, Pierre H.
"Apprenticeship in Early Nineteenth Century Montreal, 1790-1812."
MA thesis, Concordia University, Montreal, 1975.

Avenel, Georges d'
Découvertes d'histoire sociale, 1200-1910. Flammarion, Paris, 1910.

Baehre, Rainer
"Paupers and Poor Relief in Upper Canada." Historical Papers/Communications historiques (1981), pp. 57-80. Ottawa.

Basch, Françoise
Les femmes victoriennes: Roman et société. Payot, Paris, 1979.

Batts, John Stuart
"Seeking the Canadian Pepys: The Canadian Manuscript Diaries Project." Archivaria, No. 9 (Winter 1979-80), pp. 125-40. Ottawa.

Baltye, John
"The Nine Hour Pioneers: The Genesis of the Canadian Labour Movement", Labour/Le travailleur, No. 2 (1979), pp. 25-56. Halifax.

Bellavance, Marcel
"Les structures de l'espace montréalais à l'époque de la confédération." Cahiers de géographie du Québec, Vol. 24, No. 63 (Dec. 1980), pp. 363-84. Quebec.

Bergeron, Louis
"Approvisionnement et consommation à Paris sous le premier empire." Fédération des Sociétés historiques et archéologiques de Paris et de l'Île de France, Vol. 14 (1963), pp. 197-232.

Berlanstein, Leonard
"Vagrants, Beggars and Thieves: Delinquent Boys in Mid-nineteenth Century Paris." Journal of Social History, Vol. 12, No. 4 (Summer 1979), pp. 531-52. Pittsburg.

Bernard, J.-P., P.-A. Linteau, and J.-C. Robert
"La structure professionnelle de Montréal en 1825." Revue d'histoire de l'Amérique française, Vol. 30, No. 3 (Dec. 1976), pp. 383-415. Montreal.

Boyer, Paul
Urban Masses and Moral Order in America, 1820-1920. Harvard University Press, Cambridge, Mass., 1978.

Bradbury, Bettina
"The Family Economy and Work in an Industrializing City: Montreal in the 1870s." Historical Papers/Communications historiques (1979), pp. 71-96. Ottawa.

Branca, Patricia
Silent Sisterhood: Middle-class Women in the Victorian Home. Croom Helm, London, 1975.

Bridenthal, Renata, and Claudia Koonz, eds.
Becoming Visible: Women in European History. Houghton Mifflin, Boston, 1977.

British Journal of Sociology
1970-81. London.

Brown, J.B.
"The Pig or the Stye: Drink and Poverty in Late Victorian England." International Review of Social History, Vol. 18, Pt. 2 (1973), pp. 380-95. Amsterdam.

Bulletin des recherches historiques
1895-1968. Lévis.

Bulletin d'histoire de la culture matérielle/Material History Bulletin
1976-81. Ottawa.

Bulletin du Centre de recherche en civilisation canadienne-française
1970-81. Ottawa.

Cahiers canadiens de sociologie
1975-81. Edmonton.

Cahiers internationaux de sociologie
1970-81. Paris.

Calhoun, Daniel
The Intelligence of a People. Princeton University Press, Princeton, 1973.

Canadian Antique Collector
1970-74. Toronto.

Canadian Collector
1975-81. Toronto

Canadian Historical Review
1921-81. Toronto.

Canadian Illustrated News
1868-83. Montreal.

Canadian Newsletter of Research on Women/Recherches sur la femme, bulletin d'information
1975-78. Toronto.

Canadian Studies in Population
1979-81. Edmonton.

Canadian Women's Studies/Les cahiers de la femme
1979-81. Ottawa.

Charbonneau, Hubert, et al.
La population du Québec: études rétrospectives. Boréal Express, Quebec, 1973.

Chevalier, Louis
La formation de la population parisienne au XIXe siècle. INED/PUF, Paris, 1950.

Clark, Clifford E., Jr.
"Domestic Architecture as an Index to Social History: The Romantic Revival and the Cult of Domesticity in America, 1840-1870." Journal of Interdisciplinary History, Vol. 8, No. 1 (Summer 1976), pp. 33-56. Cambridge, Mass.

Clark, Melissa
"Les formes alternatives de prise de conscience politique chez les femmes." Paper presented at the meeting of the Institut d'histoire de l'Amérique française, Université d'Ottawa, 19 Oct. 1979.

Comparative Studies in Society and History, An International Quarterly
1970-81. London and New York.

Conrad, Margaret R.
"Women's Studies in Canada." Dalhousie Review, Vol. 60, No. 3 (Autumn 1980), pp. 438-44. Halifax.

Cook, Ramsay, and Wendy Mitchinson, eds.
The Proper Sphere: Women's Place in Canadian Society. Oxford University Press, Toronto, 1976.

Cowan, Helen I.
British Emigration to British North America, The First Hundred Years. Toronto, University of Toronto Press, 1961.

Daedelus
1970-81. Cambridge, Mass.

Dalhousie Review
1970-81. Halifax.

Darroch, A. Gordon, and Michael D. Ornstein
"Ethnicity and Occupational Structure in Canada in 1871: The Vertical Mosaic in Historical Perspective." Canadian Historical Review, Vol. 61, No. 3 (Sept. 1980), pp. 305-33. Toronto.

Daumard, Adeline
La bourgeoisie parisienne de 1815 à 1848. SEVPEN, Paris, 1963.
"Une référence pour l'étude des sociétés urbaines en France aux XVIIIe et XIXe siècles: projet de code socio-professionnel." Revue d'histoire moderne et contemporaine, Vol. 10, No. 2 (July-Sept. 1963), pp. 185-210. Paris.

Dechêne, Louise
Habitants et marchands de Montréal au XVIIe siècle. Plon, Paris & Montreal, 1974.

Degler, Carl N.
At Odds: Women and the Family in America from the Revolution to the Present. Oxford University Press, New York, 1980.

Délibérations et mémoires de la Société Royale du Canada
1970-81. Ottawa.

Diesbach, Ghislain de
Le tour de Jules Verne en quatre-vingts livres. Julliard, Paris, 1969.

Dostaler, Yves
Les infortunes du roman dans le Québec du XIXe siècle. Hurtubise HMH, Montreal, 1977.

Downs, Arthur C.
"Downing's Newburgh Villa." Association for Preservation Technology Bulletin/Bulletin de l'Association pour la préservation et ses techniques, Vol. 4, Nos. 3-4 (1972), pp. 1-113. Ottawa.

Drolet, Antonio
"La ville de Québec, histoire municipale; II: Régime anglais jusqu'à l'incorporation (1759-1833). Cahiers d'histoire, No. 17 (1965). Quebec.

Dublin, Thomas
"Women Workers and the Study of Social Mobility." Journal of Interdisciplinary History, Vol. 9, No. 4 (Spring 1979), pp. 647-65. Cambridge, Mass.

Duby, Georges, and Armand Wallon, eds.
Histoire de la France rurale. Seuil, Paris, 1976. 3 vols. Vol. 3: Apogée et crise de la civilisation paysanne, 1789-1917.

Dumont-Johnson, Micheline
"Des garderies au XIXe siècle: les salles d'asile des Soeurs Grises à Montréal." Revue d'histoire de l'Amérique française, Vol. 34, No. 1 (June 1980), pp. 27-56. Montreal.
"Histoire de la condition de la femme dans la province de Québec." In Tradition culturelle et histoire politique de la femme au Canada, Commission royale d'enquête sur la situation de la femme au Canada, Ottawa, 1972. Étude No. 8.

Durand, Yves
Les Fermiers généraux au XVIIIe siècle. Presses universitaires de France, Paris, 1971.

Easterbrook, W.T., and Hugh G.J. Aitken
Canadian Economic History. Macmillan, Toronto, 1956.

Ethnologie française
1971-81. Paris.

Fair, D.B.G., comp.
"Interpretation Manual for Animation in a Period Kitchen." Manuscript on file, National Historic Parks and Sites Branch, Environment Canada — Parks, Ottawa, 1977.

Faucher, Albert
"La notion de luxe chez les Canadiens français au dix-neuvième siècle." Mémoires de la Société Royale du Canada, ser. 4, Vol. 11 (1973), pp. 177-82. Ottawa.

Feminist Studies
1975-81. College Park, Md.

Fenwick, G.E.
"The Medical Statistics of the City of Montreal." British American Journal, Vol. 3 (Jan. 1862), pp. 33-37. Montreal.

Fierheller, John W.
"Approaches to the Study of Urban Crime: A Review Article." <u>Revue d'histoire urbaine</u>, Vol. 8, No. 2 (Oct. 1979), pp. 104-112. Ottawa.

Fingard, Judith
"The Winter's Tale: The Seasonal Contours of Pre-industrial Poverty in British North America, 1815-1860." <u>Historical Papers/Communications historiques</u> (1974), pp. 65-74. Ottawa.

Flandrin, Jean-Louis
<u>Famille, parenté, maison, sexualité dans l'ancienne société</u>. Hachette, Paris, 1976.
"L'attitude à l'égard du petit enfant et les conduites sexuelles dans la civilisation occidentale: structures anciennes et évolution." <u>Annales de démographie historique</u> (1973), pp. 143-210. Paris.
<u>Les amours paysannes; amour et sexualité dans les campagnes de l'ancienne France (XVIe- XIXe siècles</u>. Gallimar/Julliard, Paris, 1975.

Flinn, Michael, ed.
<u>Scottish Population History from the 17th Century to the 1930s</u>. Cambridge University Press, Cambridge, 1977.

Garden, Maurice
<u>Lyon et les Lyonnais au XVIIIe siècle</u>. Les Belles Lettres, Paris, 1975.

Gauthier, Raymonde
<u>Les manoirs du Québec</u>. Fides et l'Éditeur officiel du Québec, Montreal, 1976.

Gillis, John R.
"Youth in History: Progress and Prospects." <u>Journal of Social History</u>, Vol. 7, No. 2 (Winter 1974), pp. 201-207. Pittsburg.

Girouard, Mark
<u>The Victorian Country House</u>. Rev. ed. Yale University Press, New Haven, 1979.

Gorham, Deborah
"The 'Maiden Tribute of Modern Babylon' Re-examined: Child Prostitution and the Idea of Childhood in Late-Victorian England." <u>Victorian Studies</u>, Vol. 21, No. 3 (Spring 1978), pp. 353-80. Leicester and Bloomington.

Graff, Harvey J.
"Crime and Punishment in the 19th Century: A New Look at the Criminal." <u>Journal of Interdisciplinary History</u>, Vol. 7, No. 3 (Winter

1977), pp. 477-91. Cambridge, Mass.
"Pauperism, Misery and Vice: Illiteracy and Criminality in the Nineteenth Century." Journal of Social History, Vol. 11, No. 2 (Winter 1977), pp. 245-68. Pittsburg.

Grant de Pauw, Linda, and C. Hunt
"Remember the Ladies": Women in America, 1750-1815. Viking Press, New York, 1976.

Greenhous, Brereton
"Paupers and Poorhouses: The Development of Poor Relief in Early New Brunswick." Histoire sociale/Social History, Vol. 1 (April 1968), pp. 103-126. Ottawa.

Greer, Allan
"The Pattern of Literacy in Quebec, 1745-1899." Histoire Sociale/Social History, Vol. 11, No. 22 (Nov. 1978), pp. 293-335. Ottawa.

Grew, Raymond
"More on Modernization." Journal of Social History, Vol. 11, No. 2 (Winter 1980), pp. 179-87. Pittsburg.

Gunn, Gertrude A.
The Political History of Newfoundland, 1832-1864. University of Toronto Press, Toronto, 1966.

Hamelin, Jean, and Yves Roby
Histoire économique et sociale du Québec, 1851-1896. Fides, Montreal, 1971.

Hammerton, James A.
Emigrant Gentlewomen: Genteel Poverty and Female Emigration, 1830-1914. Croom Helm, London, 1979.

Hardy, Jean-Pierre, and David-Thiéry Ruddel
Les apprentis artisans à Québec, 1660-1815. Presses de l'université du Québec, Montreal, 1977.

Hardy, René
"L'activité sociale du curé de Notre-Dame de Québec; aperçu de l'influence du clergé au milieu du XIXe siècle." Histoire sociale/Social History, Vol. 3, No. 6 (Nov. 1970), pp. 5-32. Ottawa.

Hareven, Tamara K., and Maris A. Vinovskis, eds.
Family and Population in Nineteenth Century America. Princeton University Press, Princeton, 1978.

Harrison, Brian
"For Church, Queen and Family: The Girls' Friendly Society, 1874-1920." Past and Present, Vol. 61 (Nov. 1973), pp. 107-138. Oxford.

Harrison, Molly
The Kitchen in History. Osprey Publishing, Reading, Eng., 1972.

Helly, Denise
"Anthropologie et différentiation sexuelle." Paper presented at the meeting of the Institut d'histoire de l'Amérique française, Université d'Ottawa, 19 Oct. 1979.

Histoire sociale/Social History
1968-81. Ottawa.

Historical Association of Canada/Société historique du Canada
Annual reports, 1922-65. Ottawa.

Historical Papers/Communications historiques
1966-81. Ottawa.

Historical Reflections/Réflexions historiques
1974-81. Waterloo, Ont.

History and Theory
1961-81. Middletown, Conn.

History Workshop. A Journal of Socialist Historians.
1975-81. Oxford.

Holcombe, Lee
Victorian Ladies at Work: Middle Class Working Women in England and Wales, 1850-1914. Shoe String Press, Hamden, Conn., 1973.

Hubscher, Ronald-Henri
"Société globale et population agricole. Un essai de classification des catégories socio-professionnelles non agricoles." Revue d'histoire moderne et contemporaine, Vol. 27 (Apr.-June 1980), pp. 312-19. Paris.
"Une contribution à la connaissance des milieux populaires ruraux au XIXe siècle. Le livre de compte de la famille Flahaut (1811-1877)." Revue d'histoire économique et sociale, Vol. 47, No. 3 (1969), pp. 361-403. Paris.

International Journal of Women's Studies
1978-81. Montreal and St.Albans, Vt.

International Review of Social History
1970-81. Amsterdam.

Joseph, Isaac, and Philippe Fritsch
Disciplines à domicile — l'édification de la famille. Recherches, Fontenay-sous-Bois, 1977.

Journal of Canadian Studies
1970-81. Peterborough.

Journal of Family History
1970-81. Cambridge, Mass.

Journal of Historical Geography
1975-81. Oxford and Madison, Wis.

Journal of Interdisciplinary History
1970-81. Cambridge, Mass.

Journal of Modern History
1969-81. Chicago.

Journal of Population
1969-81. Chapel Hill, N.C.

Journal of Social History
1967-81. Pittsburg.

Judt, Tony
"A Clown in Regal Purple: Social History and the Historians." History Workshop: A Journal of Socialist Historians, Vol. 7 (Spring 1979), pp. 66-94. Oxford.

Katz, Michael B.
"Social Class in North American Urban History." Journal of Interdisciplinary History, Vol. 11, No. 4 (Spring 1981), pp. 579-605. Cambridge, Mass.
The people of Hamilton, Canada West; Family and Class in a Mid-Nineteenth Century City. Harvard University Press, Cambridge, Mass., 1975.

Kealy, Linda, ed.
A Not Unreasonable Claim: Women and Reform in Canada, 1880s-1920s. Women's Press, Toronto, 1979.

Kelley, Mary
"A Woman Alone: Catherine Maria Sedgwick's Spinsterhood in Nineteenth Century America." The New England Quarterly, Vol. 51, No. 2 (June 1978), pp. 209-225. Brunswick, Me.

Knibiehler, Yvonne
"Les médecins et la "nature féminine" au temps du code civil." Annales, E.S.C., Vol. 31, No. 4 (July-Aug. 1976), pp. 824-45. Paris.

Labour/Le Travailleur
1976-81. Halifax.

Lacelle, Claudette
"La garnison britannique dans la ville de Québec d'après les journaux de 1764 à 1840." Histoire et archéologie, No. 23 (1979). Ottawa. (Published in English as "The British Garrison in Quebec City as Described in Newspapers from 1764 to 1840," History and Archaeology, No. 23 [1979], Ottawa.)
"La propriété militaire à Québec de 1760 à 1871." Histoire et archéologie, No. 57 (1982), Ottawa. (Published in English as "The Royal Regiment of Artillery in Quebec City, 1759-1871," History and Archaeology, No. 57 [1979], pp. 3-145, Ottawa.)

Lacombe, Marthe
"La maison George-Etienne Cartier, rue Notre Dame à Montréal." Travail inédit, No. 240 (1977), Parks Canada, Ottawa.

Lapointe-Roy, Huguette
"Paupérisme et assistance sociale à Montréal, 1832-1865." MA thesis, McGill University, Montreal, 1972.

Lavigne, Marie, and Yolande Pinard
Les femmes dans la société québécoise. Boréal Express, Montreal, 1977.

Lessard, Michel, and Gilles Vilandré
La maison traditionnelle au Québec: construction, inventaire, restauration. Éditions de l'Homme, Montreal, 1972.

Lessard, Michel, and Huguette Marquis
Encyclopédie de la maison québécoise, trois siècles d'habitation. Éditions de l'Homme, Montreal, 1972.

Linteau, P.-A., R. Durocher, and J.-C. Robert
Histoire du Québec contemporain. Boréal Express, Montreal, 1979.

248

Lottin, Alain
"Naissances illégitimes et filles-mères à Lille au XVIIIe siècle." Revue d'histoire moderne et contemporaine, Vol. 17 (April-June 1970), pp. 278-322. Paris.

McCrone, Kathleen
"Feminism and Philanthropy in Victorian England: The Case of Louise Twining." Historical Papers/Communications historiques (1976), pp. 123-39. Ottawa.

McDougall, Mary Lynn
"Women's Work in Industrializing Britain and France." Atlantis: A Women's Studies Journal /Revue d'études sur la femme, Vol. 4, No. 2 (Spring 1979), pp. 143-51. Wolfville, N.S.

Mennel, Robert M.
Thorns and Thistles: Juvenile Delinquents in the United States, 1825-1840. New England University Press, Hanover, New Hampshire, 1973.

Michelet, Jules
Le peuple. Reprint of 1846 ed. Flammarion, Paris, 1974.

Miller, Douglas T.
"Immigration and Social Stratification in Pre-Civil War New York." New York History, Vol. 49, No. 2 (April 1968), pp. 157-68. Cooperstown, N.Y.

Minhinnick, Jeanne, and Elizabeth Wylie
"Extracts from the Macaulay Papers Relating to Furnishings, Architecture and Gardens." Association for Preservation Technology Bulletin/Bulletin de l'Association pour la préservation et ses techniques, Vol. 5, No. 3 (1973), pp. 34-76. Ottawa.

Mitchell, Sally
"Sentiment and Suffering: Women's Recreational Reading in the 1860's." Victorian Studies, Vol. 21, No. 1 (Autumn 1977), pp. 29-46. Leicester and Bloomington.

Moogk, Peter N.
"The Craftsmen of New France." PhD diss., University of Toronto, Toronto, 1973.

Morin, Yves
"La représentativité de l'inventaire après décès — l'étude d'un cas: Québec au début du XIXe siècle." Revue d'histoire de l'Amérique française, Vol. 34, No. 4 (March 1981), pp. 515-34. Montreal.

Murard, Léon, and Patrick Zylberman
Le petit travailleur infatigable ou le prolétaire. Recherches, Fontenay-sous-Bois, 1976.

New England Quarterly
1975-81. Brunswick, Me.

New York History
1970-81. Cooperstown, N.Y.

Nineteenth Century
1970-81. London.

Ontario History
1970-81. Toronto.

Ouellet, Fernand
Éléments d'histoire sociale du Bas-Canada. Hurtubise HMH, Montreal, 1972.
Le Bas-Canada, 1791-1840. Changements structuraux et crise. Éditions de l'université d'Ottawa, Ottawa, 1976.

Past and Present
1970-81. Oxford.

Perkin, Harold
The Origins of Modern English Society, 1780-1880. University of Toronto Press, Toronto, 1969.

Perrot, Michelle
"Délinquance et système pénitenciaire en France au XIXe siècle." Annales, E.S.C., Vol. 30, No. 1 (Jan.-Feb. 1975), pp. 67-92. Paris.

Population
1970-81. Paris.

Population Studies
1970-81. London.

Quebec (Province)
Rapport de l'archiviste de la province de Québec. Quebec, 1921-62.

Quebec (Province)
Rapport des Archives du Québec. Quebec, 1963-75.

Raddall, Thomas H.
Halifax, Warden of the North. McClelland and Stewart, Toronto, 1948.

Recherches sociographiques
1970-81. Quebec.

Resources for Feminist Research/Documentation sur la recherche féministe
1979-81. Toronto.

Revue canadienne de criminologie
1970-81. Ottawa.

Revue de l'université d'Ottawa
1970-81. Ottawa.

Revue d'histoire de l'Amérique française
1947-81. Montreal.

Revue d'histoire économique et sociale
1969-81. Paris.

Revue d'histoire moderne et contemporaine
1970-81. Paris.

Revue d'histoire urbaine
1972-81. Ottawa.

Revue historique
1970-81. Paris.

Robert, Jean-Claude
"Montréal (1821-1871). Aspects de l'urbanisation." Doctorate thesis, École des hautes études en sciences sociales, Université de Paris No. I, Paris, 1977.

Roberts, David
Paternalism in Early Victorian England. Rutgers University Press, New Brunswick, N.J., 1979.

Rodgers, Daniel T.
"Socializing Middle-Class Children: Institutions, Fables and Work Values in Nineteenth-Century America." Journal of Social History, Vol. 13, No. 3 (Spring 1980), pp. 354-67. Pittsburg.

Rosenberg, Rosalind
"In Search of Woman's Nature, 1850-1920." Feminist Studies, Vol. 3, Nos. 1/2 (Autumn 1975), pp. 141-54. College Park, Md.

Scott, Joan W., and Louise A. Tilly
"Women's Work and the Family in Nineteenth-century Europe." Comparative Studies in Society and History. An International Quarterly, Vol. 17, No. 1 (1975), pp. 36-64. London and New York.

Sébillot, Paul
Coutumes populaires de la Haute-Bretagne. Reprint of 1886 ed. Maisonneuve et Larose, Paris, 1967.

Shorter, Edward
"Illegitimacy, Sexual Revolution, and Social Change in Modern Europe." Journal of Interdisciplinary History, Vol. 2, No. 2 (Autumn 1971), pp. 237-72. Cambridge, Mass.
Naissance de la famille moderne, XVIIIe - XXe siècle. Seuil, Paris, 1977.

Showalter, Elaine
"Victorian Women and Insanity." Victorian Studies, Vol. 23, No. 2 (Winter 1980), pp. 157-82. Leicester and Bloomington.

Signs: Journal of Women in Culture and Society
1975-81. Chicago.

Simoni, Pierre
"Science anthropologique et racisme à l'époque de l'expansion coloniale: le cas du Grand dictionnaire universel du XIXe siècle de Pierre Larousse." Historical Papers/Communications historiques (1980), pp. 167-84. Ottawa.

Sklar, Katherine Kish
Catherine Beecher. A Study in American Domesticity. Yale University Press, New Haven, 1973.

Slater, T.R.
"Family, Society and the Ornamental Villa on the Fringes of English Country Towns." Journal of Historical Geography, Vol. 4, No. 2 (April 1978), pp. 129-44. Oxford and Madison, Wis.

Slone, Donald D.
"Victorian Feminism in the Nineteenth-century Novel." Women's Studies. An Interdisciplinary Journal, Vol. 1, No. 1 (1972), pp. 65-92. New York.

Snell, J.G.
"The Cost of Living in Canada in 1870." Histoire sociale/Social History, Vol. 12, No. 23 (May 1979), pp. 186-91. Ottawa.

Social Forces
1970-81. Chapel Hill, N.C.

Stearns, Peter N.
"Modernization and Social History: Some Suggestions, and a Muted Cheer." Journal of Social History, Vol. 14, No. 2 (Winter 1980), pp. 189-209. Pittsburg.
"The Effort of Continuity in Working Class Culture." The Journal of Modern History, Vol. 52, No. 4 (Dec. 1980), pp. 626-55. Chicago.

Strumingher, Laura S.
" 'L'Ange de la Maison': Mothers and Daughters in Nineteenth-century France." International Journal of Women's Studies, Vol. 2, No. 1 (Jan.-Feb. 1979), pp. 51-61. Montreal and St. Albans, Vt.

Sullerot, Evelyne
Histoire et sociologie du travail féminin. Gonthier, Paris, 1968.

Tannenbaum, Edward R.
"The Beginning of Bleeding-heart Liberalism: Eugène Sue's Les Mystères de Paris." Comparative Studies in Society and History, Vol. 23, No. 3 (July 1981), pp. 491-507. London and New York.

Technology and Culture. The International Quarterly of the Society for the History of Technology
1970-81. Chicago.

Thuillier, Guy
Pour une histoire du quotidien en Nivernais au XIXe siècle. Mouton, Paris, 1977.

Treble, James H.
Urban Poverty in Britain, 1830-1914. Batsford, London, 1979.

Trofimenkoff, Susan Mann, and Alison Prentice, eds.
The Neglected Majority: Essays in Canadian Women's History. McClelland and Stewart, Toronto, 1977.

Urban Studies
1970-81. Glasgow and Boston.

Vermette, Luce
"Les donations, 1800-1820: activités domestiques et genre de vie."
Rapport sur microfiches, No. 16 (1982), Parks Canada, Ottawa.
"Les donations, 1850-1870: activités domestiques et genre de vie."
Rapport sur microfiches, No. 17 (1982), Parks Canada, Ottawa.

Victorian Studies
1970-81. Leicester and Bloomington.

Welter, Barbara
"The Cult of True Womanhood, 1820-1860." American Quarterly, Vol.
18, No. 2, Pt. 1 (Summer 1966), pp. 151-74. Philadelphia.

Whitfield, Carol C.
"Tommy Atkins: le soldat britannique en garnison au Canada, de 1759 à
1870." Histoire et archéologie, No. 56 (1981). Ottawa. (Published in
English as "Tommy Atkins: The British Soldier in Canada, 1759-1870,"
History and Archaeology, No. 56 [1981], Ottawa.)

Wilentz, Sean
"Crime, Poverty and the Streets of New York City: The Diary of
William H. Bell, 1850-51." History Workshop. A Journal of Socialist
Historians, Vol. 7 (Spring 1979), pp. 126-55. Oxford.

Wilson, Margaret Gibson
The American Woman in Transition: The Urban Influences, 1870-1920.
Greenwood Press, Westport, Conn., 1979.

Wohl, Anthony S., ed.
The Victorian Family. Structure and Stresses. Croom Helm, London,
1978.

Women's Studies. An Interdisciplinary Journal
1972-81. New York.

Women's Studies. An International Quarterly
1978-81. Oxford, New York, Paris, Frankfurt.

Wrigley, E.A., ed.
Nineteenth Century Society, Essays in the Use of Quantitative Me-
thods for the Study of Social Data. Cambridge University Press,
Cambridge, 1972.